ISBN   978-0-9834831-3-7

TIMOTHY BARTLETT
An Australian History Story

Warren Dent

Timothy Bartlett
An Australian History Story

Table of Contents

Part One..1
1. A New Boat..1
2. Communal Interest................................5
3. Island Riches..11
4. Risky Business.......................................17
5. Lessons Learned...................................25
6. Secret Cave..29
7. Birthday Present...................................37
8. Two Partnerships..................................45
Part Two..53
9. Cell Llife...53
10. Justice Wrought...................................67
11. Sea Incarceration.................................73
12. An Arrangement...................................81
13. Wild Waves..87
14. Unrelenting Heat..................................95
15. New latitudes..99
16. Stormy weather..................................105
17. Land ho!..109
18. Ice Cold...115
Part Three..119
19. The Colony...119
20. Parramatta Town................................129
21. Upstream Fish.....................................143
22. Richmond Bottoms.............................153
23. Boat Building.......................................165

24. What Next? 179
25. Sad Acceptance 191
26. Summer Heat 207
27. Convict Madness 215
Part Four 241
28. Paths Ahead 241
29. Time Passing 257
30. Boat Innovation 271
31. Southern Islands 281
32. Life Progresses 291
33. A Visitor 301
Author's Biography 315

Part One

1. A New Boat

The rowlocks creaked in unison as Timothy wrestled the ancient oars into obedience and the boat surged slowly forward against the incoming tide. Timing was of the essence entering or exiting the harbour due to the substantial tidal swings that took place everywhere along the south Cornish coast. At low tide the quaint stone-walled Polperro harbour was pure sand, and the old trusty boats stood on special stands or lay on one side waiting for the seas to return. To the fishermen in the village the tides were a natural component of life, advancing predictably about an hour every day. Boats with the deepest drafts could leave two hours after the low tide point and could return analogously two hours before, thereby providing thirteen-hour working days, although in pilchard season the bigger boats would stay out up to five days at a time.

Historically, Polperro dates back to the thirteenth century, having been known as *Portpira* in 1303, and *Porpira* in 1379, with the chapel of *St Peter de Porthpyre* being founded in 1398. The tiny community started out as a fishing village and stayed that way for centuries, and indeed is still active today. The village was originally under the jurisdiction of two ancient manors, those of Raphael and Killigarth. Successive generations of the Killigarth and then A'Lee families occupied their farm lands above the port as recently as the nineteenth century. The original quay was built in the 1500s and replaced in the early 1700s by the current version, financed by a Mr. Long, the then Lord of Raphael Manor, which always had title to the harbour.

Polperro stands expectantly on the hills around a natural rocky inlet in the coastal cliffs. Warehouses, fishing sheds, a small processing plant, and supply stores guard the waterfront beyond a narrow dockside road. Wide enough only for simple carts, the route climbs steeply between the myriad houses dotted on the hillside and the cliffs towering over the harbour below. From the sea, the village forms a picturesque inviting sight—seemingly offering a warm welcome to any mariner looking for shelter.

Like many southern Cornish coastal villages however, Polperro has had its share of tragedy and heartbreak. The winds and storms can be incredibly fierce along that otherwise desolate and exposed stretch of coast, causing extensive, almost irreparable, damage. Nature always had her way. Yet, over time, the residents developed a resiliency that also grudgingly allowed them to experience fortune and happiness in a wide variety of ways.

The Bartlett family history included wins and losses on both sides of the experience ledger.

Tim Bartlett was in his self-designed and self-built boat. With limited draft he was leaving port some ninety minutes after the Saturday low tide point just as the church tower bells struck their midday peal.   His was one of the smaller boats owned by locals. Most were much larger and designed for serious fishing. There were a few standard rowboats around, some drying upside down on the dock, but Tim's boat had both rowlocks and a specially designed keel.   It had an apparatus underneath the centre like a giant fin, containing a narrow well that allowed a mast to be added to hold a simple but productive cloth sail.

Well, to be fair, Tim himself hadn't actually built the boat. His uncle Ben and some of the village craftsmen had built it. When his father Thomas had died from consumption three years ago, the biggest issue faced by the remaining family was what to do with their full-size double masted ketch. Thomas had earned a hard-worked, but very good living from it in different ways over the years. However, the ketch was too much for a young twelve year old to manage, even though he'd been to sea regularly in it with his father ever since his eighth birthday in 1788, seven years ago. The boat had always been kept in excellent condition and there were a number of fishermen neighbours interested in making an offer for it.

After lengthy deliberations with his mother and trusted friends in the village, they'd struck a deal.

Uncle Benjamin and two of the men who had crewed for his father would buy the boat. They would provide some cash up front to his mother and pay the remainder of the boat's value over the next ten years out of their fishing harvest proceeds. Tim would remain part of the crew but, as well, in a couple of years when he was a bit older, they would build him the boat he coveted per his own design, of which they all approved and were intrigued. His mother, Elizabeth, wouldn't have to work again at the processing plant if she didn't want to, but could keep up the house and her garden and pet canaries for the rest of her days. She'd be lonely without her man around, but there were other widows in the village just like her and she'd be well accepted into their company. In fact, she would be one of the younger widows at age forty-seven, and while the climate and work had weathered her skin and created permanent wrinkles, she still had a spark in her eye and a winsome smile and would be a good catch for the right suitor were she interested. Uncle Ben, Tom's brother, had never married and the most prevalent rumour in the village was that he and Elizabeth would make a fine couple.

They'd finished building Tim's boat just recently, and a large crowd of interested townspeople had gathered on the breakwater to watch the first major test of seaworthiness and maneuverability. The sun was high and warm as Tim leant into the task of rowing out against the current. Piercing the narrow gap between the breakwater and the cliff took a lot more effort than rowing across the harbour from the mooring position, but he'd done it many times before and his strength was in no way challenged. In fact, his strength was well recognized in the village, for he consistently held his own in arm wrestling with brawny twenty-year-olds, five years his senior, and could carry a barrel of preserved pilchards easily across his broad shoulders.

Once into the outer harbour, he shipped the oars into the special holding straps he'd created, and undid the lashings holding the slim hardwood pole that lay diagonally from port at the stern and as far to starboard as possible at the bow. It extended fore and aft two feet in each direction beyond the boat frame, and while the arrangement left Tim a small space to be centered in when rowing, its asymmetric arrangement was the part of his overall design that left him least happy. The veteran village boat builder, John Laidlaw, had spent hours shaping the mast.   It had taken ten days alone scouring the nearby countryside before he had found just the right tree. And three weeks after that to cut, shape, trim and sand it to perfection. Close to six inches square at the foot, tapering to less than two inches diameter at the top, its fifteen-foot length was designed to be approximately one hundred fifty percent of the boat's waterline measurement. The longer the boat and the taller the mast, the bigger the sail and the faster the speed, but for a one-man boat there was a definite trade-off between speed and practicality. It was only Tim's superior strength that allowed him to manhandle the mast into a vertical position and drop it into the funnel well of the extra keel. Tightening it into position and using a short paddle to push against the tide, he moved centrally between the cliffs that defined the passage out to the English Channel. He lowered the boom, undid the straps holding the sail and pulled it upward with all his might.

A loud roar of congratulatory cheers rose from the crowd on the breakwater and Tim tossed his cap in the air in response and sat down by the tiller. He'd done it! It would have been much harder had a full wind been blowing, but with practice, he would become an expert over time for sure. His concept worked! And even on this first jaunt, a couple of ideas had immediately arisen that he felt would make things easier all round.

Ah, that sunshine had never felt so good to a fifteen-year-old….

2. *Communal Interest*

Tim walked across the sand with a wire brush and metal scraper in his gloved hands. Sean looked over the pitted starboard rail on his sloop, *Zafira,* and called, "Hello, Timothy. Are you near to ready? Looks like an unusual westerly coming up, just what we want."

"Aye, Sean, perfect, and as predicted for the season. Let's hope it spends itself and we get the usual sou'wester coming back. From over yonder where I was working I noticed a few barnacles way down under your bow. Going to clean them off for you. Don't want anything to slow any of us down tonight."

"You're a fine man, Tim. I thank ye. Guess I hadn't checked hard enough meself."

"Do you need any extra rope, Sean? We've got two coils we don't really need."

"For sure and I'd be happy to relieve you of one of them. Thank ye. And in fact I have an extra lamp if you need a trade."

"I'm sure we could use it. Good exchange. I'll bring the rope over later. Let me fix underneath here for you first."

His father had taught him well. It was a small community they lived in, and in a tight community you looked after one another. Sure, folks did things different ways and needed to preserve their own values and privacy at times, but in working with and against nature, togetherness was usually far more important than competition. While each lead fisherman had his favorite grounds and kept them secret in season, when they were on a joint mission, petty differences were put aside.

And tonight six of the largest boats would be putting out together. Tim's own little convertible 'tub', as some of the sailors called it, had served him well over the past two years, allowing him to explore the coastline more closely than his peers and elders probably realized. But it wasn't a consideration of any form for the tasks ahead this day.

The wharves and jetty were strewn with nets and floats and excess fishing paraphernalia that wouldn't be necessary on the trip starting later that evening. All the sails had been carefully mended, the varied riggings checked and rechecked, the pulleys scraped, and rotting boards replaced. Rudders and tillers were taken off, examined and reassembled, and the fish storage chests had been scrubbed clean and dried out.

With the chiming of the six o'clock church bells forty men and boys and the wives of those married, along with a couple of girlfriends, headed for the church in the warren on the eastern cliff-top. There, with heads bowed, they sang a short hymn and joined their minister in prayer:

> "Heavenly Father, we thank you for the good fortune you bless upon this town and your people assembled here. Grant us guidance in the coming quest and shower your thanks upon those who have served and gone before us. We pray to you to be with those on the perilous seas and to embrace them with your mighty protection and grant them success in all their rightful undertakings. Grant them in all hours of need to see that they have a God who remembers them, and grant them grace in the hour of danger to commit their souls into your hands. O Lord Jesus Christ, who can rebuke the storm and bring it to silence, and lay the roaring waves to rest, show them who call to you out of the deep that you hear their prayer and will save them. Bless any that are left behind in the darkness.

> Finally, bring us all to the only safe port. Frail are our conveyances, and the ocean is wide; but in your mercy you have set our course. Steer the vessels of our lives towards the everlasting shore of peace, and bring us at length to the quiet haven of our hearts' desire, where you, O God, are blessed, and live and reign for ever and ever. As we partake of this food let us remember the One who sacrificed for us so we would have eternal life. As we drink let us remember His blood which was shed for us, and as we eat let us remember His body which was broken for us.

> In your name we pray. Amen."

A communal supper was served in the adjoining hall and joyous well wishes with pats on the backs, hugs, and a few tears, were shared across families and friends. Elizabeth pulled her son aside and with a secretive smile said: "I have an extra gift for you tonight when you come to pick up your food supplies. Don't be late." Tim stared in astonishment, wondering what his mother could be talking about, but said nothing in response, knowing full well she wouldn't impart any more information no matter how hard he begged. Besides which, she had immediately turned and grabbed the arm of her cousin Mildred Barnes, who was standing sullenly nearby. Usually a sadly countenanced woman, her visage brightened the minute Elizabeth stepped beside her.

Tim wandered outside, noticing the clouds building up to the southwest, grinning as he remembered Sean's prediction. The old man was always right with his weather predictions. Still plenty of sunshine left, although summer and even the autumn equinox were now behind them. He fingered his father's pipe in his pocket, rubbing his fingers along the stem, remembering the rich scent it had always carried, and which was unique to the man's specially blended tobacco. His father had taught him everything he knew about sailing, and fishing. At times he'd been unforgiving when Tim had violated small tenets of safety, and he'd felt the strap across his backside. He had to acknowledge, however, that his father, while strict, had been eminently fair, praising him for deeds well done and supporting him in taking on new challenges— both mental and physical. He'd inherited the man's broad shoulders and strength and developed a disposition that was a direct cross between that of both parents. Amiable, outgoing, and unselfish like his mother; thoughtful, planful, yet creative like his father. For years he'd wished he had a younger sister, like Michael Morrisey, who had been born exactly a week earlier than Tim. They'd grown up as best friends, and now served on Uncle Ben's boat together. But no sister, nor brother, had been forthcoming, and despite being an only child his parents had never spoiled him, bringing him up with solid Christian values and a realism of his position in life. There were days like this when he especially missed his father, for they'd gone on these multi-day trips nearly a score of times.

His reverie was broken as a pair of arms flopped over his shoulders and hands clasped tightly across his chest. No one but Clarinda would sneak up like that, and he whirled out of her grasp and said: "One day I might forget it's you who surprises me like that. Be careful lest I..."

"Lest you what?" she responded. "Turn me over your knee and spank me?   Oooh, I'm so scared..." Her sparkling eyes searched his face as she grimaced theatrically and sat down on the grass. "Sit beside me, Timothy and hold my hand. I miss you every time you go like this. Part of me worries that you won't come back, so I'm just like every other female in town worrying about their menfolk.

"I can't bear sad goodbyes, so I just hope it all goes well and if it does, why I'll have a little surprise for you when you return." With that she jumped up and ran across the church lawn to join a group of girlfriends giggling and laughing as they sauntered off down the track back to town.

Tim pulled the cap off his head and ran his hands through his thick crop of hair. What was going on? His mother had a gift for him and Claire promised a surprise on his return. What mysteries lay ahead? he wondered.

One more quick check of the boat, and a stop at the home of the trip's banker to pick up the necessary cash, which he stored in a waterproof pouch held midriff on his belt, then home for supper. He ate heartily, knowing it would be his best meal possibly for three days or more. He helped his mother wash and dry the dishes, then crammed the food and drink she had prepared into a hamper and went to pull some warmer clothes together. When he returned to the kitchen and the warmth of its log fire his mother held out a knit-frock that had once been his father's. "Here, son. It's your birthday next week and I've been repairing your father's jersey for you. I knitted this for him myself nearly twenty years ago, before you were born. I was so proud that I'd invented my own pattern and I used to stand and knit with other young wives on the path overlooking the harbour waiting for him to return from fishing. I had to go search for wool that matched the old colour in order to darn the few small holes in the back. But it's yours now. I know your father would be happy to have you wear it."

"Oh Mother. I haven't thought of this for ages. Father wore it all the time on the boat to keep warm. Thank you so much. I will treasure it. Can I wear it tonight?"

"Of course. I wanted it to be ready for this first trip after the fishing season. So there you are. Now change your jersey for this one, and be on your way. I see lanterns moving down the paths so your time is near. And give your mother a hug and a kiss before you leave."

No one had a mother like Tim's. He knew he was fortunate and the envy of several of his friends who knew the depth of her love for him. He wished his father were still alive by her side.

Along the quayside it was strangely quiet. The fires in the braziers caused shadows to flit back and forth along the docks around the abandoned equipment. The tide was high so the boats bobbed readily at an easy boarding level. Whispered goodbyes between husbands and wives were the norm, only crowded out as each captain in turn released his lines from the giant wharf cleats and pushed off with a loud shout of "AWAY *Zafira*," "AWAY *Tigan*," and so on down the list, the last one being Ben's boat with the final shout "AWAY *Vesta*."

Out through the 'gap' and along the reach of the outer harbour the six boats glided in single file. One hundred yards out in the English Channel they stopped, faced into the wind, gathered full sail, then turned around and headed southeast.

It was a hundred miles to Guernsey and they wanted to be there by noon next day.

3. *Island Riches*

Once again the group's timing was favourable. The veteran sailors in the village knew the winds and currents of the Channel as well as they knew the roads and tracks across country to the inland towns. Along this part of the coast the prevailing currents ran easterly or slightly north of east, but were mild being in the one to two-knot range. With a westerly wind the boats could set a straight line course to the southeast filling their sails from starboard. The flotilla this night consisted of Hanson's schooner *Andana*, two ketches, Ben's *Vesta* and Sean's *Zafira*, and three sloops, Biggs' *Tigan*, Higginson's *Lunamar*, and Johnson's *Pagode*. A single lamp hung high in the rigging on each as they stealthily moved forward in the dark with the moon high behind the clouds. The schooner and the ketches started to pull away almost immediately with their extra sails gathering more wind. The plan was for them to arrive perhaps an hour or more earlier than the others and to set up the initial contacts and organize berth space to make loading as expedient as possible.

The villagers were well known in St. Peter Port, where they were viewed as honest, fair, and reliable traders. Ahead of time it wasn't known locally exactly which items they might need, but recent product arrivals from Europe provided enough variety to satisfy most demands. The latest haul was a large quantity of kegs of brandy – much finer in quality than some of the previous loads. The Polperro men always took back brandy, although not for themselves. Beer, rum, and whiskey were the sailors' drinks. But in the Cornish cities and towns where the citizens were more refined, brandy was much in vogue. Like tea and gin, it was growing in popularity among an increasingly wide clientele.

The Guernsey Islands were a British protectorate, but free from the heavy taxes imposed by King George III on certain items elsewhere across the realm. Its proximity to the French coastline allowed easy access to European goods, and suppliers of such on the mainland there were happy to have extra customers only twenty miles out to sea. The traders in St. Peter Port had built extra warehouses close to the docks, sometimes converting old houses built during the earlier French occupation.   Commodity trade become a life-blood for the community, and local authorities, far removed from London parliament's oversight, were wholly supportive of increased trade and the profits derived. Many of the town's aldermen were in fact part owners of trading businesses.

Given their special status under English laws, the traders faced no threats other than those of weather affecting deliveries, theft, and misappropriation—as in any island business.   They were very conscious however, of the risks faced by the Cornish sailors as they smuggled their goods back into their small ports and sold them into the inland trade.

The merchants had been waiting for nearly a week for the Polperro fleet to arrive.   As soon as the wind turned to the west they knew they'd be on their way and so anticipation ran high. They immediately posted a lookout at Mont Cuet in the northeast lands.   As soon as the lead boat of the small flotilla was sighted, the lookout planned to ride his horse the four and a half miles into port and alert the merchants and wharfmen.

The big schooner came in sight from the northwest late morning, sailing majestically wing-on-wing across the tip of the Guernsey Island before turning south to the Port of St. Peter. Multiple wharfmen grabbed the lines thrown to them and secured the *Andana* tight to the sea wall. The tide had just started going out, and as it could sometimes drop by as much as twenty-five feet, loading was always planned for close to high tide when the boat decks were level with the stone dock surface. There was no rush for the moment.   Hanson and his crew reported how slight the seas had been and how smooth their crossing.   They expected the five remaining boats to be arriving over the next two hours.   Meanwhile, they checked their boat from bow to stern again looking for unforeseen damage or cracks in masts, railings, and rudder, and weak spots in sails which they unfurled and inspected on deck.

Hanson and Ben were the recognized leaders in trade negotiations although each of the captains held a quantity of cash to limit any risk of one man defecting or being robbed and losing the whole bank. On the stone benches in the plaza just off the wharves, the six captains and their trusted mates sat and soaked up the midday sun while they listened to the merchants and warehouse owners describe the goods they had in stock. The merchants retired to their offices, allowing the Cornishmen to chat among themselves and to grab food and drink from the surrounding pubs.

From connections in Looe and the neighbouring island, the closest settlements back home, the men had learned that the price of tea in Europe was one-sixth of what it was in England proper, and that brandy, similarly, was one-fifth of English tax-laden prices. They would try to take home twice the usual loads of both commodities but make sure there was room enough for salt for preserving their fishing catches. The tea and brandy would be split across all six ships so that if any one ship was caught by the King's Revenue men there would be back-up on the remaining ships for each product. The schooner would carry half the salt with the rest apportioned to the sloops, leaving the two ketches with space for other goods. The targets would be rum, tobacco, and lace, with the quantities dependent on leftover loading space.

During the afternoon the crews checked their boats and walked around the port, meeting with a group of like smugglers from the town of St. Mawes, some thirty miles to the southwest of Polperro, who'd also taken advantage of the westerly winds and arrived a day before. Over dinner in separate pubs the men met with the various traders they'd talked with earlier to continue negotiations on quantities and price. Late in the evening they were taken to the various depots where they inspected their purchases for quality and sea-worthiness. Cash deposits were exchanged and by midnight the sailors had retreated to their boats for a good night's sleep.

A light misty rain greeted everyone in the morning. auguring a change in the prevailing winds as hoped and as predicted by the coastal sailors. A hundred men now congregated between docks and warehouses ready to load the boats for both Polperro and St. Mawes. The barrels or hogsheads, were heavy, and in most cases needed two men to manage each one. Inevitable squabbles and mistakes occurred due to the dual loading and it was one of Tim's functions to check that the correct barrels were loaded on the correct boats. Leaking or broken barrels were identified and replaced at the merchant's cost. Tim was a stickler for precision and commitment, and had no hesitation in refusing to load any questionable crate or barrel. He ran back and forth between the two sets of boats, liaising with his counterpart from the St. Mawes fleet. Within an hour the two had worked out a process that helped keep the loading gangs lined up correctly and minimized mistakes.

By mid-afternoon the last crates were being tied down above deck, and the crews anxiously surveyed the waterlines and the impact of the heavy loads. The rides home would be sluggish for sure, although the winds turning sou'westerly would certainly help with tacking. Depending on the strength of those winds, running against the current would produce some spray from small waves, but not enough to worry anyone, even with the full loads.

The biggest concern, as usual, would be outrunning the Revenue men if they were in the vicinity. The sailors would all worry about that closer to journey's end. By leaving late afternoon they hoped to arrive back home in the dark before dawn, more easily avoiding detection from the dreaded dragoons of government. The men were well aware of the cost of being caught for smuggling, as some of their predecessors had paid the ultimate price of death by hanging. The government couldn't afford many revenue boats and the primary hope was that they were deployed along the coast or in the tidal rivers away from the fleets' home towns. Each coastal town had an elaborate signal system indicating the known presence or otherwise of the King's men. As the only means of communication they were highly reliable, but not infallible. They helped manage risk of discovery but never guaranteed one hundred percent protection.

So be it. The crews shook hands and wished each other good luck, untied their lines, waved to the haulers and merchants on shore, and moved heavily away from the wharves. The Polperro fleet headed north out of port while the St. Mawes fleet took the southerly route, destined for a more westerly crossing. The dangers lay twelve hours ahead. Every man was well aware and knew where his firearm was readily available. No man wanted to have to use it but was prepared to do so if necessary. They had thousands of pounds in cargo on board, with handsome profits waiting for all of them at the other end of the voyage. Yet, this was the part they all hated. Going out and securing the goods was exciting. Coming home was scary, no question about it. Every man had thanked the Lord on arriving home safely on previous trips, and every man hoped the current trip wouldn't be his last. Fear was a common bond, although no one would acknowledge it openly.

Into the setting sun and the unknown conditions awaiting they sailed, trepidation in every heart.

4.   *Risky Business*

Looe Island, or St. George's Island, as it was alternately known, was three and a half miles east north-east of Polperro, and only about five hundred metres off the mainland, almost accessible at very low tides on foot. Small, mountainous, and rocky, it had smuggler-friendly residents who, for a fee, would hide merchandise in inland caves authorities had never found. The Polperro fleet stood off two miles out, watching for activity. The standard signal if there were revenue boats in the vicinity was to have a pyre burning on a headland. A fire on the western headland would indicate presence somewhere to the west of the island, while the converse applied to a fire on the eastern headland. Depending on fog and marine mist it was sometimes hard to tell which hill was which from a distance, but tonight the sou'wester had blown the shores clear and no fire was to be seen by any of the sharp eyes on the boats, with and without the use of telescopes. The boats had furled their sails and tied together. Now, concurrence was quietly reached among the captains, raising everyone's spirits, so the men untied the lines, hauled their sails aloft, and turned for home five miles away.

Once again, approaching their own port, no fires were seen burning on the heads and so they proceeded up the outer harbour and past the breakwater as the first light appeared in the sky to the east. Safe at last, the crew slapped each other on the back with relief and happiness flooding their souls. Alerted quickly to their arrival by the lookouts, the townspeople arrived in throngs, dressed and ready to bring the new prizes ashore before the tide ran out. Even with all hands helping many barrels weren't able to be unloaded, but would have to wait for the tide to rise when it would be easier to get the ones stored deep in the holds. Just before lunch the church bells summoned everyone to the chapel, where once again families hugged, and public and private prayers of thanks were offered to God.

Zeb, the local banker, collected the details of the transactions from the captains and recorded them in a second set of books kept expressly for the purpose. He and the village committee then sat and decided what and how much they needed to keep for their own purposes and what could be sold for inland trade. Fees were assessed to pay the captains for the use of their boats, with a recognized contribution for the commensurate risk of running into turbulent seas and/or government cutters. The fees would be apportioned across the goods brought back relative to their value. The salt merchant in town was granted the total supply brought in, at a price that also included Zeb's fee for money lending, and on condition that he sell it back in season to the processing plants at no more than a 5% gain.

And so the trading went on. Everything was transparent so there were no uncomfortable feelings between participants. Everyone benefitted, some more than others, especially those who had put up more money, as was appropriate.

The local spirits merchant had put up enough funds to buy two-thirds of the brandy cache, the remainder being offered to anyone interested who had the cash or could get financing from Zeb. Tim's only interest, along with Ben's, was to secure some of the tea for inland sale. Once the local grocer had taken enough for community needs and his own trading purposes, Tim and Ben paid for ten large crates, and had them transported up the hill to Ben's house where they filled one of the front rooms. The townsfolk listened to the deals made and were pleased, as much because the rewards would help various members in the village, but almost as much for the safe arrival home of their friends and loved ones.

Over the next few days carts would be loaded, horses groomed and harnessed, and the long overland journeys taken to the various towns and cities where eager buyers awaited European and Oriental goods. Initial stops would be at the small towns of Liskeard and Lostwithiel, then as far afield as the larger towns of Plymouth and Newquay. Everyone in the community had a role to play, and the prosperity of the village came about from the unique understanding of the sharing of functions between families and individuals. Not every coastal village was as harmonious as Polperro, which treasured its status and position, and jealously guarded against interference from outsiders.

Elizabeth welcomed Tim home with gusto. "Okay, my son, I want to hear all about the trip. You will not be allowed to go to bed until you share every little detail. How did the boats perform? How awkward were the negotiations? Who led them? Who else was there in Guernsey? Anyone? How were the winds and the seas? Did you wear your father's jersey? And most important of all, selfish as I am, were you able to get me some new stockings?"

"Ah, Mother, will you share a drink of some fine brandy I brought back while I liquefy my innards in order to tell you so much? And here's some tea from Ceylon, never seen on these shores before. Perhaps we could try it with breakfast. And yes, I did indeed bring you stockings. Four pairs of the finest silk. You wouldn't think for a minute I'd forget, would you?"

Tim's head dipped and he shyly said: "I hope you won't mind, but I also brought some back for a friend."

"That would be Clarinda wouldn't it, Tim? I don't mind at all. You are growing up and she has her eyes on you. She's a lovely girl, albeit a year younger than you, and I'm thrilled that you would consider bringing her a gift. You remind me of the days your father was courting me. Excuse me if I get a little nostalgic. I know one day I will lose you to some fine lass, I just don't want it to be too soon."

"But there's also something else, Mother. A newly established merchant has started importing spices from the Far East. He gave me a package which has samples for you to try. See, the labels are in Chinese and French."

"How wonderful. I'll have to read in my books to see what I can learn and how best to use them. We'll cook something up at the weekend. Thank you, my dear. That's very thoughtful."

She rose and kissed his tousled hair. "Now do tell, who was the most scared coming home, and who stood most bravely?"

It was well after midnight when the two put their glasses down for the final time and headed for their rooms. "Goodnight, dear Mother. Sleep tight. I'll bring you breakfast in bed."

"G'night, son. I'm glad you are home safe."

William and Patsy O'Brien knew the mood of their town and had risen earlier than usual in order to bake extra bread and biscuits, anticipating there'd be demand for special treats on a day of gentle family celebrating. Tim was one of the first customers, buying two large still-hot rolls. He hurried home, put the kettle on the stove, and fetched down his mother's favourite teacup.

By mid-morning the docks were full of residents warming themselves in the sun and chatting about the successful haul the men had brought back. Smiles were everywhere, as were pats on the back, firm handshakes, and hugs between men and women. Life was hard in most of the fishing villages along the coast and days of sheer joy like this one were few and far between. Everyone shared in the happiness. Community spirit was well evidenced and justly indulged.

Everyone in the village was aware of the risks the men faced as smugglers. Ten years earlier when the patrols had been stepped up, the smallest boat in a returning flotilla had become separated from the others in a violent storm that had sprung up unexpectedly as they were halfway across the Channel. The larger contingent had been blown west of Polperro and finally managed to find shelter in a protected cove in Lantivet Bay, where they waited out the storm for two days before limping home. The smaller boat surprisingly had held course better and suddenly found itself at the southeast end of Looe Island where they quickly gained semi-protection in the shallow waters behind the larger of two huge rocky outcroppings. They congratulated themselves on their good fortune in surviving one of the more vicious storms any of the sailors had experienced, although were apprehensive over where their companion ships might be. The storm raged through the night and the next day, but then eased towards dusk. When the boat finally pulled clear of land they found the waves still topped ten feet and broke heavily against the planking. But the men were anxious to get home, so they pulled their jerseys and wet coats and boots tighter, lashed themselves to the bulwarks and mast, and with tiny sail headed for home, confident no one else would be out in such a storm to apprehend them.

Indeed no one else should have been out in the storm by choice, but as they steered west they were sighted through the pelting rain by the King's coast guards, who had been sheltering to leeward in a western cove on the island, having also been surprised by the unexpected storm.

It then became a race home. The Polperro crew realized that had any island fire been lit to warn them it would have been doused to ruin by the storm, so they could readily understand not seeing any signal. For now though, it was man and boat versus the elements. Rowing in ten-foot seas was out of the question and no one wanted to lighten the boat by tossing contraband overboard. So they took the last remaining choice, knowing the risk, and raised the single sail higher to gain more speed before the crosswind. Within half a mile of their harbour heads, which they could barely make out through the mist and crashing sea foam, the inevitable happened – the sail tore right through from the fierce wind, the pieces fluffing helplessly and leaving them to the vagaries of the waves. The captain and others hung on hard to the tiller while the Revenue men's boat gradually caught up and came carefully alongside. The smugglers were semi-exhausted from battling the storm and had no fight left, especially being outnumbered. They grudgingly accepted the lines thrown and secured the boats together, reluctantly letting themselves be guided into the protection of their own outer harbour.

It was there that things went from bad to worse. The officials commandeered the boat with all its plunder, and recorded the names of the men on board. A large rowboat came out from the main harbour full of angry citizens demanding that their village boat and its plunder be released. The rain still poured down and the citizens' cries were ignored, at which point they rammed the King's boat and two burly villagers climbed aboard. The lead lieutenant had anticipated same and with callous deliberation shot both men at close range. He shouted to the villagers to clear the waters and to stand to, but his actions only enraged them further. In shock at the gunfire, they initially pulled slightly back as if conforming to the captain's shouted commands. As he relaxed, sensing his response had had the desired effect, he was shot through the heart by one of the smugglers, all of whom had temporarily been overlooked while the villagers became the focus. The remaining soldiers now felt threatened by the fighting cries on both sides of their vessel and found more villagers trying to climb aboard. So they quickly cut the lines holding them to the smugglers' sloop and high-tailed it back through the rain out through the heads. The two villagers who'd been shot were tossed overboard, and although they were quickly rescued, one died of his wound on the way back to port. The other survived but was never quite the same afterwards, as the bullet had passed through his neck just under his ears.

The fellow who'd shot the officer was treated as a hero, for his action had turned the battle around. But everyone knew his days were numbered since the Revenue men would be coming back overland in force and would hang him for his deed. A collection was quickly taken up, extra clothes pushed into a sack along with food and drink, and still in the thick of the storm he was given a horse and urged to ride as fast as possible as far north as he could, and start a new life somewhere. The only saving grace was that he was single, so that no family members were left behind or slowed him down in his travels. The village never saw or heard from him again. Their immediate task was to empty the sloop of its contraband before the Revenue men returned. The chap who offered up his horse was given rights to the young fellow's lodgings.

Fast deliberations came up with a solution all endorsed. They off-loaded the cargo that had the highest taxes while the rain still poured down. The tide was going out, which meant that eventually the men were sludging across the sand, hauling crates and barrels up the slippery steps to the docks. In the morning, carts left early with the goods meant for inland trading and a fresh crew took the sloop back to St. George's Island, where they paid for the remaining contraband to be deeply hidden.

Just as the sloop returned to Polperro, the rest of the fleet turned up and the disastrous situation was discussed among the village elders. The Revenue men were stationed in Plymouth so it was clear there was no way the villagers would be able to unload and store all the goods they'd purchased in Guernsey before riders turned up.   There was nothing for it but to have the three other boats leave town and hold up somewhere along the coast for at least four days before trying to return again. It was suggested they head for Portscatho, twenty-four miles southwest and in the jurisdiction of Falmouth rather than Plymouth. The Revenue men knew nothing about the three extra boats but if they found a larger supply of contraband than one sloop could carry on the docks or in storage, the fines would go up and simply attract increased official attention in the future.

Dry clothes were gathered by the crews, supplies of food and grog pulled together, and almost as quickly as they had arrived, the boats left again. Although the wind still blew, it was nowhere near as ferocious as in the days gone by, and the rain had stopped.

No one was happy. Certainly not the sailors who had come home and who had turned around and departed almost before they could say hello to their loved ones. Definitely not the men on the sloop that stayed behind, nor the poor man shot, now fighting for his life.

Last but not least, most of the villagers, especially the town elders, were scared, nervously wondering what the morrow would bring.

5. *Lessons Learned*

The morrow dawned grey and cold with the wind whistling between the houses, slamming doors shut, rocking the boats in the harbour and bending small trees and grasses at will. As expected, it didn't take long before twenty-five men on horses and with carts arrived on the hilltop, their red coats standing out against the bleak sky. With terrifying shouts they rode down to the docks, some stopping and banging on house doors with their clubs or rifle butts. Parents pulled children away from the windows and merchants pushed furniture against their shop entry doors.

The soldiers and sailors in the group were clearly feisty and angry, seemingly spoiling for a fight, rather than just executing official duty. The sailors in the group readily identified the sloop they had chased and quickly boarded her but became incensed when they realized all the contraband had been unloaded. They went on a rampage searching the warehouses before finally understanding that the goods were now well on their way to inland haunts. One rider was sent back to Plymouth to alert comrades who would search the countryside to see what they could recover.

It was Tim's father who finally stepped forward at the far end of the dock, where he was immediately surrounded by swarthy men yelling at him. The King's Sergeant asked where the captain of the sloop was to be found, but before Thomas could answer the man emerged from a narrow alley and surrendered. He knew that the armed men would not hesitate to knock doors down, search houses, and eventually find him, so rather than see the wanton destruction he was sure would follow, he willingly gave himself up. He was manhandled and beaten to the ground while the sergeant loudly proclaimed his misdeeds and acts against the crown.

As bad as dealing in contraband goods was, the killing of an officer was far worse. In order to prevent more bloodshed, an old woman with a cane pushed her way through the throng of redcoats and told the Sergeant that it was her son who had shot the lieutenant, but that he had left town. She hoped he'd never be found, but as consolation she brought forth from under her skirts the very rifle he had used, and offered it up.

The soldiers were nonplussed at her brash action and moved back to give her more space. It wasn't in their makeup to beat women and children and they looked to their leader for advice. Some of the venom in the men had dissipated but there were some who still wanted revenge. A quick discussion brought bravado back and the group split in two, one half marching to the sloop, the other grabbing the smuggling captain and tying him to a rail stanchion at the dock steps. There they stripped the shirt from his back and to the horror of the villagers a huge soldier dealt out twenty lashes with a cat-o'-nine-tails, the sloop captain screaming in terror and pain as bloody bits of skin peeled off and fell on his britches or to the ground.

At the same time the sailors set a fire in the hold of the sloop, and watched as it blazed out of control, spreading along the old wooden deck, and flaring up along the furled sail. The rigging caught fire and flames ran up the ropes in a display that tormented the innocent villagers watching, many of whom broke down in tears at the vicious display of carnage. The crackling of burning timbers haunted all those who watched, save the King's men, who gathered up their supplies and weapons and marched up the road out of town.

Men rushed to salvage what they could of the sloop, throwing buckets of water across the hull and deck and onto the mast. Simultaneously, women rushed to the aid of the prone captain, raising his head to sip water and placing soothing balm on his raw skin. As soon as he could sit he was given rum in healthy doses to help fend off the pain. They carried him to his hut, where he was laid on his bed and finally passed out, much to the relief of those tending him.

Even when the other three boats arrived home, there was no celebration, for people were sick at the memory of the cruelty that had taken place. The old woman was heralded for her bravery, and the young captain lauded for stepping forward and so helping avoid what surely would have been broader destruction and mayhem.

The visitation was a grim lesson for all, and while most seethed with anger and wished for revenge, they realized that any retaliatory action would only bring harsher and more terrible responses on their heads. It took a year for the dark horror to be integrated into community life, although for some it never really ever went away. Secretly, a small group of citizens vowed to keep smuggling, as it was a well remunerated livelihood from which nearly all gained some value. They made plans to be more prepared, to ensure sufficient arms were on board but never to fire first, to make sure boat separation never occurred again, and to steer any interception that might occur away from their home port. Finally, if absolutely engaged in conflict mode they would retaliate with their own weapons of fire, and to that end each smuggler's boat in future carried covered pails of liquid pitch and bows and arrows with fur balls replacing arrowheads, ready to be aimed at sails to set fire to them. As a last resort they vowed to let flaming Revenue men's ships sink with all aboard, although they hoped that likelihood would never come to pass.

It was six months before a determined and brave party of men in four boats once again set out for Guernsey. Over the following years confidence gradually returned and experience grew. Twice in that period the fires on Looe Island helped avert discovery, and the Polperro villagers made sure their comrades who lived there were recognized and rewarded.

Smuggling became a way of life again.

6.   *Secret Cave*

Ten years after the tragedy, and back with the present celebration, Tim and his mother walked down to the waterfront where they met up with Ben and Sean and a number of the others who had been to Guernsey together. By silent mutual understanding it was a day of rest and relaxation. The sunshine helped with the easy-going atmosphere that enveloped the folks who gathered in small groups. Some sat on the stone benches, others sat on the dock and dangled their legs towards the water, while others took to the few chairs put out by some of the merchants. Clarinda came skipping along, her locks a glorious tumble of red-gold curls, sparkling where the sun touched them.

"Good morning, Mrs. Bartlett, hello, Tim. What a lovely day this is. I'm so glad everyone is home again. You can feel the relief in the air. What was the trip like Tim? Any pretty girls in Guernsey catch your attention? Oh, you're blushing." Facing Tim's mother directly she continued: "See Mrs. Bartlett, I knew he always had an ulterior motive for going along."

Turning back to Tim she smiled and flirted: "*Comment ça va, ma cherie?*"

"Ah, *tu es une jolie allumeuse,* Clarinda," Tim's mother replied. "It's good to see you so happy." Deliberately providing an opening for Tim, she added, "I have to tell you Tim brought me back a gift. He's such a thoughtful son. "

"*C'est quoi?*"

"Some fine silk stockings, same as his father would bring back. But he also brought some new spices. You'll have to come to dinner when I try them out."

"Oh, thank you, Mrs. Bartlett. I'd love to."

Tim was enjoying watching the sun bounce off Clarinda's shiny hair, but quickly regained focus and said: "And I have a gift for you too, Clarinda. I'll run home and get it. Wait here."

At home, he grabbed a large clean towel and wrapped his gift as best he could, tucked it under his arm, and strolled back to the spot he'd left.   Uncle Ben had joined the ladies and was regaling them with exploits of the trip. Mother had explained Tim's absence and he now laid the towel in front of Clarinda and said, "You'll have to excuse the fine wrapping and you must guess what is inside."

"Can I touch to see if it's soft or hard before I guess?"

"No, that might make it too easy. What do you think?"

"Let me think. Ah, I know, it's a French book. You've brought it to help me improve my language skills."

"Mother, she is so quick. Did you give her a clue while I was back at the house?"

"I certainly did not. I think she needs to make one more guess. Clarinda, is it a book of fact or fiction? Perhaps either a history book, or a scurrilous and pompous French mystery?"

"Ah, now you are making it hard. I think there is a bit of the romantic hidden beneath that guarded exterior Tim shows, so I'm going to guess it's a French novel. Am I right, Tim?"

"Well, I think you'd better just open it and see. Only then will you know."

Slowly, painstakingly, Clarinda laid back successive levels of the towel, savouring the anticipation. She soon realized her parcel was soft, not hard, and her eyebrows rose in confusion. Beyond the final fold the soft package of stockings lay before her and she shouted with joy. "Oh, you all played me so well. Thank you Tim, you are a sweetheart. And a trickster to boot. These are the first silk stockings I've ever owned. I will treasure them for ages. I can't believe you did this for me, Tim. Thank you, thank you, my gallant hero."

Ben interjected, "I saw him bargain his last pennies away, miss, to get these for you. We gave him a hard time when he purchased them, which tells me you must be pretty important. Because," he continued deadpan. "he didn't spend nearly as much on the ones he bought for the other girls."

Tim turned away to hold his mirth. Clarinda blushed and Elizabeth giggled and said: "Don't you believe a word he says, Claire. He's as bad as the rest of us. Forgive us for having a little fun at your expense."

"True, missy, he only bought gifts for you and his mother here, no one else. You're welcome to punch me if it'll make you feel better. I'm only half sorry, as I really did enjoy that look on your face. And now I must run before I start laughing. You folks have a wonderful afternoon."

Tim was the one who burst out laughing, and unwittingly his mother joined him. The sound was so happy that Clarinda couldn't stop herself, and soon the three were the centre of attention on the docks as their raucous joy spread along the cobblestones and brought smiles to all those in earshot.

Tim rose to his feet and looked down the outer harbour to the ocean. "I'm going to go for a leisurely sail. I sense a light fresh breeze out there. Clarinda, would you like to accompany me? You'd probably want to leave those new stockings behind, I think."

"You are a rogue, Timothy Bartlett, but yes I'd love to go out on the water. I'll meet your boat at the breakwater steps after I take this precious gift home. Bye, Mrs. Bartlett. I can see why you love your son."

"Bye, Claire." You are a delight, my girl, she thought. Every time we meet I learn something new. You and Tim would make a lovely couple. Pretty, with charming self-confidence and esteem, and now a sense of humour to match your intelligence. I hope Tim is smart enough to realize, as I don't want to push.

Clarinda admired the bulging biceps Tim exposed as he rowed smoothly down the stretch of water to the heads, sitting back letting her thoughts drift away over the cliff-tops to fold with the small cotton-like balls of clouds high in the sky. Tim smiled as he sensed Claire's reverie, hesitant to break the spell she was clearly enjoying. As he brought the oars in she refocused and asked: "Can I help you with the mast?"

"No," he replied, "but when I get the boom in place you can unstrap the sail for me. Now watch your head as we swing about." Two minutes later they were tacking west, into a light breeze that took nothing away from the warmth of the sun.

"I'm going to show you a special place, Claire, that no one else knows about. It's four miles down the coast this way, so sit back while I take us there."

In what seemed no time at all Tim dropped the sail and removed the mast.

"You can't see it, Claire but we are sitting above a ridge of rock that is only ten feet below the surface and is exposed at medium and low tide. It becomes a formidable barrier to the rocky shore one hundred yards away over there when uncovered, and even now it breaks the current and strength of the waves to almost nothing. You see how there's no splash where the water meets the base of the cliffs?

"Move up here between me and the bow so I can show you something. Look along my arm where I'm pointing. Can you see a rock that looks like a giant whale fin with the tip at the top? It's about ten feet tall, I would guess, and if you follow the sloping edge you might be able to see that it doesn't look very thick, more like a giant spear tip."

"I see it, Tim. I see what you mean. In the shape of a tent. What's so important about it?"

"As we come closer you'll see that it isn't exactly parallel to the line of the cliff but is slanted away. There's more room between it and the cliff at this eastern end than at the other end. At first I thought it was just a part the cliff itself. But there, now you can see it's like a fence hiding a hole in the cliff behind. You just can't tell until you get up this close. From any spot out further it's just another rock formation like anywhere else along the coast."

"I see it, Tim, but can you sail through that gap? It looks pretty narrow."

"Depending on the tide I can make it sometimes but as high as it is now, no, because the fence, or gate as I call it, leans too far back towards the cliff. But that's not exactly where we're headed anyway. In a minute you'll see that behind that large pointed rock up ahead jutting out from the cliff itself on our right, there's actually a very large gap. See, it's just coming into view now. It's a large hole in the cliff, protected by that whale-fin fence and the underwater outcrop back there acting like a reef. "

"It's dark in there, Tim. I'm a little scared. Have you been far inside, and do you have any light sticks?"

"In the locker at the stern there are two lamps we can use. The hole is no more than ten feet wide but goes inland maybe fifty feet. You can see there's hardly any wave action, the water is almost calm. Also it's no more than six feet deep so you can't even get in here at low tide. Hand me one of the lanterns and the paddle. It's too tight for the oars.

"Thanks," he said whenshe held up the lamps. "Here we go. Isn't this something else? I was so excited when I found it. And still the best is to come. Wait.

"Now, we steer to the right a little, and look, it's like a tiny beach here. You can see through the clear water how the rock floor slopes gently up for four feet and we can step out and pull the boat up behind us.   There's even a pinnacle rock ten feet further in where we can tie the painter and hold the boat fast. What do you think Claire?"

"It's like a secret cave, Tim. You are so smart to know about it. How wonderful. I can't believe you found it. Have you been here often?"

"No, this is just the fourth time. You can basically enter only at high tide and I don't often get away on my own. I've known about it for a year. There's one other thing to show you. Come over to this side. See that trickle of water? I've traced it back to a fissure behind that jumble of rocks you see. It's fresh water that must come from a spring. I've been dying to find time to walk the cliff top above here and see if I can find a source, but haven't done it yet. Maybe one day we could go together and see what we could find. What do you say?"

"I think that's a splendid idea. This is an amazing find. I thank you for sharing it with me. I promise to keep it secret. Do you trust me?"

"I wouldn't have brought you here if I felt otherwise, Claire. From now on this will be our secret together."

"How long can we stay, Tim? You said you can only get in and out around high tide. This is unbelievably exciting but I don't want to get marooned here. Is there more to see?"

"I'd guess we have about thirty more minutes. After that it will get a little risky. We left the harbour a bit after high tide, and it's been well over an hour so let's not push our luck. The big part of the main cave goes back further, as I said. The floor slopes up again just like here and there's another totally dry cave area at the end, but it's not as large as what you see here, and not really worth exploring."

Clarinda smiled. "What a day Tim. Yesterday you were a smuggler. I think you are still a smuggler today because now with this secret cave you could store any personal contraband you want to keep for yourself."

"You mean all the gold and diamonds I plan to steal from the wealthy travellers on ships at sea? Sorry, Claire, it would be very difficult to get barrels and crates in here single-handed. At best, I think of this as a place to hide if I ever needed to do so. Let's just hope that it never comes to that."

"Just dreaming, just dreaming. You are right, of course. In any event it's still a great day. Your mother was so appreciative of the gifts you brought home and you surprised me with the stockings. A bit daring if I may say so, but your mother didn't seem to mind and I love them so much. You are very good to me, Tim."

With that she turned, held his face in her hands, and kissed him slowly and passionately, loving the feel of his lips on hers, and the meeting of tongues. He didn't pull away but returned the embrace with fervor. They held each other and prolonged the contact until Claire could no longer breathe and she reluctantly dropped her hands and pulled back. "Thank you, thank you, Tim. You are very special to me." She turned and sat down on the rock face between his outstretched legs and leant back against his chest. It felt strong and supportive and she listened to see if she could hear his heart beating as loudly as hers was. She reached back and pulled his arms across her front cradling his hands under and around each breast. Slowly she melded into a contented wishful, mind-defined space, comfortable and thankful with a man she could trust.

Tim had a sixth sense of when it was appropriate to say nothing, and he let Claire dream on while he held her tight. But eventually he whispered that it was time to go, at which point she turned and kissed him again, lightly this time, and walked back to untie the painter from the secure hold around the pinnacle rock.

She followed his directions carefully and was somewhat relieved when they finally drifted over the outer shoal, this time more readily visible than before. He hoisted the sail and they headed back on a tack across the sou'wester towards home.

7. *Birthday Present*

Surprisingly, the sun had put a little colour in both sets of cheeks. One would think after years of working on the sunny coast of Cornwall, given frequent confrontation with the wind, that one's skin would have absorbed all the effects the climate could hand out. But nature hadn't left a pamphlet behind explaining everything and apparently there would always be things to learn at her doing. The crowds had dissipated when the pair got back, although a few friends were sitting in the sun drinking beer and sharing stories. Some of the boat owners were putting their nets and related equipment back on board in anticipation of going out fishing in the next couple of days to see what the Atlantic had brought into the Channel over the past week.

"Thank you for a wonderful time today, Tim. You've made me feel proud with both the gift and your trust in me. You may have forgotten but I mentioned I had a little surprise for you. It's not quite ready but will be for your birthday in a few days. Be good now. I must run and help Mother with some chores so I'll catch up with you tomorrow. Ta-ta." And she blew him a kiss as she turned and walked home.

Over the next few days Tim spent most of his time working with Ben and his co-owners on the boat. It hadn't really suffered at all on the Guernsey trip but he polished the brass anyway, shaved down the rail splinters, and checked the bottom paint. They hadn't used the anchor in a long time so one day they took her out, checked the depth reading knots on the chain and rope, made sure the winch worked freely, and that the anchor still held them tight in the spots where currents ran fastest and winds were strongest.

He scrubbed out the fish lockers, checked the hoses and the fresh water supply on board, made sure the limited medical supplies were intact and complete, and painstakingly went over every inch of the seine and drift nets, replacing floats and rings where necessary, and mending tears and holes in the precious nets themselves. The rigging was pulled down and every rope line checked for tautness and minuscule unraveling. Finally he worked the stays, canvas sails, looking for loose threads, weak spots, tears, and small holes. Extra planks, drain bungs, coils of various sizes of rope, the inevitable pail of pitch, the bows and arrows, and now rifles and pistols, the flags and gloves and wet weather coats; all were checked and inventoried. No item was left to chance and Tim felt proud of his work on his uncle's possession.

He was just as industrious at home, helping his mother keep their small cottage spick—and—span. They only had the two bedrooms and a large kitchen cum eating area with small bathroom, and small sitting room. But it was all they needed, and it stayed warm even in the middle of winter, encased between two larger houses with very thick soundproof adjoining walls. There was a tiny garden out back where Elizabeth grew a limited number of herbs and vegetables. Because of the shape of the roof the garden received an adequate supply of sunshine so the two of them always had fresh vegetables except in the middle of winter. Their location also avoided the common sou'westers that dominated the coastline, although in a real gale the winds would howl down the chimney.

Tim's mother and father had both been born in the village and there were more Bartletts living there from other branches of the family tree that had taken root in the area generations ago. Not that Thomas had fraternized deliberately with relatives. As he sometimes remarked, "One can choose one's friends but not one's relatives." He had more time for friends he'd gone to school with and grown up alongside than members of the Bartlett family at large. Tim was the only other Bartlett in his boat's crew.

Dawn was just breaking as Tim set off west along the clifftop path that started in West Looe and ended in Polruan over ten miles away. He was originally going to bring Clarinda along, but in the end decided it would be faster on his own. It was windy, as usual, and he wore his father's knit-frock over two shirts, with woolen britches tucked into heavy boots. A beret kept his head warm, and a satchel with food and drink was slung across his back. He figured his cave was at least three and a half miles from the Polperro headlands, so he moved energetically, anxious to learn whatever he could. The problem was that the path followed old sheep tracks, in many sections a hundred yards or more inland from the sea-cliffs per se. After traveling about three miles by his reckoning, he left the track every fifteen minutes and walked to the cliff edge, carefully leaning into the wind and searching the coast line ahead. It was on the third such detour that the sun rising behind him helped identify his whale-fin rock slab throwing off different reflections than the rocky cliff itself. He smiled contentedly and hurried forward.

Lying on his stomach forty feet below he could see the slanted 'gate' protecting his secret opening. Despite his longing there was no way to climb down, so he worked on logging rock features into his memory to make it easier to find next time. Backing away he rose and started walking directly inland. He'd gone well over a hundred yards when he realized his boots were treading soft ground. Soon a different coloured grass waved beneath his feet and he stopped. Looking around, it seemed that there was a small patch of swampy ground he'd walked into, supporting his notion that there was a spring in the vicinity that also filtered underground. A reflection of some form caught his eye, and he peered in its direction. There it was again. He walked forward and saw a rock that was revealed when the tall grasses blew a certain way before the wind. In fact, there were six rocks, almost in a straight line running southwest to northeast. The rocks were much bigger than he initially thought, for when he tried to move one he found it was buried deeply in the ground. The rocks were of a different colour and constituency than the rocks that were used further inland to build stone fences around sheep paddocks.

From history teachings at school he knew the Romans had rarely travelled southwest of Exeter, so perhaps these stones had had some significance to the Dumnonii tribe of British Celts centuries before. Now I'm reaching, he thought to himself. More likely this marks the spot where some enterprising mining surveyor drilled for evidence of tin or copper. Certainly, productive mines were not too far away. I'll have to ask some of the elders back in the village before I get too excited.

Late in the afternoon Clarinda found him working inside Ben's boat. "Tim, after supper tonight can you come to Betsy Anne's place? She has a new jigsaw puzzle with two hundred and fifty pieces and it would be fun to put it together. It's a scene of an inland town with a river running through it. A painting with many colours but a lot of sky and water which will make it extra hard to do."

"Of course, and I have much to tell you from my walk along the cliffs this morning. You are so good at puzzles, it's no wonder Betsy wants you to help her. I'll be there once it gets dark. See you then."

Clarinda could hardly conceal her excitement. She had plans she definitely could not share with anyone. She wondered how much attention she'd give to Tim's revelations from his cliff walk when the time came. Not much, she thought. She and Betsy Anne were best friends, just as Tim and Mike Morrisey were. The four of them had always played together as children and still went on picnics together or spent time in other joint activities. Betsy was a year younger than Claire but a great companion anyway. Age never seemed to matter.

The wind had picked up at supper time and was making whistling sounds through the rigging of some of the boats. It could be heard all round the harbour, but no one took any notice. It was as common as the tide changes. Even so, Tim pulled his jersey a little tighter and crammed his beret lower on his forehead. It was getting colder.

At the far end of the warren, yellow light shone through the window of Betsy's house. The wind was stronger up on the cliffs and Tim wouldn't have minded staying at home and reading. It was that kind of night. But he had made a commitment and was looking forward to working on a puzzle—something he hadn't done in months. He knocked on the door and was quickly let in by Clarinda, who'd clearly been waiting close by. The room was warmed by a blazing fire and she helped him take off his jersey and cap and hang them on the nearby pegs.

"Where is everyone, Claire? No Betsy, and what about her folks? I thought they'd be here."

"No, just you and me, Tim. This is your birthday surprise."

His eyebrows knit in misunderstanding. "You mean the puzzle is for me?" he surmised.

"Well, partially. See, here it is on the kitchen table. I already started working on it. Come on, help me out."

Tim was clearly still a bit confused, but sat down and spread out some of the errant pieces. "Well, this certainly could be a challenge when I look at that painting, but where's Betsy?"

"Oh, you silly. I thought you'd be smarter. This is Betsy's night for choir practice. She'll be at the church for ages. And her parents are having dinner with my parents. They are talking about going into a new business together and I knew Father didn't really want me around. So I made an excuse to be gone.

"But more than anything, I wanted some time alone with you, Tim. Our togetherness in your cave made me realize how much you care for me, and how much I care for you. You shared a great secret with me, and the more I thought about it I realized how special that made things. When we kissed it made me feel dizzy and warm all over. It was a sensation I liked very much. I know you did too. And frankly I didn't really want to stop. But had to. You held me intimately and when you did, strange feelings flowed through my body.

"I want your hands on my body again Tim. There, I've said it. I'm both scared and excited to have those feelings again. They were new. I'd never felt them before, and they felt so, so good. Do you understand?"

Tim nodded his head up and down, and love shone from his eyes. He opened his mouth to speak, but Claire interrupted him before he could start.

"No Tim, hold on for a minute and let me continue before I lose my nerve and clam up. I promised you a birthday present. I not only want to kiss you again, and again, I want you to touch me as well."

Standing, he reached across the table and took her hand in his, his voice raspy as he whispered: "Yes, I understand. I have new feelings too." Facing her, he reached up, and with his hands in her hair, gently pulled her face to his. The softest, tenderest kisses were shared, but this time they progressed to passionate, hungry, sensual exchanges that kindled internal fires in both of them. They moved to the sofa in front of the fire hugging and canoodling joyously.

Exploration led to education and they shared new findings and secrets previously unspoken and unrealized. The learning was mutual and the time together forged a new bond of caring. Afterwards, Claire rose and lit two more candles. She sat back down and snuggled on the sofa with Tim's arm across her shoulders, his other hand holding hers in her lap.

"Do you think Betsy's folks would mind if we drank a little brandy to celebrate, Claire?"

"As long as it's a tiny sip I doubt they'd miss it at all—look at all the bottles in the cupboard there."

"Okay, I'll get us some. But you know, it might make sense if we drink it at the table and work on the puzzle a bit more. Won't Betsy expect to see more of it completed when she comes home?"

"Oh, you are so wise Tim. She knows I just wanted to be alone with you tonight, but I hope she hasn't guessed the full reason. We share talk about girl things all the time. Things you don't want to know about. She senses that something happened when we went sailing last time together, but I've held back talking about it, especially as I don't want to mention the cave. I know she'll want to know about tonight and I'll have to tell her bits, I hope you understand. I trust her as completely as I trust you, and I know she'll keep yet another secret. We have a number between us already. Perhaps one day she and Mike will need the same sort of privacy we just enjoyed. She's a little more mature physically than me so I don't think it will be long. Will you tell Mike?"

"I don't think so. We boys don't tend to talk about intimate feelings and behavior. We just lie and repeat stories we hear. Although Mike is more sensitive than other boys, probably because he has a younger sister, and hence knows more about girl body functions. I think I know what you mean when you say

Betsy is physically more mature than you. It means she started becoming a woman earlier than you did."

"You learn quickly Tim, and I'm delighted that you have kept your knowledge to yourself and not made rude comments to us girls, as some of the boys in the village do.

"Now," she said, that's enough brandy or I'll be sick. It's not my favorite drink I must say, but we daren't open a wine bottle. Here, let me rinse the mugs and return them to the shelves. I must wait for Betsy, but do you need to go home?"

"I told Mother I wouldn't be out late and I can stay a little while. I don't want to leave, Claire. I want to hold you and love you some more."

"You mean touch me, and have me touch you again, Tim?"

"That would be truly enjoyable and hard to resist, but no, I meant I'd just like to hug and softly kiss you some more. That was the most loving and meaningful part. Everything else was extra."

"You make me want to cry, Tim. You are so gentle and thoughtful. I see your mother in you. She's such a sweet soul, and you hold the best of her attributes inside as well. Come round this side of the table and kiss me again before you leave. I need some time to compose myself anyway before Betsy arrives. You are such a loving man."

The wind was nowhere near as biting on the way home and the sounds from the rigging seemed more symphonic than needling. There was no moon lighting the way, but there was a new energy in Tim's steps and a smile on his face that he knew he wouldn't be able to keep from his mother. She could see through him with ease at any time and he'd given up trying to conceal his feelings from her. She knew when he was angry, when he was brooding, or contemplative, or excited, or happy, or anxious. How did she do that? he wondered. How did he give himself away so easily? Maybe he'd never know – it was just a mother's instinct.

What an evening!

Happy Birthday indeed.

8.   *Two Partnerships*

Even in the cold weather the boats went every day or so to see what they could catch.   The big hauls were in summer, but demand for pilchards stayed constant year round and the processing plants liked to keep busy.   The men would return with their fish boxes full, their nets torn, and their muscles aching. Which was when the women took over, helping transport the spoils to the nearby huts where stray items in the nets were removed, the fish were checked, and then packed in the hogsheads with salt to preserve them for the trip to Looe or inland markets.   Donkeys and horses would pull the carts along ancient narrow tracks and wider roads, leaving daily, so that the fish were as fresh as possible when they reached market.

Once in a while a shark would end up in a net.   There was always widespread interest in such a large creature.   School was suspended and the children watched in awe as the huge animal was pulled up on the dock.   The boat owner and his crew had first share of the fresh meat, with the remainder going next to those most needy.   In some rare instances the whole shark might be kept by the boat's crew and placed on a cart and sent off to market.   The payment coins returned would usually be spent wisely on repairs and upgrades to the boat itself.

The prevailing sou'westerly winds coming off the Atlantic varied by season.   The experienced elder sea-faring men developed a sixth sense in predicting their strength and direction and the possibility of squalls or storms.   Only in the fiercest of storms did the boats not go out in season.   Wind was the sailor's enemy, and when it blew against the current, conditions could become mightily unpleasant.   This often happened on the homeward journeys, for the fleet fished well off the coast and while the wind was often behind them on return, the current was not.   The boats were not as maneuverable when heavily laden, and every sailor was glad to see the headlands in his sight and to reach the relative safety of the outer harbour.

The village routine of fishing and smuggling continued over the years leading up to the turn of the century, although two new facets of sea life had recently emerged. Large cargo barques returning to England from India or China would sometimes hover off the Cornish coast and sell untaxed items directly to the merchants of the coastal villages. Out of the blue, unheralded, small foreign boats would arrive in the outer harbour with examples of the goods their 'mother-ship' had available. The villagers would send out one or two sloops with local merchants and Zeb, the banker, aboard, and purchase selections of spices, fine china, silks, and cottons.

Always anxious to protect and ensure the payment of taxes on imported goods, the practice didn't escape the attention of the Revenue men, who started to resort to a change in tactics. The number of boats they commanded was small, and if they were operating along one specific region of the coast, activity elsewhere would proceed in earnest, and unabated. The King's boats could not patrol long distances quickly.

In order to mitigate this deficiency the officials added more mounted troops who patrolled the roads across the moors and who, unannounced, would ride into a village and survey the boats in the harbour, looking for crates of contraband stashed above deck. Alternately they would ride out on the headlands and watch for the returning fleets through telescopes, sometimes poised beside the very fires burning to announce their presence to the smuggling fleet. Their actions were more of a nuisance than a real threat, just something new that the residents had to be prepared for.

Among a number of the villages there were some men more desperate than others, living at the fringe of society, not well integrated into the mainstream, but still contributing to the mainstay of fishing activity and industry. These men owned boats, licensed by the Admiralty, to attack, and even capture, enemy ships. Often they would return from plundering with valuable contraband of diamonds, coffee, pepper, and indigo dye sticks, the latter from India, and destined for industry and art across the country. In some cases this privateering would be combined with smuggling, abusing the Admiralty privilege and raising the dangers of detection for others. In 1799, four men from Coverack, some thirty-five miles away as the seagull would fly, were caught red-handed and convicted in court for smuggling and obstruction.

To increase the chances of avoiding future detection, small groups started blasting caves out of the sea-cliffs, and digging tunnels inland. These served the purpose of storing contraband away from existing ports, but providing access from the land side for distribution to inland towns.

In the middle of February just after the year 1800 had been rung in, the small Polperro township celebrated two weddings. Despite the fact that it was winter, the season had been decidedly mild, and so on one special Sunday morning, at the end of regular service, the minister officially tied the knot between Timothy Bartlett and Clarinda Hinson, and between Elizabeth and Benjamin Bartlett. The Bartlett's were uniformly popular throughout town, and a gala luncheon with free-flowing liquor was held on the docks in their honour.

Ever since Tim's seventeenth birthday he and Claire had become inseparable. Their physical and emotional love had grown, and finally they'd been prompted to form a union after Tim's mother had surprised him with an announcement at dinner not three months earlier.

"Tim, we'll be having a visitor a little later this evening, and I have something joyous to share with you beforehand. As much as I dearly loved your father, and his memory haunts me daily, since he left us I've been fortunate to also be loved by another. We have money to live on for many years, but I miss the daily companionship I became used to with Thomas. No one can take his place totally but I long for the protection and care that can be provided by a man my age..."

Tim interrupted with a grin on his face: "Mother, if you and Uncle Ben are coming together, I couldn't be happier. He has been a wonderful uncle to me, and it's obvious to all how much he cares for you. It might be a bit strange to think of him as a half-father, but you deserve one another. I know how well he will look after you."

Tears glistened in Elizabeth's eyes as she and Tim hugged. "I'm so glad you approve, son. You are so very, very important to me. As you grow I see more and more of your father in you. You are strong and generous, level-headed, smart and reliable, and so much more. Thank you for understanding. We'll break out a bottle of wine when Ben comes by later."

When Ben arrived and the handshakes and hugs were over and the first sips of wine had started warming the three souls, another surprise came tumbling out, this time from Ben. "Tim, you've been on the *Vesta* crew with us for some eight years now. Your contribution is as much as any partner's. As a group we still have a few more payments to make to your mother, so it's hard to have you buy in just yet. But, given your mother's and my new circumstances, we have an offer for you. No strings attached. I'm giving you the key and deed to my small house, and your mother and I will live here. That is, if it's okay by you."

Tim's thinking had not reached quite that far. He'd just assumed Ben would be moving in, but this was a totally new input. Before he could react Ben continued: "You are nearly twenty and at some point you will need your own place. Also, it's not very difficult to imagine that you and Clarinda might soon want to be together permanently."

"Ben, and Mother. You are too good to me. That is a wonderful gift. I'm not sure I deserve it. No doubt you could find a good buyer for it, Ben. Are you sure you wouldn't rather do that? Something will work out for me when needed. I love the idea, it would be so much fun to own. But are you sure you are sure?"

"We've talked it over extensively, Tim. Our minds are firm. You are very welcome. I know your father loved you, but in some ways you are also the son I never had. I'd be proud to know that the little house stays in the family as it has for the last hundred years. It's yours."

"Oh my, how incredible. Thank you, thank you, both of you. I can't believe it."

The night drifted on, a second bottle of wine emptied, and two unseen shooting stars crossed the heavens.

Within a week, Tim and Ben had exchanged lodgings. Tim had far less to move than did Ben. Clothes, books, a few journals his father had kept, bed coverings, a minimal number of fish carvings, and just two ornaments hanging on a wall. On reflection his life was indeed pretty simple. They each kept their own beds, which required carts to move.

Tim had been in Ben's hut many times, but his first night alone felt strange. The creaking of timbers and the sound of the wind were slightly different than what he was used to. The colour of the walls was different, the layouts of the eating area and bathroom were different, and there was something else amiss that was less definable.

It took a while to identify it, but eventually he put it down to the absence of his mother. There were no feminine touches around. The kitchen curtains were plain linen, not lace. There were no small vases to put pansies and roses in when blooming. There was no apron hanging on a hook by the stove, no woman's jacket thrown over the back of a chair. The smell of tobacco replaced the smell of vegetables and herbs hanging in string bags, and there was no lingering aroma of the lavender soap that Mother sometimes used.

The tobacco smell reminded him of his father's pipe lodged firmly in the pocket of his britches. Time to be his own man. The new lodging was a catalyst for a new life. He placed the pipe on the mantle above the fireplace next to the giant shark's tooth his dad had gifted him at a very early birthday. Tim didn't smoke at all, and Ben only rarely. So Tim hoped the smell from Ben's odd pipeful would disappear before too long.

On the first day without boat chores he scrubbed down the walls and the floor, and washed the curtains. He emptied all the cupboards and scrubbed the shelves. The cushions on the sofa and the chairs were set outside in the sun to air. And while Ben was out Tim asked his mother for some of her special soap to add the familiar fragrance.

Michael, Betsy, and Clarinda gathered around and admired the work Tim had applied, and the small changes he'd wrought. Michael was envious of Tim's new arrangement but was gallant enough to be highly supportive and complimentary. Clarinda eyed things differently, hoping fervently that she would be asked to be the lady of the new home. She and Tim had played new love games immediately after he had told her about his gift. They'd run to Ben's house to check it out. She'd parade through the kitchen acting like a playful maid asking "And how would you like your eggs cooked this morning, fine sir of the manor? Will his lordship be wanting the carriage to travel into town?" They'd laughed and he'd thrown her down on the bed and tickled her sides until she could stand it no further. He'd pulled her up and whispered: "I liked the view under your skirts," whereupon she turned him around and delivered a soft kick to his backside. "Behave young man. I'll tell you when you can take liberties."

The romantic in Tim had good things planned. The whole village had stayed up for the New Year's Eve celebrations. Being the start of the next century, the main bonfire pile of wood was larger than ever before, and several folks had procured clandestine fireworks. The grass had been flattened for a dance area and a small stand of low wooden crates put in place for the accordion, fiddle, and mouth-organ players who would emerge after a few drinks. Tables of food and drink were nearby with nearly everyone contributing something. Clarinda had baked some biscuits, and Tim donated a flask of brandy.

The rain had held off and the whole evening had been a terrific success. The music had brought almost everyone onto their feet dancing or clapping in tune. At midnight they lit the giant pyre and set off the fireworks. The heat warmed them all, and as the coals settled, folks lay in the grass close-by, watching the flames and embers sparkling in the darkness.

Tim pulled Clarinda into a spot outside the main circle and whispered: "Happy New Year, my lady. I have a gift for you." He handed her a tiny parcel wrapped in soft leather.

She carefully opened it and held the small object up to the light. "I know what it is, Tim. It's an amulet. And it's called The Excalibur, representing King Arthur's times. Oh, it is so delicate.

Is it silver, Tim? Where did you get it? I love it. Thank you, thank you. I shall treasure it forever. I must buy a chain to hang it around my neck." She hugged and kissed him and he struggled to tell his story.

"About a year ago I was sailing home from the secret cave when another small boat with an oriental man in it came in from the Channel. He was off a freighter carrying exotic cargo to London, and was on his way into our harbour. He showed me some of the things that would be for sale on his big boat. One of them was this very talisman. I thought of you immediately and I followed him into our harbour, got some coins, and bought it there and then. And yes, it is made from silver. It's very delicate so be careful. I'm so glad you like it. I've been saving it for a special occasion."

"You are just so thoughtful, Tim. And this is indeed a special occasion. How wonderful."

"Well, I hope to make the occasion even more wonderful, Clarinda. You see, I talked to your father yesterday and he gave me his blessing to ask you to be my wife. Will you let me love you forever, and come live by my side and bring us children we would cherish? I'd be the happiest man alive here if you would say yes."

"Oh, Tim! You know there's nothing I could want more. Yes, yes, yes. I would love to be Mrs. Bartlett. I do love you so." She leant forward and smothered him with kisses. "We must find my parents and your mother and Ben, and Michael and Betsy and all our other friends, and tell them the news. Come on, follow me."

Part Two

9.   Cell Llife

The metal door clanged behind him as he was pushed once again into the moldy cage. It seemed he could argue until blue in the face and nothing would change.   It was a pure accident; why couldn't that be recognized? He didn't deserve this at all.

"Welcome back, cobber. Looks like you failed again. Don't you get it yet? We're just like animal fodder for the wealthy citizens of the country. To be hidden away and dispensed with as quickly as possible. When will you realize? Look at me. I stole a man's handkerchief in a dare. I probably had more money on me than he did at the time, but look what I got. I didn't need to pawn the damned piece of cloth in order to buy food. But here I am. Sometimes I think the constabulary is just too eager to meet quota. No empathy or understanding at all. What is my wife doing now, with no money coming in from my job? And where are my two mates who were in the dare with me? No help forthcoming from them. They make me sick. Clearly they could care less. I'd thrash them within an inch of their lives if I ever caught up with them. Fat chance of that, of course. Same for you. Get used to it, mate. Neither of us will be going home unless we do something stupid and then it will be in a pine box."

"Ahhh, shut up, Lennie. You are a pain in the back end. Try to think as if there might be hope. Maybe one of our gaolers will take pity of us. Maybe the judge will die of smallpox and we'll be set free. Maybe a smart lawyer will come up with a new argument, or maybe a priest will appeal to the human side of the police."

Lennie laughed. "You don't believe that bullshit for one second, I know. How long has it been now? A full month you've been stuck with me in this cell and I have no idea where you were before. The chances of any of those brilliant ideas happening is about the same as an earthquake tumbling the walls and letting everyone go free. Just ain't gonna happen, friend. No way, no how. If you want to think positively as you say, I'd be practicing your words for the judge. See what appealing idea you can come up with. I'll listen and tell you how you are doing. Not that anything you say will have any impact anyway. You stabbed a man. That's life for sure if you don't hang."

"Such a cheery soul they gave me for a room-mate. How long before the judge arrives? Have you heard? Do you know what town he's in at the moment, how far away he is? Has anyone escaped from this gaol, I wonder, or the courtroom itself? Sure would be nice to see the sunshine again. And to shave. This beard is scratching me and driving me crazy."

"So your beard is driving you crazy. Unbelievable. What do you think this is, a fine hotel? You are lucky you haven't been whipped yet. Twenty lashes or more. Must be some regard for you upstairs. Nearly every other man in here has felt the cat. I have. And simply because a guard didn't like the way I looked at him. Miserable oaf. Not worth spitting on. Go on, tell me your story one more time and I'll see if I can catch any glimmer of hope. I've got plenty of time in here and I'd rather keep awake so I can see the rats running over my shoes than simply feel them in the dark after lights out."

"Have you even heard of Polperro, Lennie? It's a fishing village about twenty-five miles west by south-west of this famous city. To think that Captain James Cook, and Admiral William Bligh, two great sea-men who discovered and mapped so much of the South Pacific Ocean, sailed from Plymouth Sound to here. I'll warrant that they probably had never heard of our village either. So be it. We fish pilchards—big sardines—and pack them in hogsheads with salt as preservative and ship them to the big cities. It's a hard living but we augment our limited income with one other activity—smuggling in European and Oriental foods and commodities. Like tea and brandy, which have heavy import taxes applied otherwise. It's risky business because the penalties on being caught are horrendous—the King doesn't like being deprived of revenue. I'm the latest victim."

"Sort of ironic, isn't it, chum? Right from next door to your village those two men you mention had a lot to do with Australia, right? If you don't hang I bet that's where you'll be going. Me too. Too bad. Bligh had that mutiny thing going, but Cook was a discoverer, right? Might have been a lot more fun to have travelled with him."

"I wasn't even born when he discovered Australia and Botany Bay in 1770, Lennie. But if I can't get out of here I fear you may be right and I'll be sent there anyway. Arrrrggghhhhh!

"But back to my story. I think for once that the King's dragoons finally outsmarted us. My suspicion and that of others was that they had paid someone off in our village to inform on us, as they hadn't found any other way to catch us. I remember it was almost exactly a year after I got married that we had some visitors from East Looe come to the village by boat. We usually traded goods from our carts in West Looe, as it was a long way around to cross the Looe River to the eastern part of the town. So we didn't really know the folks from that side of the river.

"This family that arrived wanted to move further down the coast they said and so we let them rent one of the unoccupied shacks up on the west cliff to see how they'd fit in. Turned out James was a pretty good fisherman. Taciturn, rarely smiled, never went out of his way, but did his share. There was a small girl but we never saw much of her. Always clinging to her mother's skirts, thumb in her mouth, face dirty, clothes old and ill-fitting, hair a mess. We felt sorry for her but her mother, whose name was Ruth, kept very much to herself. Good reason, as we felt he was a wife-beater when he got into the grog. We'd hear a woman screaming every once in a while and when Ruth did appear she always had a scarf around her face. I remember one day it blew off in a strong wind and the womenfolk on the wharf noticed lots of bruises on her cheeks and neck. Never did understand men like that."

"He sounds like a lot of men I've heard about. There must be something else that made you wonder about him though."

"You are right. At some point we realized small items had gone missing. A coil of rope, a landing net, a shovel, a small statuette from the church hall. No one had seen James pilfering but we were pretty sure. Every now and then he'd take off alone in his boat early morning before anyone was about, and be back at end of day. We figured he'd taken the items to sell back in Looe. It was on those days that we'd see more of his wife. She and her daughter would come down to the docks. One time when she was there a couple of us checked in his hut and found nothing incriminating. But our suspicions remained strong and we never totally trusted him again, as you'll hear.

"The issue was that he contributed well to the pilchard catch and was a natural on the boats, so we let him be. It was last month, October, when something very odd occurred, however. At least it was odd in the view of many. I remember the timing well because my wife had just told me she thought she was with child and I was as happy as could be because we'd been trying for a while to have a baby. It was a Sunday morning and I immediately went down to the docks to tell my mother and uncle, who were sitting out having their usual morning tea together. Clarinda had already confided in her mother. This small boat came through the outer harbour late morning and pulled up by the sea wall. The sailor had come off a Chinese cargo ship that was heading for London with a load of silks, tea, and oriental spices, temporarily anchored out in the Channel. We'd actually done business with the shipping company before, which is why this chap was visiting. No one had brought in any smuggled goods from Guernsey for a while as we knew the Revenue men were working around Cawsand and Kingsand, so we were waiting until they decided to go much further afield towards the Falmouth area, which was their usual pattern.

"As much as we were all a little nervous, we thought a good load of tea would be very helpful to our village bank account, so one of the boat owners with two crew members took his sloop out to bring back twenty or more cases to be sold inland. Soon after he'd gone James left in his boat. Not that unusual as he often went out on Sundays, but he seemed a bit more hurried this time. I didn't think that much of it, just put it down to his wanting to beat the tides. Turns out that others also had noticed and on recollection thought it more strange than I did.

Ramon and his crew came back about four hours later with a nice haul of cases of tea. We worked hard at unloading as the tide was going out quickly. We got them all off except the last three, which remained on the deck waiting for the morrow's high tide."

"Wait a minute, had this James fellow come back?"

"Oh yes, he was there, in fact he helped with the unloading although he seemed hesitant – this was the first time we'd let him join in helping with any merchandising run, but we needed the manpower.

"We were all feeling pretty good when suddenly ten redcoats appeared on horseback and our spirits sank. What rotten luck, especially with three cases of tea still obviously sitting on the deck of the sloop. And in fact five other crates were still dockside and hadn't been transported to our hidden storage spot yet. We knew we were in deep trouble, and the lead lieutenant of the group made it very clear.

He marched to the five crates and stood on one of them."

"'This is illegal contraband as you are well aware, and the King does not look favourably upon those who would deceive him. We will be assessing the tax due on these and any other crates we find, you scum, and then doubling the amount as penalty. Furthermore, the perpetrators will be detained at his majesty's leisure. I advise you to identify them immediately or we will conduct a search of the village and make young children tell us what we want to know.'"

"Such an incredible uproar followed, with mothers particularly shouting against this threat. A large group of them rushed forward to where the lieutenant was standing—hoping to dislodge him from his stand—but the other dragoons formed a protective ring and the women were pushed back. I will admit, when it comes to children, the women of our village are incredibly protective. Any abuse of children above and beyond the norm is one of the worst sins possible. Offenders are ostracized immediately. I think it startled the King's men to come up against such vehemence. A couple of them looked very uncomfortable.

"In any event, similarly to an incident years before, Ramon bravely came forward and was seized roughly by the guards. We all knew what was coming next. The lieutenant would want to set an example, and before we knew it, Ramon's jersey and shirt were pulled off and he was tied over a railing on the dock.

"This enormous brute of a fellow ripped off his red jacket and from nowhere produced a nasty looking whip. Not a cat-o'-nine-tails, but something just as ugly and evil and murderous. A whipping was totally unnecessary and beyond any need. Ramon had come forward voluntarily, knowing he would be taken off to gaol. But the lack of success this redcoat group had been having with detecting smugglers had increased their frustration and they aimed to relieve it in their own ways. We were all sick to our stomachs. The lieutenant kept on raging like a maddened bull about how punishment was deserved and would be administered to his satisfaction. He berated us all in mocking terms.

"I couldn't stand it anymore. I was standing just behind one of the dragoons. Without thinking I pulled the knife from his scabbard and ran to Ramon, and quickly cut the ropes tying him to the rail. Others apparently saw me and jumped in front of the redcoats, stopping them from coming forward. But the big brute with the whip was still there holding the weapon in his hands and looking at me with the most malevolent eyes I'd ever witnessed.

Hate just poured out and I could see him thinking how he was going to cut me into little pieces. He brought the whip down, but I moved aside and it went between Ramon and me, thank heavens and caught around the rail. That surprised him and as the end of the leash wrapped tighter around the railing he was pulled a little off balance, and was propelled forward straight at me.

"You can guess the rest. He fell directly on to the knife I was holding, which sank into his chest as he went down half across me, half on the stonework. Everyone, including the dragoons, was stunned. Even their leader said nothing. Just stared at me with the same sort of hatred I'd seen in the eyes of the man with the whip. More of our men had now gathered and far outnumbered the redcoats. One of them picked up the whip, and several had followed my lead and pulled the knives from other soldiers' scabbards. Two Revenue men had raised their firearms and fired shots over the crowd, but our young men swarmed them and wrestled the rifles away. Suddenly, we were in charge of the situation, not the redcoats. We made them stand on the edge of the dock, backs to the sea, where it was at least a ten-foot drop to the sand below. Such a sorry looking lot.

"Some women had moved over to tend to the big brute who was stabbed, but it was too late. He was dead. There was no denying my action had led to his demise, although there were plenty of witnesses as to exactly what had happened. They knew I had definitely not stabbed him deliberately. But, no matter how you looked at it, it was an awkward and confused situation we were in."

"Oh my, what a problem. What on earth did you do?"

"Thank the Lord there were cooler heads around than mine in the village elders, who got together and formed a little council. After about thirty minutes of deliberation they came up with a proposal which our defacto leader, a senior named Graham Jenkins, presented to the lieutenant. I don't remember the exact words he used but the gist of it was as follows. Six of the dragoons, along with the dead man, would be permitted to go back to their quarters in Looe. Three men would be held at Polperro for security purposes. I would be sent with the six redcoats, along with five men from the village to safeguard my welfare and to ensure the situation was appropriately and adequately explained to the authorities. A lawyer would be hired to represent me. The village would pay the appropriate fines on the eight cases of tea identified. The captain of the vessel that had brought in the tea would be allowed to stay in the village without being charged.

"Frankly it was an outrageous and audacious proposal to put before authorities. Usually one is in no position to bargain, let alone dictate a process with them. The lieutenant was going red-faced as the elder talked to him, and eventually exploded. 'Who do you think you are to tell me what I will and won't do?' he yelled. 'We are the King's men with full authority to uphold the law on tax receipts. You cannot bargain with us.'

"Meanwhile, I'm of course shaking at the knees and my wife is hanging round my neck crying her eyes out, anticipating I will be going to gaol or worse. I'll come back to what happened to me in a bit.

"Our elder very calmly continued: 'Lieutenant, you know, and I know, that you have no authority to exact punishment. That is the courts' mandate. But here you seem to feel you are above the law and can do what you want. But all you can legally do is assess the situation and apprehend potential criminals who have the right for a trial. We are volunteering to send an upstanding member of this village with you, and are not avoiding the notion of some responsibility for the events that have occurred.'

"'Irrelevant. I could have you all hung, you ancient venom. This will not do. We are the authorities, not you.'

"'Oh my,' said the elder. 'I thought we were offering you a realistic compromise that both maintains your integrity and has us face our responsibilities. I really am very sorry if you don't see it that way. I forgot to add that the three men who remain here will be treated respectfully and not hurt and will be released with payment of the appropriate fine when you return with our men. Do you still find this suggestion unreasonable?'

"'Yes, you ignorant peasant. We shall have none of this. I demand you and your men step back and let us go immediately.'

"The elder was unfazed. 'Perhaps I should point out something more, lieutenant. We are all sea-faring men, not peasants per se. The sea is our second home. A couple of your group look like they might be sailors, but the vast majority look like they are more comfortable on horseback than they would be on the heaving deck of one of our boats. That's obvious from the way they keep looking behind them and shuffling their feet at the dock's edge. Men who can't sail and can't swim really are at very high risk on the seas out in the Channel, especially when storms are brewing. You're probably aware of men lost out there whose bodies have never been recovered. If ten horses even managed to make it home rider-less, don't you think the presumption would be that the riders fell over a cliff edge or into a harbour and were washed out to sea with the tide?'

"'You miserable, ridiculous cur. No one would believe you for an instant.'

"'You may think that, and you are welcome to do so, sir. From the looks on the faces of your men I don't think many would vote with you. And in any event, we would deny that you were ever seen here, were anyone to ask. I wonder if we should see how your men feel.'

"'Be quiet, you insolent dog. I shall see you in irons for this.'

"'I've tried to peacefully offer you a solution, Lieutenant, but it seems you are either a total imbecile who doesn't recognize his position or you think bravado in front of your men will intimidate us.'" Turning to the villagers behind him, the elder called for my best friend, Mike Morrisey, to come forward. 'Mike, I think some limited persuasion might be necessary. Can you oblige?'

"And with that Mike pushed a large broom against the chest of one of the men in line who turned and screamed as he pitched to the sand behind.

"'Lieutenant, I don't think he's hurt much. A few bruises perhaps and an ego sorely dented. But notice how the tide has already started to come back in. Somehow I don't think anyone will help him up any of the steps to the wharf or dock. Can he swim, do you know?

"'Perhaps,' the elder continued, 'I should add that we are all patient people. We men wait hours for the fish to fill our nets, the women wait hours for the boats to return. We've sent men to take your horses back topside and look after them, and I know those horses can also be patient. But I suspect it won't be long before some of your men need to pee at the very least. In fact, it looks like a couple have passed that stage already. Would you like to hear my terms again so you can agree to them in front of your men, or shall we just wait a bit more until extra persuasion is required? It's up to you.'

"Finally the situation seemed to register with the foul-mouthed lieutenant. He asked to hear the arrangements again. They were re-iterated and it was made clear that no negotiation was possible and that any form of retaliation would create rebellion among all the sea-faring ports, which would provide increased harassment to the Revenue men's efforts. Our leader ended by saying: 'We've shown you we are just men, but confident enough to stand up to you. We could just as easily have turned on you with our numbers and had each of you flogged, but we didn't. The whip will be confiscated and chopped into pieces. The message of this exchange will spread quickly along the coast, so be careful how you respond. I will just add that we sincerely regret the death of your comrade, which was clearly the result of an accident. We hope the judge will also see it that way.'

"It was not a good time. Ramon came up and volunteered to go with me since he'd been the one to bring the contraband in. But the village didn't want to send two men away to court and there was no way I could avoid going, since the man would not have died had I not picked up the knife and used it. We felt pretty confident I would be let go since his death was clearly an accident, so we kept to the deal as proposed. My wife, of course, had her doubts, and she continued to weep and wail. I think it hurt doubly since she'd just told me she was pregnant. I tried to comfort her but frankly I was feeling scared myself. What if I got an unsympathetic judge? What if the Revenue men had more influence in the courts than we realized? How long would it be before the next Plymouth Assizes? Lots of questions. No answers.

"While I was trying to comfort my wife and be brave for myself, things were being organized. Three dragoons, including the one down on the sand, were taken away and locked in a shed. Five men volunteered to travel back with me to Looe, and then on to Plymouth. But something else was going on and it took me a while to realize what it was. There were still a lot of men on the dock, both young and old, and a few of the older women were in the background. The newest man, James, was in the centre of the throng, and it was evident to me he was being prevented from leaving. His wife was at the back waiting for him. Suddenly he was pushed to the rail where Ramon had been tied, and Graham, the soft-talking elder, stood in front of him.

"'James, this village can't stand wife-beaters. You've contributed to our catches and received appropriate payment in response. But your time is up. Not only because you abuse your wife, if that's what she is, but also because you are a thief.'

"James started to sputter and tried to move away but he was hemmed in. Graham turned to the women at the back by the shops and called out: 'Bring his woman here.'

"She was brought out crying and made to stand beside James. They didn't touch. And now old Graham's voice got angry.

"'Not only are you a thief and a woman abuser, but you are also the lowest form of human possible. A traitor!'

"At this there were a number of strong unpleasant murmurs among the men. Obviously they'd all come to the same conclusion I had.

"'It was you who sailed off today and informed the authorities about the tea coming in. For that there is no redemption. The people who took you in, worked with you, shared their boat and hut, and tolerated your indiscretions have been betrayed. You are as worthless as any old crab on the rocks that is fodder for the gulls. You will leave here immediately. You may take your boat, for we never want to see it or you again. Or, if you prefer, you may travel back with the lieutenant to claim your filthy bounty. If you do we will burn your boat.'

"Turning to the woman he continued: 'As for you, lady, we have no grudge against you. If you wish you may in fact stay here. You can remain in the hut rent free for a year, after which you will be expected to contribute. We shall also expect you to become a full member of the village by helping with the pilchard processing like everyone else. Your girl may go to school.

"'Or, you and your daughter can stay with this man. It's your decision.'

"Huge tears rolled out of her eyes and down her face and onto her pinafore. She held her face in her hands, but through the sobs she plainly said: 'Thank you. I choose to stay.'

"At which point the village women bundled her away, taking her back to her daughter, who'd been left behind at the hut when the King's men came."

Lennie had been listening attentively but now interrupted. "Wait, wait a minute. How did you know for sure this James character was the one who turned you all in to the authorities in Looe or wherever? Surely you had no real proof?"

"Yes, and no. You are right in one way. We had no direct real proof, true. Unsubstantiated suspicions at best, but the timing of his trip back and forth, and the arrival of the redcoats, was just too coincidental. I didn't learn until I was on my way to Plymouth here that the nail in his coffin was actually provided by his woman. Once the redcoats arrived she confided in one of the village women that James had come home very agitated, and had beaten not only her but had walloped his daughter hard as well. He'd muttered something like 'I'll teach you all, including those would-be fishermen here who look down on me. You watch what will happen.'

"She was scared that he'd find out she'd reported his utterances, but she'd finally had enough, especially in light of how reasonably well the villagers had tried to treat her over time. Her story was passed on to Graham, who got input at the little council meeting, which is why it took so long. No one was surprised when she elected to stay.

"The final act of the night occurred when six men picked James up and threw him into the harbour. The water was about a foot deep at the dock by then, and he took off for his boat as fast as he could. Didn't say a word, just turned and ran. Had to push the boat out of the harbour. I had to commend the men on their restraint. I'm sure some would have liked to have caused him much more pain than what he received.

"So there's my story. I have no idea what fine was paid, nor when the last three dragoons got back. All I know is that I miss my wife and friends and hate this damned cell and the waiting. The police don't want to even listen. This is a rotten pickle, in my view."

Lennie scratched his beard, thought for a couple of moments, then declared, "One thing your lawyer will have to do is cut down the length of your story. I hear the judges are pretty impatient and have many trials to work through. If the dragoon had fallen on his own knife I don't think there'd be any problem acquitting you, although they may turn around and want to trade you for the captain of the boat that brought in the tea. They'd still view that as a crime against the crown. In a way I'm a bit surprised the elders didn't send him too. But no matter now. The thing you really have going against you is that the knife was in your hand when the chap fell on it. And you were interfering with the crown's work. Your lawyer will want to be darned good is all I can say."

Exactly how Tim saw the situation himself. It would be up to the lawyer and the judge in the end. Probably little he could do about it except plead leniency in the face of his wife being pregnant and alone. One more time, he questioned himself. Was I so foolish in trying to save Ramon from a lashing? Should I have stood by while that animal flailed him? I don't think so. I sure wish I'd dropped the knife after cutting his ropes. I sure wish lots of things. I wonder how Clarinda is managing back there. Hopefully she will come to my trial and I'll see her again. Meanwhile I should concentrate on surviving here, I guess. I wonder what fate is ahead.'

10. *Justice Wrought*

It was mid-December when the Plymouth Assizes were called into session. Timothy's case was scheduled as the third on the docket after lunch of the fourth day. He'd spent considerable time with the lawyer who had been hired by the village banker, and was pleased with his understanding of the facts and the arguments he was proposing to use with the judge. His wife and three villagers, plus Uncle Ben, Mike Morrisey and Graham Jenkins, were present and he'd spent a tearful reunion with Clarinda during the luncheon break. He was not surprised to see the redcoat lieutenant in court, accompanied by a small lady with five small children noisily complaining that they were hungry and tired.   His lawyer was most unhappy to see them and Tim wondered why.

The judge was clearly tired of hearing the cases presented through the morning. He had acquitted four of the prisoners and handed out sentences, ranging from seven years to death by hanging, to seven others. One of the death judgments was for a murder at one of the copper mines to the west.

The police had formally charged Tim with manslaughter based on the input from the Revenue men.

When his time came, Tim's lawyer responded to the description of the incident and the charges that were read out with an eloquent and impassioned recital of his own version of what had happened. He argued that to call the incident a stabbing was inappropriate. It was an unfortunate accident which the dead man had brought on by his own actions, as umpteen witnesses could be brought forward to corroborate. When he made a plea for consideration due to Tim's wife's pregnancy, the police prosecutor interrupted and yelled: "What about the dead man's wife? There she is with five of her ten children. Who will look after her and her kin now? Will she be forced to the streets and to set a terrible example for her children? Her plight is far more desperate than that of the prisoner's wife."

The judge nodded and Tim's lawyer had no rebuttal. It was at that moment Tim realized his fate was doomed. There was a poignant silence and a hush across the courtroom, broken only by a couple of tiny sniffles emanating from two of the children. The judge lifted his head and pointed directly at Tim. "A good man and father is dead. It was the knife you were holding that killed him. You didn't drop it, or try to prevent injury by turning away as he slipped. His death is squarely on your shoulders. The charge of manslaughter is upheld and you are sentenced to hang until you are dead.

"Case dismissed."

Tim was bewildered. His premonition had been correct. What would life mean now? He was ushered from the prisoner dock and allowed time to say goodbye to his wife and friends, but he was hardly aware of what was being said. His lawyer was telling him he would appeal and at the very least see if the death penalty could be commuted to life imprisonment. But it was Clarinda Tim clung to. Their joint sobs broke the hearts of the viewers, for the couple was well regarded and liked in the village back home. The final ignominy for Tim was to see the smirk on the lieutenant's face as he passed them in the corridor.

Just before he was led away he whispered to Clarinda: "You must show Mike our secret cave, because you will have to go there sometime. Remember the trickle of water coming in at the back? Right where it meets the cave floor I've buried a tin with money my father gave me long before we were married. Each year for my birthday he would give me several shillings that I suspect even mother didn't know about. He also gave me money from any profits due to smuggling. I often wondered if he knew he was not going to be long on earth to give me so much. You'll find there is a very substantial amount hidden there. Mike will have to help you retrieve it when the time comes.

"I'm sorry, my love. I do not know what is in store for me. Pray for me. I will pray for you and our baby. Perhaps if it is a boy you might call him Thomas after my father. But if it's a girl then you choose the name you like best. I love you dearly. I'm so sorry."

His words faded as the constables pulled him away and escorted him back to the gaol. He was thrown into a different cell, which was colder, filthier, and smaller than his old one. A burly guard jeered in his face. "Welcome to living hell, son. The next time you see sunshine it will be through a noose."

Shock and despair would not let Tim sleep. He even refused the swill that was offered as food, drinking only the meagre amount of water provided at the start of each day. There was no one to talk to, although he heard wailing from other cells further into the dungeon interior. He wondered what had happened to Lennie, whose trial was scheduled after his own. Would he ever see him again? For that matter would he ever see anyone he knew again?

Three days later he did in fact receive a visitor – his lawyer, who had somewhat encouraging news. Tim would not hang, as his sentence, along with those of many others convicted for life, had been commuted to life imprisonment through His Majesty's good graces. He was to be transferred that very afternoon to one of the floating prison hulks in Plymouth Bay, there to await transportation to Australia, where his term of imprisonment would be effected. He would never be allowed to return to England and would serve his time at the Botany Bay penal settlement in a manner to be determined by the authorities there.

What Tim registered most was that he would stay alive. He was so thankful that he vowed there and then to do everything in his power to live as full a life as possible, to help and thank his fellow man wherever he could, and to stay healthy, fit, and productive, no matter what. His lawyer held out one more faint hope that Tim clung to desperately. It might be the case that in time, he could send for his wife to join him in the new country. There was talk of allowing this by English officials, but no guarantees yet.

Accordingly, Tim was transferred to the hulk *Chatham*. Hulks were old retired navy ships, anchored along the banks of the Thames in London and at ports such as Portsmouth and Plymouth. As the prison population increased, it was decided to use them as gaols. Parliament had originally authorised their use for a two-year period in 1776, yet they continued to house prisoners for almost another eighty years. Generally a hulk was demasted, and the rigging and rudders were removed, as were any other features that might make the craft seaworthy. Inside, the decks were restructured to include cells for the convicts. On each of the decks which housed the convicts, a passage ran down the middle with cells on either side containing from ten to sixteen men. The cells opened onto the passage by means of barred doors in order to ensure that the activities of the convicts were always visible from the passageway. The cells were capable of containing from eight hundred to one thousand men. Hammocks were supplied in place of berths, which, through a slinging arrangement, accommodated the higher number of men if required.

The conditions on the hulks were terrible, especially in the early days, and far worse than in the prisons. The standards of hygiene were so poor that outbreaks of disease spread quickly. Typhoid and cholera were common and there was a high death rate amongst the prisoners.

During the day the convicts were put to hard labour. In London they dug canals or built walls around the Woolwich Arsenal, other days they drove in posts to protect the riverbanks from erosion, and on others they added infrastructure in the form of wharves, pathways, and roads along the banks. In Plymouth the prisoners laboured on fortification works. They received an issue of clothing, including shoes. Convicts could be punished for crimes on board flogging or being placed in heavy irons.

The officials were always keen to keep down the costs of these floating prisons. They wanted to avoid giving prisoners a better quality of life than the poor had outside the hulks, and accordingly the quality of the prisoners' food was therefore kept as low as possible. The monotonous daily meals consisted chiefly of ox-cheek, either boiled or made into soup, peas, and bread or biscuits. The biscuits were often mouldy and green on both sides. Two days a week, the meat was replaced by oatmeal and cheese. Each prisoner had two pints of beer four days a week, and poorly filtered water, drawn from the river, on the others. Sometimes, the captain of a hulk would allow the convicts to plant vegetables in plots along the banks. This attempt to add something extra to the poor diet of the prisoners depended on the goodwill of the individual in charge. In Tim's case, no such extra privileges were experienced.

Some leniency was shown at Christmas time, when batches of prisoners were allowed to receive family visitors on shore under watchful eyes. Clarinda came with her parents and Tim's mother and half-father. They started to reminisce about the incident that had led to Tim's demise but he shut the conversation down quickly, saying he preferred to leave alone what couldn't be undone and to concentrate on the future. Clarinda was into her second trimester and glowing, just the slightest mid torso bump evidencing her condition. The four adults promised to look after Clarinda and their grandchild and to write as soon as they heard from Tim in his new environment.

They'd all heard stories about Australia, as sailors and officials of the First Fleet, which had arrived there in 1788, finally returned and told their tales. Some were fanciful, some seemed more realistic. The only things consistent were the descriptions of the animals and birds and Sydney Cove and the Parramatta River. In some cases the aborigines were projected as pure savages, in others as helpful ambassadors of their tribes. It appeared that inland exploration was going on but that food production was unreliable and the penal system was being adapted from that originally planned. It was Ben who wondered out loud whether the uncertainty and newness of the culture being established might in fact provide unforeseen opportunities for smart, energetic men like Tim. How prophetic his words would turn out to be was totally unpredicted in the ensuing conversation.

The family promised to visit again at Easter when further dispensations would be permitted by officials. Those plans never materialized. In the second week of January 1803 Tim was summoned to the main deck before normal rising time, and placed in line with sixty other men. They were marched down the gangplank and along the shore to a small wharf. In groups of twelve they were then rowed out to a large barque, the *Coronation*, where they joined up below decks with another hundred men. They quickly learned that the ship would leave on the following morning tide for Australia. Tim and his fellow prisoners rushed to secure spots in the hold, although the more favourable spaces had already been taken by the convicts who had been boarded at Gravesend a week before. It was obvious that still more prisoners were to be boarded later as the guards and soldiers steered the newcomers away from an area near the bow that was partially walled off from the rear quarters.

It was late afternoon before they heard the arrival of the small delivery boat again. From the first voices raised it was clear what the partitions were for. The men cheered and whistled as eighty women were herded into view and taken forward. Most were in their twenties and thirties, with a few widow types and a couple that could be grandmothers. The males on board were generally ten years older, Tim thought. At twenty-two he was at the younger end of the age spectrum. There were a few youths around, and a couple of dozen who were probably aged around twenty, he figured, but most would be headed towards thirty or even forty. He wondered what variety of crimes they all represented. He'd probably learn much in the days ahead.

Many bemoaned the fact that they had had no prior inkling of their departure, regretful that they had had no chance to say goodbye to their loved ones. Tim thought it would probably be weeks before his departure would become known back in Polperro.

Sad, but recognizing that there was nothing to be done, he made himself busy getting to meet the men in nearby spots who would be his neighbours during the months ahead.

11. *Sea Incarceration*

With his years of sailing involvement, Tim was one of a select few who did not become seasick shortly after leaving port. He was used to being on deck observing the ocean surface ahead, anticipating the boat's movements in response to the waves, currents, and wind. Beneath deck he had to go by feel, but experience allowed him to anticipate and understand the boat's behavior better than others. He'd chosen a spot between two men who'd come from London and had had a week of acclimating themselves to the motion of the barque. They'd overcome their seasickness, for which Tim was very thankful.

Elsewhere, by the end of the first day in the Channel, newcomers were regurgitating their last meals and moaning in discomfort. Many turned ashen, and the quarters reeked disgustingly. The smell was bad enough anyway with elementary latrines contributing to the close-in conditions. Only those with cast-iron stomachs or the week's prior sailing behind them could manage the swill handed out for dinner. The sounds and wretchedness were just as bad in the women's quarters. Tim wondered how some of the women who were obviously pregnant were getting along.

On the second day out the boat's captain and surgeon addressed the prisoners, accompanied by the commandant of the soldiers whose duty it was to oversee the prisoners on a daily basis. Convicts were brought on deck in groups of about sixty at a time since it was impossible to address everyone simultaneously. Initially, after the prisoners had arrived on board, the guards had given them brief instructions. Now, using the captain's words, more 'detail' was to be shared. 'Detail' really meant the 'rules' of behavior, and the 'punishment' if the rules weren't observed.

The major difference now for all of them was that their prison floated and that small cells no longer applied. Instead, they were housed in large groups. They would continue to be under guard, as a militia troop had been expressly boarded for that purpose. Escape was pointless as they would be surrounded by miles and miles of ocean for as long as it took to reach Sydney.

The captain, Mr. James Clavell, then offered an interesting and unexpected perspective. He announced that his job was simply to get all aboard safely to Sydney in healthy condition. To that end he and the surgeon would insist that all convicts work with each other to ensure discipline and cleanliness, both of their quarters and themselves. They would be divided into 'messes' to help this come about. Select representation of the prisoners would be determined in the case of grievances. He and the surgeon would interview each prisoner individually and any with disease or illness would be inspected and treated by the surgeon.

Group behavior above and below deck would be watched and overseen by the Royal Marines. Punishment would be the province of the militia unless a committed crime put the ship in danger. There was a separate confined prison on board for offenders. Lashings and deprivation of rations were standard punishments. One of the men in Tim's group yelled out, "What about the women?"

The captain surprised them by quickly responding: "The same." His mistaken view, consistent with that of many authorities, was that convict women were the most depraved of all society's criminals, most in gaol after selling their bodies for survival. While untrue, it was the case that most had arrived at the boat in filthy condition, near naked in rags, having been held in prisons managed by male guards who did what they could to entertain themselves and to make their own jobs more acceptable.

The captain made it clear in so many words however, that as far as he was concerned, the crimes that the prisoners had committed onshore were of no interest to him. He would record behavior in his log book as required, but nothing would be added unless a prisoner misbehaved onboard. He then asked the surgeon to read out the rules.

Dr. Colin Keithly read from a pre-prepared set of guidelines for behavior and discipline. His seven basic tenets were:

1.   You are not to curse or swear, use obscene or filthy conversation, fight, quarrel, or steal from one another, use provoking words, or call anyone but by his proper name. You are to be respectful and obedient at all times to the officer and guards.

2.   Cleanliness being essentially necessary to the health, comfort, and well-being of every person on board, it is particularly desired that the strictest attention be paid to it on every occasion.

3.   Those to whom the management and care of the messes may be entrusted, are desired to be careful in attending to their duties, as they will be held responsible, and, in case of failure, punished severely.

4.   Anyone refusing to obey the directions of those who have the charge of messes, etc. will, on being detected, receive such punishment as the circumstance may deserve. A faithful report will be made of every man's conduct; and those who behave well, though they may have come here with bad characters, will be favorably represented.

5.   The prisoner that shall dare to break through the above rules will be punished in proportion to his offence; and anyone so offending must never expect to be recommended to the notice of the Governor of New South Wales.

6.   Consorting with the opposite sex below decks is prohibited.

The men booed and hissed at the final rule but in general seemed to accept the others. Copies of the guidelines were printed and placed in conspicuous places above and below deck, with the additional written threat that any convict found defacing or destroying the rules would be punished severely. The heaviness of the latter proclamation was balanced by Mr. Keithly's distribution of a number of bibles and prayer books for the convicts' use. Later, he sought out the fourteen convicts less than nineteen years old, one being only thirteen, and set up a school under the care of a convict appointed as schoolmaster.

The school operated for the whole hundred and fifty plus days of the voyage, at the end of which all the youngsters were literate.

The surgeon's theory was that by providing appropriate discipline and keeping the convicts active, it would not only limit them from dwelling too much on their past or the unknown future, but also provide healthy exercise. He was to insist on enforcing cleanliness in every part of the ship, including the prison, by having the decks regularly scraped, scoured, and washed.

The primary diet consisted of salted and preserved meat, ship's biscuit, flour, oatmeal, and dried potatoes. The usual ration of potatoes was six pounds per adult per week. Treats included raisins, sugar, tea, and coffee. The diet was coarse, monotonous, and offered poor nutrition, but it rarely ran short. There was an allowance of fresh water—just under a gallon per day. But water stored in barrels often deteriorated and could become undrinkable in a couple of months. Prisoners would learn to attempt to catch rainwater to drink or for washing.

Tim's interest wandered as the captain and surgeon made their speeches. The fishing fleet at Polperro had no ship anywhere near as big as this, the largest having only two masts. Here there were three. But the overall length was proportionately much greater and the masts much taller, with far more extensive and complex rigging and more sails of a totally different shape designed to catch the wind. Rectangular sails were hoisted aloft, several on each mast, with traditionally shaped sails at the bow and stern. He envied the freedom accorded to the sailors climbing the rigging to furl or unfurl the sails per the commands from the helmsman.

Just as his group was being herded to the stairway to go back below deck, the boat slammed into a huge rogue wave which first threw the bow up and then crashed it down into a far deeper than normal trough. The jarring force as the boat bottomed out threw everyone to the deck in bewilderment and surprise. One man fell headfirst down the hatch, others slid towards the ship's rail as the bow careened upward again but with the deck no longer horizontal. The captain and surgeon, being more used to the vagaries of the sea, were two of the first to recover, the surgeon rushing to the companionway in response to the screams of the man who had fallen through. Some of the marine guards had trouble getting up as their guns had become entangled with their legs. One enterprising convict had sought to grab one but was hit over the head by a fellow guard's gun butt and fell to the deck a second time, moaning heavily.

Tim had been bounced towards the second mast along with four others who had been at the fringe of the group with him. He looked up and was stunned to see a sailor twelve feet above him swinging back and forth from a thick line. The rope he'd been handling was now wrapped in a double tight loop around his throat and his own weight was preventing him from uncoiling it. Without thinking, Tim grabbed a nearby boathook and started climbing the closest rigging. As soon as he was high enough he reached out with the hook and caught the rope above the sailor's head. Using his strength, and with some help from the natural swing due to the boat's motion, he hauled the poor chap to the mast, onto which he immediately grabbed. Tim helped lift him with his free arm, so taking off the pressure the noose exerted on his neck.

The man's face was a brilliant red and his breath came in huge gasps as they both worked to loosen the coils which had left ugly burn marks. Two seamen had scrambled downwards from higher up and now helped Tim steady the young fellow and release him from his death trap. Close up, Tim realized the chap was just a lad, probably no older than eighteen. He looked closely at the rope marks on his neck and said, "You'll be okay, son. You were lucky your windpipe wasn't crushed. You'll have some heavy bruises for many months yet but in time they'll disappear." The four men carefully descended to the deck where the surgeon immediately took over and inspected the young lad. He checked the victim's breathing and applied a salve on the burn marks, coming up with a similar assessment to Tim's. "You are lucky this prisoner acted so quickly," he told his patient. "Another minute or so and I don't think you'd be with us anymore.

The two sailors who'd helped patted Tim heartily on his back and shook his hand. "Thanks, mate. You done good."

"Agreed," said the captain as he squatted down beside the surgeon. "What's your name, fellow?"

"Timothy Bartlett, sir."

"Well, you did a fine job there, Mr. Bartlett. Where do you hail from?

"Polperro, sir. It's a small fishing village southwest of Plymouth in Cornwall."

"Ah, I actually know it. My home as a young boy was East Looe. I am sure you've been there. You handled yourself pretty well on that rigging. I presume you've spent a lot of time on the boats?"

"Yes, sir. Although the biggest in our harbour was a two-masted schooner, not quite like this lady."

"We don't see many sailors among the convicts. How come you're here? Sell some bad fish?"

"Not quite sir. It's a long story."

"Right then." Turning away he continued, "Commander, bring this prisoner to my cabin tomorrow at ten o'clock, I'll do his interview then. Dr. Keithly, are the rest of that group okay? Any injuries that can't wait for your attention? I'd like to move on and get the next group up here to give them your rules."

"Lots with bumps and bruises, sir. A couple with lacerations. The man who fell down the stairway will need more treatment. I don't like what I see. Any chance to talk to your helmsman and the lookouts? We should have been prepared for those waves."

"Commander, get the next batch of convicts up here. Let's get this over and done with so I can check on my crew. You're right, Dr. Keithly. I want to know what happened too. Damn them all. More training needed, I'll warrant."

Tim was returned to his spot downstairs, where several men approached him with supportive comments for his good deed. "As long as you don't save any of the guards who get us in trouble," one of them added. "Them sailors have gotta get us to Australia, but those curs of guards just stand around thinking they are important. Too bad none of them got hurt." The sentiment brought forth nods and grunts of agreement. There was definitely a rebellious attitude among some of the men who'd been flogged by guards in land gaols.

The Londoner who had space immediately to Tim's left piped up: "You seem to have your wits about you, fellow. I suggest you be the leader of our little mess here. Anyone have any problem with that?" No one spoke up, and so it became so. Men from further amidships drifted back and helped create other messes in a surprisingly orderly fashion. Apparently the surgeon's rules and actions had had an impact. Tim had no doubt, however, that not everything would be smooth sailing in the months and weeks ahead.

12. *An Arrangement*

Early in the morning the guards handed down more pails, brushes, and bars of soap and indicated they'd be back in two hours with the surgeon to inspect the clean-up efforts. Tim was glad of the exercise. When stationed on the hulk he'd been working outside every day and his muscles had firmed up nicely after having gone a bit flabby when he was underground in the gaol. Scrubbing the deck and the stanchions wasn't quite what he would have preferred, but he did it vigorously, working up a sweat as he did.

Once their efforts were approved by the surgeon, several messes at a time were allowed topside for fresh air and exercise or relaxation as they chose. Guards were in position around the deck to maintain order. Tim moved towards one of the cannon emplacements only to find a guard blocking his way. "What do you think you're doing?" he gruffly challenged.

"I want to use the cannonballs as weights in my exercises," Tim replied. "I'm not going to fire the cannon or jump overboard. You're welcome to watch." The guard grudgingly moved aside and Tim looked over the monkey holding the balls in place. He knew that cannon-balls came in different sizes ranging from small shot at four pounds weight, up to the largest size at forty-two pounds weight. The ones on this ship appeared to be about eighteen pounds in weight, and five inches in diameter, able to be held in one hand. The balls were made of cast iron and were very dense. Launched from a cannon at a speed of nearly one hundred miles per hour, the balls could easily penetrate wooden hulls and cause massive damage to another vessel. Pirates were known to operate in the Atlantic Ocean, and so all the convict ships had protective armour aboard.

With a ball in each hand Tim started his squats and other exercises designed to build leg muscles and strengthen his abdomen. He was soon joined by others, although not many could hold the heavy balls in one hand for as long as he could. The guard watched enviously as Tim's strength became more and more apparent. After a twenty minute workout Tim replaced the balls and ran around the deck several times to warm down. It was a routine he was to follow whenever he had the opportunity in the journey ahead.

Just after ten am a guard came and collected him and marched him to the captain's cabin. On being ushered inside he found the surgeon and the marine commander also present, a somewhat daunting trio of authority.

"Sit down please, Mr. Bartlett," the captain intoned. "We've been reading what little we know about you, but we'd like to hear your story in your own words as there seems to be some small discrepancies in the recitals here."

Tim minimized any background and started with the arrival of the redcoats after Ramon's sloop had returned with the crates of tea. He was highly conscious while proceeding that the commander seated beside him represented the King also and so was careful in his choice of words to describe the Revenue men's statements and actions on the fateful day.

"So you maintain the death of the man with the whip was an accident?"

"Yes sir. Nothing was to be gained by killing a guard. Only more harassment and punishment. We lived in a peaceful village, taking our advantages from the sea and other opportunities as they arose. We were not bloodthirsty pirates, plundering for the sake of plundering. We eked out a living as best we could."

"Yet, you defied the law by trading goods without paying taxes," the Commander interjected.

"Yes sir, as I said, we were opportunists, like many others, and believed, as they did, that the taxes were unfair and deprived citizens of goods they wanted and needed. We tried to help our fellow man where we could."

"But you stabbed a King's guard in the process."

"It was an accident sir. He fell on the knife as he slipped. I made no move to thrust the knife towards him whatsoever, and I sincerely regret that he died. His wife was left with ten children to raise."

The surgeon spoke up. "You acted pretty confidently yesterday, Mr. Bartlett, grabbing that boathook and scrambling up the rigging. How many years have you been sailing?"

"Well, sir, I'm more of a fisherman than a sailor, although I did build my own boat which has both oars and a sail. I have no fear of the water and have been out fishing in heavy storms. When I was young, as one of the lightest in the crew I was often sent aloft on my father's ketch as lookout for the rogue waves, and to help us stay on course for our headlands. The rigging was not nearly as extensive as here but the needs and principles of sailing were the same." He paused.

"May I ask how the young lad is who got caught in the line?"

"Thanks to you he is alive and well," the surgeon replied. "He's only seventeen, one of the last-minute recruits we took on board at Gravesend. The problem is that the experience has soured him completely and he refuses to have any sail duty whatsoever. We understand, but it doesn't help."

"Which is why we're contemplating something highly irregular," the captain said. "We were short of our intended manpower complement when we left London, and unfortunately had a few crew desertions on arrival in Plymouth. We were able to find a few replacements, but many are younger and less experienced, like the lad who fell, than what we truly need. In fact we are short of sailors, cooks, carpenters, and animal managers.

"The surgeon and I have been working with the commander of the troops here on a new idea. And that is to 'borrow' select convicts with the right skills to help with our manpower shortages through the length of this voyage. We thought you might be a candidate to help out as a junior sailor."

Tim nodded. "Please tell me more."

"The overall idea is this. The smoother we can make this passage for all concerned the better off we'll all be. Some of us have to look after the vessel per se – the sails the ropes, the rudder the hull, the facilities etcetera, etcetera. But the vessel also serves to look after you prisoners. We need to feed you, and keep you healthy. To that end the supplies of food need to be managed. The sheep and cows and pigs and hens need to be fed, watered, and kept healthy. The cabbages growing in the soil plots need to be checked frequently. When stanchions or steps or hatches break they need to be repaired by a carpenter. Do you see what I'm getting at?"

"I see, sir, but what would it mean for me if I agreed to become a sailor under your command and not a convict anymore?"

"Well there's a bit of the rub, my man. You'd still be a convict. We can't change that. But for the extent of the journey while you perform appropriately you'd be housed with the crew and participate in activities with them. There'd be some minimal pay. On arrival in Sydney, or if problems occurred before then, you would immediately revert to your convict status. The commander here has the responsibility to deliver a certain number of convicts, and your name is on the list. The name can only be removed through death.

"However, as captain and surgeon we have to report the details of our voyage and our take on the crew and our prisoner wards to the officials in Sydney. The officials have to determine the disposition of each convict who arrives. Unless there's something unusual about a female convict the women will all be sent to Parramatta, where they will make clothes for the chain gangs. But men with skills and trades, 'mechanics', as they are called down there, are in demand. I assure you that good, supportive words from the surgeon and me can help you land a favourable position very readily with settlers who need skills at their plantations or in city residences."

"Ah, but what settler would need the services of a sailor and fisherman, sir? There must be a hundred sailors with experience already living in the colony."

"Possibly so. Maybe not. But first, they may not be fishermen, and food is desperately needed there. And you mentioned something a minute ago that I did not know but which could be useful. The last time I was in Sydney there were a couple of gentlemen who were about to start a boat-building business near Green Hills. They may well want to hire you."

Tim thought for a moment. "I don't see that I have anything to lose captain, except that I imagine the men downstairs will be very suspicious of my role. I doubt there'd be much trust, rather resentment at my treatment. Not that I'd be part of their groups anymore but it will be impossible to avoid them on deck."

"Absolutely correct. It will be up to the surgeon and the commander and me to make sure your position is understood. I think it will help if we also add others into similar arrangements. Have you been on board long enough to know anyone you'd recommend for any of the jobs I mentioned – cook, animal manager, carpenter etcetera?"

"One of the older chaps from west of London, Mr. Grant Higgins, used to run a mixed farm. He seemed far less temperamental than the others, not rushing to judgment, resigned in a mature fashion to serve his time. He's the only one I could suggest at this moment."

"Well, thank you. Remember you are on trial, Mr. Bartlett, but we wouldn't have approached you unless we thought you could contribute. Perhaps you could return to your spot, but the next time your group is on deck for any reason, seek one of the guards to escort you back here, and we'll introduce you to the crew."

Tim smiled. "Thank you, sir. I appreciate the chance."

With that, a guard escorted him back to the hold, where he sat for a long while with his head in his hands wondering at his good fortune, but not daring to say anything to those about him. Fate certainly had strange ways of making its presence felt.

13. *Wild Waves*

Tim's first test came quickly as the *Coronation* encountered a fierce storm his second day on the job. In response to the captain's bellowed commands he climbed to the lowest cross spar of the foremost mast and helped furl the sail there. The five men involved in that task then climbed higher and furled the next sail. Another team was already working on the topmost of the five sails —the smallest one. They all met at the third spar and quickly completed their task there. Two other teams were working the aft mast similarly. When done, twenty men moved aloft on the middle mast. At the same time other teams were reeling in the bow and stern sails. The jobs were completed as the rains grew in ferocity and swept the decks clean. Buckets and ropes went flying, and sailors raced to corral them and tie things down as the wind picked up. The hatches were battened and the animals locked inside their shelters. Sheets of canvas were pulled across the gardens and staked down.

The storm had come in from the west and relentlessly drove the boat more easterly than desired. The brunt of the rain passed in six hours at which time some of the sails were unfurled and the captain tacked across the remaining winds to get back on course. The next day they sighted the Madeira Islands of Portugal in the distance. A large whale about forty feet long was seen not far from the ship, and all those on deck could follow his track quite well for some distance. Grampusses and flying fish appeared during the afternoon, along with Portuguese men-of-war. It was an entertaining day for sure.

Tim made sure he obeyed all the rules and didn't flaunt his sea-faring knowledge even though he knew much more than some of the junior sailors from London. His presence wasn't well understood and there were a few men who avoided him, no doubt because of his convict status and the rampant knowledge that he was convicted for manslaughter. At the trestles where they ate dinner he made his mark in arm-wrestling, for there was no one who could match his strength. It was a harmless enough sport.

Even a couple of the more senior crew couldn't beat him, although most kept their distance, unsure of his temperament due to his conviction. They never heard his version of the incident, too uncertain and hesitant to ask.

And rather than become irritated with him, his neighbours in the hold seemed to think his presence upstairs might increase understanding of the convicts' needs down below. They were envious that they didn't have the same privileges but seemed to understand and accept his position. It helped that other men were also chosen to be part of the crew, with one immediate result – that the food served down below improved overnight. Tim wondered about fishing for fresh meat, but generally the boat moved too fast to throw nets out. Line fishing was the best option and he worked with several sailors to prop up lines off the stern, using heavy hooks on a few large preserved fish 'borrowed' from the cooks. Fortunately he was able to repay them with a porpoise caught one day and a small shark the next. Before cutting up the porpoise it was paraded on deck so that the convicts could see what one looked like. They'd seen them swimming and jumping through the air alongside the ship, but never up close. The fishermen kept up their efforts and were rewarded often enough that they more than made up for what the cooks offered for bait.

Just as the Cape Verde islands came into view they experienced something even the captain hadn't seen previously. And that was flying fish. The captain had heard of them but not seen any. The sailors yelled with mirth as flying fish flew across the deck in huge numbers. Some hit the seamen directly. Others simply landed on the deck. Pails were quickly gathered and fish loaded into them. The 'shower' went on for fifteen minutes, at the end of which there were twenty-five pails of fresh food taken to the cooks. Even the prisoners dined better that evening than any previous time on the trip.

As they proceeded south the weather started warming. They were heading directly southwest now towards the equator. Conditions below deck were not pleasant and the surgeon constructed air-sails to help bring air from above deck down the companionways. A brilliant sunset one evening provided false expectations because shortly after breakfast the following morning the clouds rolled in and heavy rain started to fall. There was no wind, so the surgeon allowed all the convicts on deck to wash off in the semi-warm water. It was crowded with one hundred and sixty men on deck all at the same time. Clothes came off and they were happy to be able to wash totally. Soap bars were handed out and passed from man to man. They laughed and sang and there was only minimal shoving as they threw their arms about, rinsed the soap from their hair and helped scrub each other's backs.

Some paraded with their manhood at full tilt, advertising their attributes to anyone who may be interested, but most seemed oblivious to the show. Camaraderie had never been so evident. The more astute ones then started washing their clothes, holding them horizontally above their heads to rinse, knowing that by mid-afternoon, given the heat downstairs, they'd probably be dry, assuming the rain would stop. The hardest task for the marines was getting the men to head back downstairs. Most of them hadn't enjoyed themselves so much in months and months.

Then it was the women's turn. They'd heard the men's shouts from above and were just as anxious, if not more so, to wash. They had no shame or embarrassment, stripping off quickly to take advantage of the rain, still coming down in bucketsful. It was a treat sent from above, literally. They were more social than the men and made short work of teaming up and helping wash each other's hair, since it was generally longer than the men's. Tim was on duty that morning, and from his perch on the lowest spar couldn't help enjoying the view below. The only thing he found disturbing was the state of the women's clothes. In essence they were rags. Very few complete chemises or dresses were to be observed, and even on, they hardly offered any modesty given their thinness and openness.

Like the men, the women rejoiced in the warm downpour, scrubbing themselves with vigour, and using makeshift combs to work the tangles out of their locks. One young lass with red hair reminded him of Clarinda and for a moment he felt lonely and abandoned. He'd experienced the loneliness a couple of times previously but deliberately didn't dwell on the past, as he knew he couldn't change anything. And he had his own dreams for the future—to save enough and bring Clarinda to Australia to be with him when he was settled. But the mass nudity, including young, firm, shapely breasts readily evident, and the slim triangular patches below with their secret delights, did cause a certain natural reaction. To stave off its impact he quickly busied himself climbing the rigging to a higher viewpoint where the view was far less distinct.

Each day at midday, as per regulations, the captain posted their longitude and latitude plus the distance they had travelled in the previous twenty-four hours. Their speed slowed and the heat increased. Tim headed for the stern and the steps on either side of the tiller where he knew individuals were recording their movement through the water.   Back in Polperro they'd just estimated their speed, as the exact number rarely mattered. He'd been told how speed could be calculated precisely but had never seen it done. It was time for him to learn.

The sailors at the stern held a wooden object shaped like a kite, and about the same size. It was tied to an especially long but lightweight rope that had a knot at every six feet, and was fastened at the other end to a reel. They also had a sand glass, or so-called egg timer, in which the sand took fourteen seconds to empty. The men threw the wooden 'kite' in the water, where it tended to stay put, like a floating anchor, and played out the rope while the boat moved forward away from the kite and the timer ran through its sand. Mathematicians had calculated that for approximately every four fathoms of rope played out while sands slipped through the narrow glass neck, the boat's speed was one knot. If twenty fathoms played out as the sands finished then the boat was doing five knots.

Tim's curiosity wasn't idle. For the last two days the crew had noticed sails on the horizon behind them. Their ship was in international waters hundreds of miles from land and the crew was concerned about pirates. On the first day the captain had had the marines fire every cannon on board to test their worthiness. All but one performed flawlessly. The commander of the troops also arranged target shooting practice. It was clear from the concerned faces on some of the younger guards that they'd never seen combat and hoped they wouldn't now. The ship following them was clearly gaining, and increased nervousness was evident as the crew all speculated on what country it might be from or whether it had any allegiance at all. The sharpest eyes were sent aloft with telescopes.

At about seven miles apart one of the lookouts declared he could identify a British maritime flag. An hour later a second lookout confirmed the sighting. Even so, nerves were still taut and the captain and commander ordered the marines to battle stations around the ship. What was most disconcerting was that she stayed on a path directly behind, never veering to right or left as would boats with an African or South American destination. Pirates had been known to fly the flags of friendly nations in order to maximize their surprise, and this was the prevailing assumption.

The prisoners were informed, and hysterical outbursts from the women became more frequent as time dragged on. The men seemed calmer, although many stood and walked up and down relentlessly to release their tension. Everyone wondered what would become of them if pirates took over the ship. Based on old tales from back home the men expected their throats to be cut or made to walk the plank. The women figured they would be raped and strangled or taken hostage for some unknown purpose. Many were terrified.

Finally, the barque that was following veered slightly westward and the crew got a better glimpse of its size. It was much larger than the *Coronation*, and had many more armaments. But it soon signaled its colours as a cargo vessel out of Plymouth destined for Rio de Janeiro. Tension eased throughout the boat and cheers were heard from the prisoners down below. A party from the *Marsden* rowed across the hundred yard gap when the two boats eventually hove to. The captain and his party were warmly welcomed and were offered rum and cold chicken, which they accepted gratefully. They'd left Portsmouth nearly four days after the *Coronation* had departed from Plymouth, but with the far greater sail area had made excellent time.

Tim was able to catch the surgeon's attention just as the visitors were preparing to leave. He hurriedly presented two ideas he had, and the surgeon brought him forward to meet and address the *Marsden* captain.

"Sir," Tim began, "I'm wondering first whether you have any spare cats. Our rat population is minimal but two of our cats recently died and we'd like to keep the rodents under control. Second, we are carrying eighty women convicts whose clothing is basically rags. I was wondering if you might have any spare material of any form in your cargo that we could purchase to help them out.   I know it's a strange request, but we have no idea what goods you might be carrying. For example, we could trade some fresh fish for a few bolts of English cloth if you had any. We have a little spare canvas but that's not exactly suitable for what the women need, and even if it were, we still have thousands of miles to travel and storms to survive where replacements may be warranted."

"Well, young man, I understand and commend your intentions, but we don't carry any cloth, I'm afraid." Turning to his men he asked: "Do any of you have any suggestions?" Silence and
"No, sir" were the immediate responses and Tim backed off, a little disappointed. He'd thought the cloth bolts had been a feasible idea.

"But we do have more than enough cats. If you want to come and catch some you are welcome to them. We won't miss a few." As the captain turned to leave, one of his sailors piped up: "On reflection, perhaps we might be able to help the women, sir. Now that I think of it, there are some cases of English tea in the aft starboard section of the hold that we had to cover with sheets before we left. When we were going to store cases of industrial fittings on top, the agent went crazy and insisted on covering the tea so dust wouldn't infiltrate the cases and destroy the purity of his product. Given the storms of the Atlantic and the battering the ships take, his concerns were probably valid. I remember he rushed away and came back later with twenty large muslin sheets in a cart pulled by a donkey. I wondered at first if he'd stolen them from a hotel, but he insisted he'd bought them for a few shillings from a warehouse further down the docks. They were the sort of large covers you drape over tables and chairs and other furniture in unused rooms in a large home. He said the cost was so trivial compared to the value of the tea that he wouldn't add it to his bill of lading, but make it up on a later consignment."

The captain frowned. "I'm not aware of this specific cargo sailor," he responded. "But if the sheets are serving a purpose I don't see how we could dispense with them in any event."

"Well, sir, I also remember that when we received the cases of industrial fittings only half the consignment was delivered. Apparently the wagon bringing the remainder from the factory had turned over when it hit a rut in the road and most of the cases were smashed. Because of that it turned out we didn't need to stack any on top of the tea. That tea is still there covered but the sheets are no longer protecting them in any way. Perhaps the covers might work?"

"Captain Clavell. Here's a deal for you. Send one of your longboats back with us with ten pails of good porpoise pieces and you can have the covers off our tea chests. One good meal like the lunch you served us will be well received by our men— we don't have the ability or the time to do our own fishing."

"Actually I'll go one better, sir," Captain Clavell replied. "We caught two porpoises yesterday. The smaller one is still wrapped in canvas with water poured over him so he won't dry out. You can have the whole animal. I'm sure we can afford that in order to make the women happier. It's a deal, and I salute you. Mr. Bartlett, please explain the situation to the cooks and tell them I'll be along to validate the order shortly. We'll have a longboat waiting for you.

"Good-bye gentlemen. May the remainder of your trip to Rio be smooth and fast. We wish you well."

And so once again Tim became a hero. It was becoming a habit.

14. *Unrelenting Heat*

The wind died and there were days when the boat was essentially stationary. The convicts' quarters, even with the ventilation chutes wide open, were oppressive. Women readily fainted, everyone sweated freely. It wasn't that much better on the main deck. Every sail was fully deployed trying to catch any breeze possible. The sails created shade spots but the deck planking was so hot it was hard to stay long in one place.

The newly arrived cats helped out but the next time one of Tim's convict comrades was on deck he sought Tim out and indicated they were now being invaded by cockroaches. Cockroaches had been in evidence since the first day out but tropical heat encouraged breeding, growth, and aggression. They apparently waited until nightfall before they came out of the cracks and crevices seeking whatever tiny crumbs of food were about. The mess leaders had led a specific campaign to get rid of the critters. As many as possible were killed on sight by a heavy boot, and during the day the floor was swept clean and food dishes were routinely washed. But it wasn't enough. Tim went and talked to the cooks and provided jars of sticky molasses to the prisoners. The syrup was laid on the floor where well-known cockroach trails were observed and trapped many of the bugs as they sought the sweet liquid. Giving up the molasses as food was hard, but it worked, and after five days the number of creatures seen had dwindled significantly.

In the forward section a young baby girl was born but lived only three days before dying of heat suffocation, despite the surgeon's persistent attention. This was an extremely sad happenstance and seemed to affect both male and female parents. Captain Clavell invited all those interested to a memorial service on deck.

The church service pennant was raised and the little girl was wrapped in her blanket and some heavy canvas. Weights were attached to the canvas, and she was laid on a plank suspended at the rail. The captain empathized with the child's mother, recognizing her sorrow, devastation, and sense of helplessness, then read a psalm of comfort. He asked the mother to step forward and state the name of her daughter out loud for everyone to hear. He then intoned,

> "We therefore commit this child's body to the deep, to be turned into corruption, looking for the resurrection of the body when the sea shall give up her dead, and the life of the world to come, through our Lord Jesus Christ; who at his coming shall change our vile body, that it may be like his glorious body, according to the mighty working whereby he is able to subdue all things unto himself."

At this point the surgeon, Dr. Keithly, tilted the plank, and the little body slid gently into the sea.

After the Lord's Prayer and the Benediction, the captain attempted to console the distraught mother with kind words, but nothing could really shake the despair she felt. A small set of friends crowded around in support, but there was little in reality to offer. The men in attendance were stiff and uneasy. The mother had carried her baby for over eight months through trying conditions in gaol and on the ship. Now there was only emptiness left behind. One second her daughter was still with her, in the next she was gone. Gone to a grave with no headstone, in a place never to be revisited. Her wrinkled visage would exist only in memories.

The burial bothered Tim more than he expected as he wondered how Clarinda was managing back home. He'd even lost track of when their baby was due and that bothered him more. He realized that attention to his job as seaman and focus on survival had dominated his thoughts for a long time, and he felt ashamed that he had forgotten his wife and family so quickly.

He was pulled out of his reminiscences by an unexpected movement of the boat, and he and others suddenly became aware that a northwesterly breeze had arrived. There were cheers across the deck and in the rigging as the boat fairly surged forward. They immediately changed course to the south and the next day reached that mythical line in the sea called the equator.

Ordinarily the captain would have held an elaborate ceremony in which King Neptune initiated newcomers to the Southern Hemisphere. The child's death the day before and the stifling heat of nearly one hundred degrees in the shade however prompted him to bypass the somewhat standard event. It was simply too hot still to spend hours on deck. The convict men asked the surgeon if he'd supply them with scissors to be used to cut each other's hair and trim back beards. Under supervision of a marine guard, nearly three-quarters of the men had their locks cut off, which helped substantially with tolerance of the heat but raised the specter of scalp sunburn. On hearing of the exercise a number of women also volunteered for the analogous treatment, although vanity over looks kept most away.

Perhaps it was the new chemises or dresses most were wearing that made them feel more attractive. The tea case covers received from the *Marsden* had been used judiciously to create simple shifts in various sizes. Under the leadership of a young woman named Laura, eight seamstresses had worked together to skillfully create outfits and coverings of various forms. They used the material sparingly, ensuring priority was given to those among the complete female population clothed in the skimpiest rags. Cotton thread was supplied from the boat's stores through Tim's insistence. In essence, the resultant chemises were underwear, but afforded comfort and decency better than some of the skirts and tunics they replaced. With impressive creativity the discarded bits of dresses and torn rags were turned into berets, belts, and even little slippers and ankle stockings. Many a newly dressed woman muttered her thanks to Tim in passing.

In general the women had managed their incarceration well. A month out of port one of the elder women had thrown a fit and had had to be restrained. She ranted and raved and threw objects, to the point that ultimately the captain had her removed to one of the isolated prison cells. She seemed permanently dazed and while the surgeon attended her diligently he was unable to make much progress.

Most of the female prisoners had been convicted of stealing, in one form or another. Their stories were dreadfully similar. Hungry, and jobless, when they didn't steal food directly, they stole money, or goods to pawn and buy food. They often teamed up in pairs to distract and pick pockets, or to lure men into dark alleyways with false promises of fraternization only to relieve them of their silk handkerchiefs or wallets and top hats. As the population in the cities had swollen from the flight of rural residents driven out by exorbitant landlord rents, job expansion couldn't keep up, and crime festered due to the desperation many felt.

About ten of the women had been prostitutes when picked up. They were the most vulgar and blatant about their interests, and an embarrassment to some of the others. But a recurring discussion among all the women was concern at the unknown fate that awaited them at the end of their journey. The prostitutes reckoned appropriately that the men in Australia would be no different to those at home with needs they could service. In fact, four of them boasted that they'd already been paid in rum shots by some of the sailors and would continue to do so. Women who had left husbands or children behind wondered if they would ever see them again and what sort of sin it would be to take up with another man in the Colony. From all the stories they had heard, having a man around provided protection and a better way to live than did staying single. Three of the more realistic women in that regard had already started developing relationships with men on board. Not with sailors per se, but with one of the cooks and two of the lead guardsmen. Their ideal was to be married onboard or soon after arrival and they schemed continually as to how they might effect those ends. True love seemed not to matter. Survival was the pre-eminent goal.

Just under the two-month mark on the seas the captain announced that they had reached the most western point of their journey. His charts showed that they were three hundred and twenty miles east of Recife, Brazil, at latitude 8° 14' south, and longitude 30° west. They would now head for the southern point of Africa running before the northwesterly winds which were picking up nicely. The slowest part of their journey was over, and while still hot, the temperature would slowly improve as they traveled southeast. It was a significant mark for crew and prisoners alike, although their journey was not even half over, and the perils ahead were as dangerous as those behind.

15. New latitudes

Nothing was really different. The water didn't suddenly change colour, the sky stayed blue, the sun rose in the east, and life on board was just as monotonous as before. Although on the second day on their new course a huge cloud started to build up behind them in the morning, heralding rain again. Everyone looked forward to its arrival. The fascinating aspect was that it was indeed a single dark cloud perhaps two miles across. There was a grey curtain extending between it and the ocean, covering a wide area that would clearly encompass the ship. Given the speed with which it approached the captain anticipated it would not stay long in the vicinity. He had the sailors round up every empty barrel and set them out to catch the fresh water, and in an unprecedented move, invited all convicts on deck at the same time to take advantage of the shower and the free wash coming their way. Once again bars of soap were handed out and pails made available. As the sky darkened and the first drops pelted the deck a great cheer went up as folk reached upwards and turned their faces into the wind and the misty curtain that suddenly enveloped them. The rain was fiercer than expected and the convicts quickly turned to let it pummel their heads and backs. But it was refreshing and exhilarating. Clothes came off and there was some playful touching between sexes that both parties enjoyed. And as suddenly as the rain had arrived, it passed on just as quickly. Steam rose off the bodies as the sun rolled out and the full pails were used to rinse soap out of hair and elsewhere.

The captain smiled at how successful nature could be in creating goodwill. The mood of the prisoners once again was euphoric. It was amazing how one twenty minute splash could offset the grumblings and malcontent that was the daily norm of prison at sea.   This was the second time rain had had had a soothing effect. 'Thank you Lord', he thought to himself.

Two hours after the storm had moved on another unusual event occurred. All around the ship there appeared small crabs – hundreds, maybe thousands, three to four inches across. The sailors on deck tied ropes on the pails and lowered them hoping to snare some. But the pails just bounced on the water and had no impact. Tim realised the problem and picked up an iron peg which he placed in his pail. The weight so added helped the pail drop beneath the surface and soon his bucket was full of the small creatures and he hauled them up. The process caught on like wildfire and soon bucket after bucket was bringing new food to the deck. Dinner that night for both convicts and crew was a treat.

The boat sometimes now made over one hundred and fifty miles a day running before the strong winds. The captain was pleased with progress. His ship continued to stay in good condition, the prisoners were well behaved and his crew was showing improved capability.   He wondered how long it would all last.

For nearly three weeks Tim had been aware of an apparent resentment towards him by a couple of the male prisoners. On deck they would look at him malevolently and pass comments under their breath about the favoritism he enjoyed. During the last rain shower one had thrown a bar of soap at him, catching him squarely high up on the back between his neck and shoulder. He checked with the surgeon, who told him that both men were from Wales and were murderers, two of the six on board. He decided he'd better keep his wits about him whenever the two were around.

As one would expect, not everyone got on well with everyone else. Few of the convicts knew each other before coming aboard and all had been raised in different environments and with different backgrounds. Plus, they came from all over England, with just a few from Wales and Scotland. There were no Irishmen on board. Their individual beliefs reflected the values they had grown up with as children and those they'd adopted after they left home. Many had come from rural backgrounds, and by and large were simple folk with hard-work ethics. None of the men would label themselves sophisticated, although most had a basic education and could read, if not write. Many of the women had been maids of some form or other, or farmers' wives. Many of them could neither read nor write. There was one pair of sisters who had been caught stealing money from a tavern and they were enrolled in the special school the surgeon had instigated. They seemed excited at what they were learning.

When disagreements arose and escalated, the men usually fought one another. One would invariably come away bleeding from the nose or from cuts elsewhere on the face, and would have a display of bruises for the following week. The two murderers Tim was watching itched to fight at the slightest provocation, and the others were wary of their taunts. Both were big and swarthy and packed iron fists. As much as possible they were avoided. It was impossible to stay permanently out of their way however.

An older prisoner, moving slowly, was in their path one day. Instead of waiting for him they kicked the man's legs from under him, causing him to fall and twist his ankle seriously. Voices of nearby squatters rose in protest but no-one offered to help, fearing similar treatment. Someone called the surgeon, but all he could do was bind the chap's ankle tightly and advise him to stay off it for two weeks. The surgeon had no tolerance for the attackers as he'd responded to similar incidents they had instigated before. He admonished them to adjust their attitudes and behavior or they'd find themselves in isolation. They scoffed in his face. The surgeon reported to the captain that the pair were born trouble-makers and that he feared they might get out of hand at some point.

Women, on the other hand, weren't nearly as vicious as the men although there were two prostitutes who weren't above scratching, spitting and pulling hard on the hair of anyone who crossed them. In the altercations that arose, among others it was name calling that predominated in spite of the surgeon's rules.

Some would get in their opponent's face and not back down until dragged away. Others would make snide comments of a derogatory nature, and keep at it for hours, annoying those not involved.

Despite Tim's intention to be ever vigilant for the two thugs who seemed determined to accost him, it was impossible to be on the alert every single minute of the day. There'd been signs of a good storm brewing all day and the captain had ordered the two topmost sets of sails furled on each mast and the bow and stern sails taken down. Evening had come faster as dark clouds moved swiftly overhead and Tim was busy setting one of the lanterns by the starboard rail when he heard his name called. He turned to see the big brutes heading his way. "Bartlett," they called again. "We'll have your head this time, you high and mighty prick. You scum. That's what you are. Think yourself so much better than the rest of us who have to live down below, while you get the captain's favors. We'll teach you."

Tim had learned to take the offensive when threatened, preferably before his assailant was ready. Which was what he did now. Before the pair could advance further, he hurled the lantern with one hand into the lead man's belly. Not that it was a dangerous weapon per se, but it had the effect of surprising him and slowing him down. With his other hand Tim reached behind, and unseen, picked one of the cannon balls off the monkey. He tossed this at the midriff of the second chap. It takes a lot to just hold eighteen pounds of cast iron, let alone throw it. Tim's regular workouts had only served to increase his strength, however, and the heavy weight ball slammed into the man's privates, dropping him to the deck shrieking in agony.

The first brute brushed the lantern aside and punched Tim hard in the stomach, knocking the wind out of him. Tim crashed backward onto the deck and his aggressor leaned over and threw another punch at Tim's face. Tim rolled on his side just in time and took the force of the blow on his left shoulder. It hurt, and as the big man pulled back readying another blow Tim rolled back again and delivered a hard kick at the man's crotch. Clutching his groin and swearing, he toppled on top of Tim, pinning him in place with his great bulk. As the man's face came up to gloat Tim drew back his right fist, straightened out his first two fingers and drove them as hard as he could into the bully's eyes. Unbearable pain registered immediately and he rolled off covering his face with his hands and howling like a banshee.

His accomplice meanwhile seemed to have found a second wind, and as Tim scrambled to his feet he felt two hands wrapping tightly around his throat. He didn't hesitate for an instant but quickly reached up, grabbed the man's two pinkies and snapped them back with a ferocious twist, breaking them at the first joint with audible cracks. The man staggered back, this time whimpering as he dared to look at his hands. Tim's shoulder ached but he had a new idea.

At the spot where they were fighting, part of the rigging to the mast in the form of a multi-strand shroud was anchored at the ship's rail. Practiced as he was, Tim jumped up and secured a grip in the netting where it angled upward to the first cross spar. Adding momentum to his swing he wrapped his legs around the neck of his attacker and hurled him six feet across the deck where his head hit the base of the mast and knocked him out.

Staying aloft Tim turned his attention to the blinded man who was now standing up, dazed and bewildered. Tim's anger had never risen to such a violent level before. He could have stopped and walked away, but he wanted to extract one last act of vengeance. Swinging again, he gained momentum and pummeled both boots into the man's neck, just under his chin. He went down with a thud and stayed down, not moving.

Tim was shaking from the encounter as he let himself drop from the rigging. It was as if he had made up for all the negative and unfair things that had happened to him so far in life. A purging of all the resentment and hate he didn't realize he had absorbed internally. The wrong types had gotten in his way at the wrong time.

Swinging from the rigging had only added to the pain in his shoulder and he held it with his right arm across his chest. He sat against the rail catching his breath.

Two militia men suddenly appeared from the bow area. Tim told them he'd been attacked by the thugs now lying on the deck, but had gotten the better of them. The soldiers were wary, wondering how one man had bettered the other two, but when they shone the discarded lantern in Tim's face and recognized him, they understood. They were nonplussed, however, as to how the two convicts had eluded being shepherded back downstairs after their exercise period. It didn't take long to find out as some of their fellow guards came running up. A younger guard had just been found dead, his body stashed behind a pile of crates aft of the kitchen. He'd had his throat cut, presumably with his own knife as it was no longer in his uniform.

A quick search of the man with the broken fingers found the knife tucked into his belt. Tim shivered at the find, realizing that he had been meant to meet the same fate as the soldier just discovered. Why the thug had decided to choke him rather than use the knife directly had been a bad choice. Perhaps the pair had planned to torture him a little before slashing his throat too. He shook uncontrollably as he thought about his intended misfortune.

The guards now became angrier and man-handled the murderers, dragging them roughly across the deck to the prison cells near the stern where they clapped them in irons. They reluctantly called for the surgeon to assess the rogues' physical state.

Tim was shepherded to the guards' meeting room where he was made to repeatedly tell how he had beaten his attackers. Once again he was elevated to hero status, as awe registered on many of the listeners' faces. He was toasted in rum, but eventually was allowed to repair to his own quarters where he quickly fell into a troubled sleep.

16. *Stormy weather*

The trip now grew even more monotonous, and crew and prisoners alike longed for something new and different, as much as they were making fast progress across the southern Atlantic. They were rewarded, in a sense, when a massive storm hit from the west in the middle of the night. The boat started rocking markedly as a major gust of wind tore at the sails. Prisoners were thrown from their bunks and articles of clothing and crude furniture slid back and forth across the floor. The ship heeled then straightened, then repeated the movements, only more violently. The plywood partition between the male and female holds splintered as two men crashed into it on one side and a stout woman did the same on the other side.

Topside, every sailor was woken, donned whatever protective gear he had and rushed out to furl sails. There'd been precious little warning of the storm and the winds were already far more ferocious than any previously encountered. By the time Tim climbed to his station, two of the sails higher up had already been ripped. It was slippery, dangerous work as the rain pelted down, driven almost sideways by the wind. Bits of hail were included and stung the skin as they hit. He and his team struggled mightily but managed to furl their sail and immediately climbed higher to the next one. The mast swayed perilously as they slowly but steadily hauled the sail down and wrapped it in the guide ropes. Each man was soaked through and could hardly hear the commands issued from below on the main deck. The men working above them shimmied past, racing to the deck to head to another mast. Tim and his crew followed closely behind.

One of the three bow sails ripped as the crew rescued the other two. It flapped helplessly in the wind, slashing against the bowsprit and the railing. The stern sails were rescued. Now the boat was completely at the mercy of the wind and the waves. The only positive aspect was that the wind was actually driving them east towards the African coast. The militia had helped by closing the hatches and ventilation shafts to the prisoners' quarters and by tying down anything loose on deck. They locked the animal enclosures although there was no doubt some would die from fright and the buffeting. This was a very serious storm.

It ended up raging for three full days, forcing the ship nearly one hundred miles off course. During that time only limited rations were served to the convicts since it was dangerous to move across decks to the companionways. Whenever they were opened a deluge of rain fell inside, drenching the folks anxious for food. Water flowed in through cracks in the deck anyway and the quarters were wet everywhere. Men and women alike were bruised as they stumbled into stanchions or slid on the slippery flooring. Cuts and abrasions abounded and the violent pitching had many feeling seasick again. They didn't eat and became dehydrated with the lack of fresh water.

The splintered partition separating the sexes drew attention on both sides and willing hands applied to the cracks pulled back the plywood and created large enough holes for people to climb through. Human nature being what it was, it didn't take long for sexual appetites to come to the fore. Some of the more promiscuous women quickly marketed their services for sale and had no embarrassment providing public fornication to men who could offer hidden rations or artifacts in payment. For the men and women who had spots near the partition it was a challenging time.

When the storm finally abated and the captain had assessed the topside damages, the hatches and ventilation shafts were re-opened and all the prisoners were allowed on deck to stretch and dry out. The sun was weak and shone intermittently between clouds. The breeze was sufficient to help blow clothes and hair dry in a couple of hours. Three of the fat lambs had perished during the melee so the captain promised a hot roast lamb dinner to both crew and prisoners. His announcement was greeted with loud cheers. Thirsty prisoners drank from a communal mug at the water barrels, and relief spread across the ship.

As the prisoners were being corralled to go below, a lookout called, "Ship ahoy," and everyone looked for sails on all horizons, but saw nothing. Two seamen climbed up to the lookout basket and came back with a perplexing tale. There was definitely something on the starboard horizon, looking like a giant floating hulk. There were no sails, just one vertical strut that looked like a short mast. But the visage was so indistinct that it was impossible to be sure of what they were seeing. Given everyone's curiosity and with no sense of any threat apparent, the captain permitted everyone to stay on deck if they wished. He steered the ship towards the floating object. An hour later and two miles distant he declared it was a small barque that was probably a victim of the storm they'd just been through. It rode low and sluggishly in the water, at the mercy of the waves and wind. The vertical strut seen from afar was a broken mast. As they got closer, another mast could be seen, broken at the base, lying at an angle across the deck. There was a pile of debris at one corner of the stern, but no hint of life of any form.

They maneuvered within one hundred yards of the hulk, and the captain asked for volunteers to take a longboat across. Four men came forward and rowed the short distance. They were able to throw a small rigging net onto the deck which was only about six or seven feet above them. On the third attempt it caught enough for one man to scramble up and secure it better, whence his comrades followed. The men were seen wandering off in different directions. One bent down and pulled open one of the hatches, but went no further. Another checked the base of the broken mast. The remaining two went back to the pile of debris at the stern and after walking all around it, started pulling it apart. Boxes, small crates, sections of rope, a sailor's shirt, and the carcass of a chicken were visible to the watchers but nothing of great interest. The cabins on the deck had been sheared off near their base and the men poked into what corners were left standing, again with no serious find. The four then went around and opened more hatches.

On the far side away of the hulk, away from the watchers, one man called his comrades over and then, with their support, stepped down a couple of steps into the companionway. Together they hauled a bloated body up on deck, checked the clothing, and removed a belt. Two of the men then went back to the stern and disappeared for a couple of minutes. The four regrouped, climbed in the longboat and returned to the *Coronation*. Their story was simple. There were a number of bodies in the hold, all male. Their dress suggested they were seamen working on a cargo vessel. The belt they recovered was of leather with a silver buckle engraved with a bull on it. At the stern, as best they could decipher, the boat's name was *Moreno*. They could see crates and barrels stored in the hold but the water level was well over the top of them and not enough light penetrated with the hatches open to see any labels or indication of contents. As the water level was still slowly rising they decided not to linger further but to leave and get back to safety.

The general consensus was that it was a freighter most likely out of Buenos Aries traveling up the coast possibly to Rio or some other Brazilian port. They'd never know for sure. A quietness settled on the group for a mixture of reasons. Sadness at the knowledge that many lives had been lost on the freighter, and the realization that they clearly had been incredibly fortunate to have survived. A few prisoners with ingrained sensitivity sought out the captain and thanked him for getting them through the perilous storm.

Not only did the captain and the cooks follow through on the promise of a hot lamb dinner, but the captain magnanimously offered rum to all takers as well. Perhaps the man wasn't too bad after all, many surmised.

17. Land ho!

In the southern hemisphere it was now autumn, although that seemed pretty meaningless to the travellers well east of Greenwich in the Atlantic.   The days rolled on.   Minor storms that lasted a few hours, not days, came and went. Some days the seas were rough, on others they were calm. Speed still kept up and one day in early April the first albatross was sighted. The giant birds were regarded as a signal that land was not too far away although the birds' range was hundreds of miles.   Day after day they became more prevalent until at last there were enough circling around that the sailors tried to catch one. They strung lines between the masts with dangling hooks, each of which held a good sized fish as bait.

Amazingly, the lines caught two, and the sailors were somewhat surprised that their ruse worked. The birds were laid out on display on the deck. They were the largest birds any of the prisoners had ever seen. The bigger of the two had a wingspan just over ten feet and weighed nine pounds. His chest was white, as were the undersides of his wings, although the topsides were brown. The bill was very strong, the upper half ending in a large hook. The feet had no hind toe but the three front toes were webbed. From the little the surgeon knew, the birds could stay airborne for days due to the way they rose and descended on the wind. They'd been observed six hundred miles from land.

The cooks offered them up to the sailors and guards but no one found them very appetizing. Enthusiasm for catching more waned readily.

But now making over two hundred miles per day, whenever the convicts were on deck exercising they would scan the port and forward horizon hoping to see a brown smudge of land. Just how far from land had these now-constant aerial visitors flown? At latitude 33° S, a bit north of CapeTown, the coastline finally came in sight.   The lookout's cry of 'Land ho!' reverberated around the ship as everyone repeated it. It had been three months since they left Plymouth and to know South Africa was nearby was rewarding, even though they knew they would not feel terra firma for a long time yet.

The captain warned them that once they turned east past the Cape of Good Hope the weather would gradually deteriorate as they entered the Indian Ocean, so they should enjoy what they could while it was available. He also warned them that rounding the Cape itself would be a turbulent experience and to be prepared.

By now Tim had become an experienced and hardened sailor, excelling at his job and on good terms with the members of all the teams he worked with. Most didn't think about his convict status, their judgments governed more by his reputation for strength and fighting skills. He never flaunted his strength with derring-do feats and refrained from requests to box with some of the bigger sailors. He would still arm wrestle but once in a while now he'd let one particular chap win with feigned indignation. All but one of the men were single, even the older ones for whom life on the sea had become more rewarding and fulfilling than life in a small cottage back on land. Several had left wives behind and had never looked back. The main laments of the men were the length of the journey and the absence of women.

'Absence of women' was really a euphemism for 'absence of sex'. With no strong family connections or interests, they took it wherever they could find it. Male to male relationships were taboo. With female convicts on board their creativity was brought to the fore. A number had found willing participants during the open-air exercise periods. In some cases women had even ended up in the sailors' compartments sharing themselves with several men, in orgiastic fashion. Their reward was usually glasses of rum, and a number were quite drunk by the time they had to return below decks. The talk of the men's conquests made Tim uneasy. On the one hand, he was married and it was now several months since he and Clarinda had coupled. In fact, by his reckoning he probably now had a son or daughter and that realization weighed on his mind. On the other hand he could feel the heat and desire rising through his body.

His team members sensed his hesitation and decided to help him out. As he descended from the cross spar that evening he found a girl waiting deliberately for him. "They tell me you are lonely," she offered coquettishly with a tilt of her head. "I'd be happy to keep you company for a bit. My name's Elizabeth. I've seen you around." Her approach was obvious, but as her hand brushed across the front of his britches Tim's resolve weakened, and he reached for one of her breasts. She responded by saying, "You can take me here against the mast or we can move up by the forecastle if you want, mister."

Tim's wants had become urgent with her simple goading, and it didn't take long to fulfill them with her help. During the whole encounter he said not a word, and it wasn't until he got back to his bunk that feelings of guilt arose. How would Clarinda respond if she found out? Would she rant and rave, or understand? Would she still want him? Were there past incidents in the village that could be precedents? He struggled to remember. And then he surprised himself with the obverse thought. What if, in her loneliness, she had another man? She certainly had enjoyed doing it with him until he had to leave. He wondered whom she might select if she did. Tormenting himself with various imaginary scenarios, he eventually dropped into a fitful sleep.

The delights of sexual pleasure, however, out-balanced the feelings in his heart and the thoughts in his mind, and for several nights following he and his paramour extended their tryst. Tim's mates encouraged him, but also suggested he might like some variety with other willing partners. He was ready to try when they started their turn to the east heading to change oceans.

The Indian and Atlantic oceans collide somewhere south of a line between Cape Pont, twenty-five miles south of Cape Town, and Cape Agulhas, one hundred miles as the seagull flies, to the southeast of Cape Town. Coming straight from Antarctica, the cold Benguela current flows northwards up the west coast of Africa, while around the east and south coasts the warm Mozambique current flows from the equator, and almost doubles back on itself when it meets the Benguela current.

Seafarers over the centuries have regarded the area as one of the most dangerous stretches of coastline in the world. Wrecks have littered the shores and rocks beneath the waves since the fourteen hundreds when Portuguese sailors first attempted the passage. Originally known as the Cape of Storms, the edge of the African continental shelf here contains a sharp drop in the sea floor that can cause rogue waves big enough to sink the sturdiest ships. The meeting of the two currents causes the waves to hit one another at oblique angles and then join to form a single, larger wave. Coupled with fierce winds circulating from the west, it is an area all mariners accord the greatest respect.

It was all crew hands on deck as the *Coronation* veered well south of the coastline with the wind behind her. The sails were full hoping to catch the maximum breeze in order to generate as many knots as possible. The main concern was the potential frequency and size of the waves ahead. Extra lookouts were added to help spot rogue waves or any other unanticipated issues as far ahead as possible. Not that they would be easy to avoid, but even being more prepared would make the transition less dramatic. As it was, the hatches and ventilation shafts were battened down and the prisoners were told to find something sturdy to hang on to. A rough ride over the next ten hours or so was fully expected.

And, true to legend, that's exactly what occurred. The boat was tossed around like a cork, the strong westerly providing the main force helping the boat retain stability and direction. Two huge waves came on nearly broadside in the first fifty miles, heeling the boat well to starboard and scaring even the most experienced sailors. The shouts and screams from below exacerbated their concerns. Through it all Captain Clavell stood resolutely firm behind the helmsman, radiating a sense of confidence that was an inspiration to all those watching. But it was a tense time. Hour after hour, eyes searched the horizon as well as the close-in distance ahead. Sometimes warning shouts would turn out to be false. It was when there were no warnings but a problem occurred anyway that was the bigger worry. A couple of smaller rogue waves went undetected in this manner.

They caused a stir below decks, as people not holding on banged their heads, but at least no serious injuries occurred.

Land could be seen to port for a while but gradually it receded into the distance as the coastline angled northeast. Night fell and the sailors were thankful that the moon was three quarters full and there were limited clouds. None of the crew was permitted to sleep. All eyes were needed to watch the waters ahead. The cooks kept up a supply of hot soups and bread, but no spirits were allowed. And all through the watch the captain stood calmly.

As the sun broke through, tensions eased, for the sea was running calmer and they were being propelled by both the wind and the Mozambique current. Part of the crew was sent to get some sleep, the remainder to check for any damage that might have occurred. The hatches were opened and the convicts allowed on deck in groups, although many stayed below and slept, having been awake for far more hours than usual. The captain set a course due east. Next stop – Australia.

18. Ice Cold

The winds were less predictable in the southern Indian Ocean. So too the storms. There could be none, or there could be any number including markedly violent ones. Some three hundred miles above the Antarctic Convergence zone where cold, northward-flowing Antarctic waters sink beneath subantarctic waters there are two islands discovered by Portuguese traders in the sixteenth century. Amsterdam and Saint-Paul are both volcanic, among the most remote islands in the world, more than eighteen hundred miles from any continent. The captain had hoped to use Saint Paul, the more southerly of the two, as a navigation check, but it was not to be. A hundred miles west of its location a rain-filled storm pelted them for two days and the accompanying winds drove them well to the south of their intended route.

The only positive aspect of their new route was the frequent sightings of enormous sperm and blue whales. There was a corresponding negative offset, however, in that it was cold. Two months earlier everyone had had a miserable time in the exhausting heat of the tropics. Now many wished they had more clothes to wear. Small isolated coal burners below deck were watched carefully lest they throw sparks, and full pails of water were maintained close by. But they never generated enough heat and small groups gathered around trying to get warmer. At night bodies would huddle together trying to conserve warmth.

The winds were so strong it was difficult to get back on track and the best Captain Clavell could do was keep an easterly heading. The prisoners received a shock one morning when the hatches were opened and snow covered the deck. Few ventured topside that day. Conditions worsened the next day as ice formed on the deck and the rigging, and visibility plummeted. Sailors were kept busy all day chopping the ice away and the hatches were kept sealed.

Ice was incredibly dangerous. Coated masts could become brittle and crack. As sails stiffened, their flexibility and usefulness decreased, and the overall weight of the ice added significantly to the weight of the boat, slowing down its progress. The presence of ice in the air also suggested that they could be heading for iceberg territory.   Appropriately wary and anxious, the captain tacked tighter and harder to the limits of wind and boat, and slowly, ever so slowly, over the next twenty-four hours, they moved out of the clutches of the foggy ice-storm.

There was no rejoicing. Sailors, and militia, were too tired, prisoners too cold. They were in the middle of nowhere where few boats had gone before. There was nothing to see, no sails, no land, no albatrosses, just a whale every now and then. The mood of the prisoners was one of defeat. Beyond resignation, they had given up. This was the worst period of the trip to date. Cold, no chance of seeing land for a month, food now tasting old, if not mouldy sometimes, they had been at sea far too long. Even drink didn't help. There was no laughter, and instances of fornication were few and far between, providing warmth more than anything else.   Despondency permeated the convict quarters. People started reminiscing about previous lives back home, deploring their crimes and capture, some wishing they hadn't been born. Despair fed despair, appetites dropped, and misery was rampant.

The cooks made a valiant attempt to help out. Weevils had owned the flour barrels for a month or more but the cooks recruited off duty sailors and marines to help painstakingly remove the little black beetles. They then baked fresh bread, and distributed vast quantities of loaves downstairs. The smell, the warmth, and the surprise had a marked impact and the cooks and helpers were applauded.

While there were definite distinctions between the types of passengers the boat carried, sailors, militia and convicts, there were times when their commonality as humans over-rode the distinctions. Everyone was cold, everyone was sick of being at sea and the length of the trip, everyone's patience was wearing thin, and everyone knew there was nothing they could do about it. They were all in the same boat – literally and figuratively. It was a miserable time for all.

The captain, the surgeon, and the commander worked hard to keep up positive outlooks, but even that became tiresome in the face of widespread pessimism. The bread had helped momentarily, and they anxiously sought other remedies. At the surgeon's suggestion a thorough search of every cupboard, nook and cranny was undertaken to find hidden board games and packs of cards hitherto unused. Behind the captain's hanging uniforms they found a chess set, and elsewhere they came up with boards for checkers, trictrac, backgammon, and the game of the Goose, as well as several decorative card decks. Why they hadn't thought of this notion before was lamented, but the prisoners grabbed the boards and cards happily and were soon distracted with new pastimes.

East across the great Australian Bight they sailed, day after interminable day, until finally they reached Bass Strait separating the mainland from Van Diemen's Land. Here another storm beset them, but it was brief and the captain was able to easily avoid the small islands in the Strait. It was the first of June when they finally turned to the northeast on the final leg to the Colony.

Dichotomous behavior became the norm as convicts worried about their future. The captain performed three marriages. One where a cook was married to one of the convict women, the other where a pair of convicts felt they had a better chance to prosper in the new land if they were together, rather than single. And one where a guardsman and convict came together. Other women with similar interests used their sexual wiles in last-minute acts to no avail. Tim's playmate promised all kinds of satisfaction but cried on his shoulders as he denied her requests for permanent company. She wasn't alone. One of the men, distraught at the notion of being on a chain gang for the rest of his life, jumped overboard. A sailor dived in and supported him until the longboat rescued them both.

They hugged the eastern coast as they proceeded north, close enough at times to see fires burning at the back of sandy beaches. Presumed to be the fires of natives, their curiosity grew, but they were too far away to distinguish any details of the few figures they saw. Tim and the few other select convicts were called to the captain's cabin. He indicated they were a day away from entering the Heads outside Sydney and would be returned to be with their fellow inmates the next morning. They would be paid for their work, but would receive their wages when they disembarked so that the risk of having coins forcibly taken away would be minimized. He also reiterated how he would be putting in strong recommendations to the authorities for special consideration for each of them. He then thanked them warmly for their service and shook each man's hand earnestly, wishing them good fortune in the new land.

As predicted, the next afternoon, the boat turned west and sailed majestically between the Heads that defined the entrance to Sydney Harbour. Lining the rails, convicts and militia viewed the lush land, small inlets, rocky cliffs, and sandy beaches with a mixture of awe and trepidation. The captain fired a signal gun and dropped the anchor two miles east of Sydney Cove. After nearly five months at sea they had finally arrived.

Part Three

19. The Colony

Tim observed the harbour through eyes with different interests than all the others. He was a fisherman at heart, and wondered what the harbour might offer under the surface. If at all possible he planned to find out. The ship was guided to a spot right in front of the quay with its single jetty poking out into the water. Once anchored, a bunch of local officials and authorities came on board and spent time with the captain, the surgeon, and the militia commander. When they left they took the inmates from the onboard prison and the three married couples, promising to be back the next day to unload the other convicts.

Transferring everyone to land took a long time. The women went first, ensconced ashore in communal tents and huts until they were simply put on another boat to take them up the Parramatta River to the township growing there. Those detained in Sydney had references from onboard and had experience as maids in better English homes. The men stayed onboard another night before offloading, at which time they were corralled in large tents with guards.

It was an unusual arrangement to say the least. In England they'd been housed first in stone-walled prisons, often underground, then in tethered wooden hulks floating on rivers and bays, then in the ship for nearly five months, and now on terra firma again, in tents no less. As such it was impossible for guards to watch every man at every moment. During the day they were marched to an appointed spot to cut down trees, build or tend gardens, clear fields, create paths and tracks, collect water, or even help build administrative edifices. They were at the edge of native bushland and many attempted to escape and travel north where it was rumoured they could get to China. Some perished at the hands of the aborigines, some simply died of starvation, others came stumbling back into camp on realizing their foolhardiness.

Tim and others were surprised at how primitive conditions in Sydney were. It was some fifteen years after the First Fleet had arrived and progress on creating the town of Sydney seemed very slow. Expectations that had been formed in Britain surrounding the potential ease of settlement had of course been way off the mark. Pioneers, both convicts and officials, with the First Fleet, had nearly starved due to a number of factors including the delay of the Second Fleet's arrival, the heat, the poor productivity of the soils yielding scant edible produce, and harassment from the natives who did not welcome strangers invading their land and treating them as unsophisticated savages. Poor planning over the management of resources such as the freshwater in the Tank Stream, cattle and sheep stock, and fishing in the harbour, accompanied by incompetent prisoner control, had seriously compromised orderly progress. Sydney was nothing more than an immature settlement that couldn't decide if it was to be just a penal colony or the underpinnings of a new town destined to be attractive to free settlers as well.

Prisoners outnumbered militia ten to one or more and set their own rules for how many hours they would work before downing tools. At night the farce continued as some men snuck out and headed for the women's camp located in a separate part of the shoreline. The guards quickly beefed up their detail, yet illicit liaisons still took place between willing partners.

In the Governor's plans, a major brick and mortar barracks was to be constructed, but that was years off. Simple wooden structures were being erected as temporary containment shelters, the first already occupied by several women. Later on, in fact, select convicts built their own houses, or rented them from private individuals. For now the situation was characterized as a prison 'without walls'. It was freedom of a never-to-be-repeated form. The convicts soon controlled a part of the cove shoreline called 'The Rocks' where eventually businesses of a lower nature thrived. The only effective form of government control was severe thrashings for convicts caught flagrantly disobeying the rules.

As much as Tim was an attractive target for the younger women, and was tempted to engage, he had other things on his mind. At the end of day after work was done, he would wander the shore east of the township, daring to go beyond the recognized boundaries. For some reason he had no fear of the natives. His attitude, contrary to that of many officials, was that he was an intruder in their land, their country. As such he treated the land and its inhabitants with respect. He watched their activities and interactions closely, never confronting them directly. He watched how they made fire, and sought to understand the different roles assumed by men and women. He wondered what they thought of these newcomers, pale in skin colour, their bodies eighty percent covered, wary of the bright sunshine, creating wooden structures that were not transportable, planting things in the earth instead of digging them up, and making loud noises with things they knew not, be they bells or rifles. These newcomers marched in line, whipped animals pulling conveyances piled high with unknown items, drank from containers, both fixed and portable, and employed things to hold their food while they used implements other than fingers to eat. How different these visitors were.

Of most interest to Tim was how the Aborigines fished. The members of the coastal *Eora* tribe of Sydney were saltwater people. Fish and shellfish were a major part of their diet, and they excelled in fishing, swimming, and diving. The men stood motionless in the shallows, watching for fish that they speared with long multi-pronged fish-gigs. The women used hooks and lines. The line was shredded and twisted very closely, made from any number of sources, including kurrajong tree bark, the inside bark of the cabbage tree, flax plant, animal fur, or grasses. The hooks were honed from turban shells. But what were truly unique were the fishing vessels the women used. Called 'nowies' or 'nawis', they were made purely of bark. From the narrow-leaved eucalyptus tree called 'stringy bark', in August after the early spring rains, great sheets of thick bark rich in sap could be peeled off whole, then cut and fired to firm up the final shape and size. The bark at the bow would be folded tightly to a point while the stern had looser folds.

Women fished and paddled with fires lit in the nowie for warmth and cooking, and infants at their breasts or on their shoulders, their fishing songs carried on the breeze over the water. Surprisingly, the delicate-looking craft could be maneuvered in quite large waves. Tim was fascinated, and although he wished he could see a nowie actually made, it was not to be. After five days of constant propinquity he asked through sign language if he could use one of the canoes. The men and women of the tribe conferred, clearly suspicious of his intentions. He brought forth a line and hook that he had liberated from his five-month floating prison and attached a large worm he'd dug out of the moist bank soil. This they seemed to understand and led him to a canoe, making it clear that others would be in canoes alongside him on the water.

He paddled out less than twenty-five yards and cast his simple line into the depths. In ten minutes he was reeling in a twelve-pound mullet to the grins of his appreciative audience. He caught another two smaller ones then handed his line to a woman in an accompanying canoe. To his delight and that of the others she had no trouble emulating his performance. Back on land he made a gift of his three fish to the man who seemed to be the group leader. In time he anticipated he may be allowed to keep one, or possibly be invited to share in eating one cooked over a fire. For now he wanted to ensure them that he understood the harbour was their fishing ground, not his.

At roll-call the next morning he was told to stand aside while the others marched off to the appointed task of the day. A sergeant led him to the Prison Warden's office in a wooden hut south and away from the waterfront. The warden had a number of papers strewn untidily across his desk. He puffed on an old pipe and a wisp of steam rose from a cup of tea off to one side. The smells made Tim's nostrils twitch in anticipation. The warden seemed not to notice.

"Mr. Bartlett, it appears that you performed a valued service on the *Coronation*. Saved a sailor's life, helped capture and subdue two murderers, and took the place of a deserter by working the riggings for all but a few weeks of the journey. Unusual arrangement by Captain Clavell, but it seems to have worked well with several men beyond yourself helping out in other areas. Yes, a very enterprising captain indeed.

"He gives you great credit for awareness, prompt and decisive action, intelligence, and a positive outlook. Hmmmm, we could do with more men like you around here. So tell me, what have you learned so far since arriving?"

"Well sir, I think you and the Governor and other officials are going to have an awkward time until more substantial quarters for us prisoners are built. There's too much freedom on our hands, and the men relish it because where we come from it was much much worse. We're not used to it. Dr. Keithly's ideas of planned exercise through work discipline worked well with the men on board ship, and probably would do so again.

"On the personal side I've been spending most of my spare time observing how the *Eora* tribes-people fish. They have these strange canoes, but are very adept in them. And they certainly know how and where to catch their meals. I think the government fishermen could learn well from them."

"Speaking of which Mr. Bartlett, I understand you are a Cornwall fisherman of some renown."

"Not renowned for my fishing sir."

"Whatever the reason I wish we had more fishing boats and fishermen to increase our catch and offer more fresh food to all of us here."

"From what I've observed, sir the longboat is not the best vessel for fishing. It is heavy to maneuver, built for moving through heavy surf, not for exploring shallow coves and rocky inlets. Smaller boats would be much more useful."

"I don't disagree Mr. Bartlett. But we don't have any smaller government boats and the Governor's restrictions prohibit private ownership of any boat."

"Why is that, sir?"

"To prevent escape, of course. Many men here have a sailing familiarity, perhaps not as strong as yours, and escape is uppermost in many minds. It wouldn't take that much. Although, as we spend more time between here and Parramatta I think that will have to change. We'll probably want private boats to ferry supplies between here and there at the very least."

"Why is Parramatta so important, sir?"

"It seems that the land thereabouts is much richer than here and may be used to grow better crops. Also the river is navigable up to that point, but no further. And at just fifteen miles away it's close enough to reach quickly."

"How are the natives in that area then? More or less friendly than here?"

"Not quite as awestruck because they can't see our big scary ships, and are more dependent on living off the land rather than the water. Their name for Parramatta is *Burramatta* which means the eel place. They throng there where the fresh water in the river meets the salt water from the Harbour. All I know is that *matt'* means 'eels' and *Burra* means 'place'. What amazes me more than anything else is the fact that the tribe there, called *Dharug*, speaks a different language to what we hear here, yet they are so close to one another."

"Maybe I'll get there one day."

"Much sooner than you think, Mr. Bartlett. Much sooner. How does tomorrow sound?"

"I don't understand, sir."

"Well, the way things work, son, is that landowners, business proprietors, and officials can request that labourers with certain skills be assigned to them to help with various needs. A few days ago we received a request from a chap in Green Hills who wants help building boats. The captain of the *Coronation* indicates in the log book that you have some experience in that capacity."

"But sir, I thought you said boats couldn't be owned privately. And while I know a lot about boats and have indeed built a very small one, I have much more experience as a fisherman."

"Don't argue, son. We have no spots or demand for more fishermen at the moment. Do you want to stay on a work gang in Sydney or start participating in an honest occupation? This man is planning on building large boats that could sail to England, or elsewhere, not rowboats prisoners could escape in. I think you'd be smart to join his team."

"Where is Green Hills, sir?"

"On the Hawkesbury River northwest of Parramatta, maybe twenty miles as the crow flies. Much longer of course via the meandering tracks across country. We have a wagon load of government supplies heading to Parramatta tomorrow. Be here at 6am sharp and you can travel with them. You'll have to wait in Parramatta till some group of soldiers is headed to Green Hills. Got it?"

"Yes sir, and thank you, sir."

"Oh, one last question. Do you have a woman you have some arrangement with that you'd like to accompany you? We can accommodate that according to the rules. One less mouth for us to feed."

"Ah, no sir. Although there could be one in Parramatta who came out on the ship with me."

"You'll have time there so have one of my men take you along to the various abodes holding the women convicts. I'll organize it in the morning. Now be gone and the best of luck to you. Dismissed."

The road to Parramatta had more traffic on it than Tim had expected. He'd been taken at daybreak to the local stores where he waited over an hour while the goods were loaded. Two bullocks were hitched in front of a huge dray piled high with furniture destined for an official's residence, along with numerous crates and bags of food for the Commissariat. He and the guards walked at the slow pace of the bullocks which were driven by two convicts seated awkwardly on part of the load. No-one seemed to have any enthusiasm for their job and whenever Tim tried to make conversation he was rebuffed. Even the two convicts managing the bullocks showed no interest in sharing any information, just kept swearing and whipping the beasts up front along the narrow track. Whenever a cart coming the other way approached, a stop was made and then they very carefully maneuvered past each other. Poultry and eggs seemed to be the most prevalent commodities moving in the opposite direction although milk in enormous jugs and small carts overflowing with vegetables also were headed to the main town. Horses, bullocks, and a few donkeys pulled the loads. Stopping was always loathed as bullocks were notorious for resting and needing extra inducements to get started again. It took a long time to get to the inland town.

Not that there was much to see along the way beyond forest and vast meadows. No serious hills, just a few minor creeks to cross that wound their way to the Parramatta River and thence the Harbour. The only excitement was seeing a small mob of kangaroos grazing in one of the open fields. Tim wanted to get closer but was denied the opportunity, the guard indicating that as soon as he would move toward them they would certainly bound away. And they were too far away to shoot. From all accounts the land was filled with the animals and he'd have plenty of chances in the future to observe them. Here he was anxious to learn more about them yet the guards were so nonchalant about their presence that they couldn't care less. He hoped he never got that way.

The other aspect of travel that most caught his attention were the bird calls. Some were melodious in the form of lengthy songs. Another in particular sounded like bells or chimes, and yet another was like a sharp cracking sound.   Once in a while he'd see a brightly coloured bird of parakeet size, akin to some he'd seen at the frontier edges of Sydney. And at one point a giant black cockatoo sat high in a pine tree cracking nuts, parts of which fell to the ground. It was fascinating and entertaining, although none of his traveling companions seemed to care. He got the feeling that his presence was not welcomed, although just why he could not discern.

It was late afternoon before any bark slab huts were seen. They were incredibly primitive affairs with giant cracks between the vertical boards that were either uneven striplings or irregular cuts from larger tree trunks. The roofs were made of bark and hanging sheets of cloth served as doorways. Gangs of men were busy clearing fields of trees and stumps. Tim was not surprised when they stopped at the first pub they came to. He used a coin from his boat wages to buy a pint of lager, and sat outside in the shade of an acacia tree that was showing yellow buds. He figured they were lucky it was a dry day since the road they'd just traversed would surely be a muddy nightmare after rain. As it was, the ruts they had experienced were bad enough. He wondered how often carts broke down and how easily damaged wheel-rims could be repaired. Strictly a do it yourself job he figured, which explained why they had carried a variety of spares in their load.

Finally arriving at the Commissariat, a number of soldiers helped unload the dray in relatively short time. Tim was shown a spot where he could bunk down for the night, and warned not to try to escape, or he'd be hunted down and likely shot on sight. The law was less readily enforced away from the main settlement they'd come from, even though the Governor was thinking of establishing a second home here. The apparent ruthlessness of some of the guards bothered Tim until he inadvertently learned that some convicts had 'gone bush' and had become outlaws of the worst form.   Not many, but these escapees hated their gaolers and vowed revenge. They lived in semi-hidden groves in thick forests. Some had stolen guns along with food from outlying farms, threatening the farmers with severe beatings if they resisted. Some had indeed paid the price. The militia, acting with the local police, would chase after the criminals, often employing the tracking expertise of helpful aborigines.

One story described an incident where a group of militia and police came across an escapee camp seemingly abandoned shortly before their arrival. A fire was still burning and a dog was chewing on a fleshy bone. The militia guards had split into pairs, setting off in different directions from the camp, anxious to confront the wild convicts. After an hour's searching, two pairs met up back at the camp, but the third pair never returned. The four men followed the obvious trail their companions had forged, hoof marks being evident in the soft soil. They eventually found the pair butchered on the bank of a small stream. Their clothes and boots had been taken and it was clear the horses had been led into the water and taken downstream. After half a mile no tracks were found that would indicate they'd left the safety of the water so the men turned back and buried their friends before returning to their depot.

The atrocity goaded the mounted troopers into a wide-scale multi-man search across miles and miles of bushland, this time with several native trackers involved. It took two weeks but eventually three men were captured, one wearing the belt and boots of one of the dead militia. They were roughed up but brought back alive to the Parramatta gaol. There they suffered repeat whippings as different men exacted their revenge for the death of their comrades. In the end, hardly able to stand, their backs raw from the thrashings, they were taken out deep into the Blue Mountains. There they were stripped and each shot in one knee, left to fend as they could. They were never seen again.

It was clear to Tim that in this new land, rough justice was definitely a way of life when those supposed to uphold the law could bend it to their will. He vowed never to cross the militia in any future interaction.

20. Parramatta Town

Parramatta, originally named *Rose Hill*, had been founded in 1788, the same year as Sydney. The harbour-side Colony had only enough food brought from Britain to support itself for a short time. The soil around Sydney Cove had proved too poor to grow the amount of food that fifteen hundred convicts, soldiers and administrators who had arrived in the First Fleet needed to survive. In an attempt to deal with the food crisis, a Cornish farmer convict named James Rouse was granted land at Rose Hill on the condition that he develop a viable agriculture. The area was deemed the most likely place for a successful large farm as it was the closest land to Sydney that could depend on large volume fresh-water irrigation. There, Rouse became the first person to successfully grow wheat in the new land. His success prompted other farmers to follow and the area also became recognized for the pioneering of the Australian wool industry. In the 1790s a young soldier named John Macarthur managed six hundred sheep on his farm, and years later produced stunningly fine wool after introducing Spanish merino sheep. His efforts, unheralded at the time and later moved to the Camden area, were to lead to the creation of one of the world's richest export industries of Victorian times.

Under the notion that Parramatta, not Sydney, might become the center of civilization in the new land, Governor Phillip built himself a small house there and supported government work on local infrastructure and administrative housing. The limited number of free settler residents followed suit, building homes and renting them to female convicts brought to the area. Similarly to the situation for male convicts in Sydney, initially there was no particular government place set aside to house women in Parramatta. The majority of women were originally from rural areas back in the old country, though they generally had already moved at least once, to towns and cities, in the search for work. A large proportion were domestic workers. But beyond these broad commonalities, convict women came from different backgrounds and regions, had different skills, inclinations and dispositions. In the early period, these factors, rather than their convict status, shaped their colonial experiences. Some had to 'spin for government', while others were set to make shirts, frocks, trousers, etc., for the male convicts at a certain number per day. There were plans to create a Female Factory above the current gaol, but it would take another year for that to come about. Before that, women, like men, were told to find their own lodgings. A very strange prison arrangement indeed!

As such, Tim had no idea how to really find any of the women who had been on the *Coronation* with him.   A guard walked with him to the section of town where most of the women resided in large groups in make-shift buildings. In the sixth dwelling he recognized some of the women cutting designs in cloth, but when he asked about Laura they had no information. They seemed depressed and resigned to their tasks. At the twelfth house one of the women suggested Tim might find Laura working in a warehouse at the docks where clothes were bundled before being put on a packet ship headed for Sydney. His pace quickened as the guard led him to the river.

He was surprised to see several small packet sloops tied to the wharf. From earlier conversations his understanding was that private boats were discouraged and that the government owned only open longboats. How had he missed seeing any of these in Sydney, and who owned them? He hastened to ask questions of an old man sitting in the sun outside one of the warehouse buildings. The fellow explained that the warehouse owners and other privateers had been given special dispensation to build and own the packet boats and that in Sydney they unloaded in the Cove west of Dawes point, where Tim had never visited. Pushing on, Tim talked to a couple of sailors on the second boat and learned that it had been built a year before in Green Hills, where he was destined to end up. When he asked how the boat had gotten from Green Hills to Parramatta he was told it had sailed the whole way.

The Hawkesbury River flowed northeast from Green Hills in a twisting route to a place called Wiseman's Ferry and then southeast to the coast at Broken Bay - nearly seventy miles in total. Boats would take shelter in Pittwater, a large volume of salt water protected behind a long peninsula, and wait for good weather to continue another thirty-five miles or so south along the coastline to the Sydney Heads and up the Parramatta River to the docks. Roads in the Hawkesbury region, like much of the colony, were to be almost non-existent for twelve more years, and horses and other beasts of burden were few. Transport of bulk commodities to Sydney from the Hawkesbury region had to be by water.

The third Governor of New South Wales, Philip Gidley King, recognised the need for commerce to develop throughout the fledgling colony and turned a blind eye to the building of a few ships for private traders. And so the boat-building industry began. One of the leaders was Henry Kable, who had arrived as a convict with the First Fleet and set up a boat-building business with James Underwood and Samuel Rodman Chase about 1800. Others were encouraged to follow, and a small fleet of packet boats was gradually built.

Tim wandered among the warehouses with his guard lagging behind. No-one denied him entrance, anticipating that he was either a buyer or seller of goods. In a tumbledown shack he finally found the woman he knew as Laura folding and packing clothes into a large box. He stood watching her for many minutes, a plethora of challenging thoughts tumbling through his head. Was this a woman he wanted to spend time with? What about Clarinda? Did she still have a potential role in his future life? He was disturbed by the rough, seedy nature of the colony and its environment. Would Clarinda be able to stand it? Was it too ugly and primitive to ask her to even think about joining him in it? By being untrue to her would he feel guilty the rest of his life? Would he be able to live with himself after breaking the promises he had made to her and her family? And what did he know about Laura other than her seamstress skills? He had learned she was born in Edinburgh and that her family had moved south to York, then Manchester, looking for work when she was a little girl. Her mother had washed clothes for families and her father had looked after pigs at the stockyards. There were no brothers or sisters. To help bring money in, she and another girl she'd befriended had established a pickpocketing process. While one sweet-talked a gentleman and promised enthusiastic gratification, the other would relieve him of his wallet. It was an old con game that others also played. One night, however, an intended victim suddenly realized what they were up to and grabbed Laura by the hair and dragged her screaming for two long blocks until he came across a constable and turned her in. Behind the bland façade she had presented on board their ship Tim sensed a goodness that had been crushed by circumstances. And she was here, Clarinda was not. She had survived a ride across perilous oceans. Would Clarinda, far more delicate, manage the same?

What about the child he'd fathered back home? He still didn't know if it was a boy or a girl. How was Clarinda managing without him being around? He'd promised to write as soon as he arrived here. Why hadn't he done so? Others at the Sydney camp had bought paper and pencil from enterprising merchants. Some who couldn't write had even paid others to write for them. Was he too proud? Had his special status aboard ship gone to his head in some way? Perhaps he thought he was better than other convicts? Or was it something else? As much as life was primitive here there was an air of opportunity. He sensed that with hard work and some smarts he could make a good life. If that were true did he really need a female companion to keep him company while he moved on? He was only twenty-three; many, many years were in front of him.

He turned away and sat on the bank of the river shaking his head back and forth, going over and over his thoughts. With his mind thousands of miles away back in Polperro, at first he was unaware of the voice softly mouthing his name. Only when he felt a touch on his shoulder did he turn and find Laura standing behind him, a look of puzzlement on her face.

"I knew it was you, Timothy," she said. "Why are you here? How did you find me? What do you want?" The semi-brusqueness of her questions belied the gentleness of her touch and the tears eking out of her eyes.

She sat down beside him and continued, "It's good to see you so soon. It's so boring and futile here."

Tim turned and reached out for her as a male voice boomed out, "Laura Stewart, get back in here to your station. That crate is to be boarded in an hour. Get on with it."

Pointing at Tim, he bellowed, "You, whoever you are, move on, we've got work to do here."

Tim yelled to Laura's back, "What time do you finish? I'll come back."

"Seven p.m." was the faint reply.

The guard, who had been standing off a distance approached. "So you've found her I see. I tell you what. Give me threepence and I'll leave you be. Against my orders, mind you. There won't be a ride to Green Hills until Monday of next week, so you can have two days to do what you want. Just be at the gaol that morning by six a.m. or we'll come looking for you and there'll be hell to pay when you're caught. You seem like a decent fellow so I'm trusting you. I can always say you simply ran away from me and I couldn't find you if you cross me. Got it?"

Tim nodded yes, dug in his pocket for the bribe, and wandered away from his guard.

He roamed the simple streets of Parramatta and admired the new Governor's mansion on the crescent, then sauntered out into the countryside, filling in time. Back in town he crossed the bridge that had been built upstream and explored the opposite bank. He could see the eels in the clear water and watched a native spear two of them and wander off into the bush, no doubt carrying home the evening's supper for the family.

His mind played with his emotions. Why was he even interested in any way with Laura? Had his commitment to Clarinda never been sincere, just a sham based on propinquity and availability? True, there weren't many eligible girls in the village. Did he not care about the baby? His own flesh and blood that he had helped create? Was he a coward at heart with no real sense of family and dedication? No, he didn't believe that for an instant. So why had he come here looking for Laura? Was his body so weak that its wants overruled his heart? Was that what he really wanted even now? Or had something significant and not well understood happened? Had the terrible journey over so many months caused a fundamental change in his make-up and outlook? Had it made him more bitter in some ways? Had it made him realize he had only himself to depend on? That there would be no Mike Morriseys, no Uncle Bens, no Ramons for support and care when needed? Would even Clarinda need him now that she had a baby? Maybe the baby was enough to fulfill her life and he would always be second fiddle? He'd seen it before. Especially since the fishermen were so often gone for long periods, the wives banded together and doted on their children. The men came home with their catches, wives responded in conjugal games, then packed the fish in hogsheads as the men headed out to sea again. Was that all there was to life in Polperro? Was that all he could have looked forward to? Was that what he wanted, or had this journey to the other side of the world changed all that?

Now that he knew he was not bound by the walls of a sleepy harbour, the timing of the tides, the smell of fish and the slap of canvas in the wind, had some new sense and awareness arisen that changed everything? He was mightily confused. He debated whether to even go back to the warehouse at seven p.m., but realized if he didn't he might never know the answers to some of his questions.

He had no watch, just a sixth sense that brought him back with time to spare. Laura came skipping out of the warehouse entrance with a smile on her face and a girlfriend clinging to one arm.

"Timothy, this is Mary, my best friend here. We work together. She was on the boat with us."

"I well remember," Tim responded. "With red hair like that Mary, you were easy to spot in a crowd."

"Aye well, I was born with it. It's part of me, anywhere you look." And she giggled. An image of Clarinda and her red hair flashed through Tim's mind and he looked away quickly.

"Come on then, Tim. Mary and I were going to make a thick vegetable soup for supper. How long since you've eaten?"

Disappointed he couldn't be alone with Laura, Tim followed as they headed back to the house where he'd found she resided.

"Come through to the kitchen, the others have most likely finished eating by now. Maybe they've left some bread for us. Yes, there we are, and let me get you a mug of ale. Now, while we chop the veggies and boil the water tell us what's happened in the last month since we all arrived in this country. And don't spare any details, good or bad. What is Sydney like?"

For the next hour Tim regaled them with what he had observed and the tales he had heard. They listened with rapt attention, frequently interrupting to ask for clarification or details.

"What are the women like?" Mary wanted to know. "We hear they seek out the men fiercely, competing for their attention. Did you lay with any of them Tim? You could lay with me you know."

Ignoring the suggestion Tim said: "There were a limited number of women who worked in the government stores, and who owned or ran some of the shops and businesses. The toughest ones were the publicans, but there were also some more gentle ones who ran the bakeries and general stores. We only saw them in the evening and Sundays as most of the time we were away from the settlement clearing land or putting up a building. Every now and then we'd see aboriginal women at the edge of the forest, and as I've mentioned I went out fishing with one tribe."

"Do they truly all go around naked as we've heard, Tim?" Mary asked. "Some of the native men in this area have learned to wear loincloths at the insistence of the authorities. And some wear cloaks made of possum skins. I hate it when they cover their good parts. The women wear nothing that we've seen, but they don't seem very attractive. Maybe you men might like seeing their breasts and muffs but they often have bumps on their heads and cuts on their faces, so we think they get beaten at home. They sure look wild."

Laura interrupted. "Tim, it will be lights out here in a few minutes. The authorities will come to check on us, so you must go. I have to work tomorrow like all the women, but Sunday we have off. Maybe we can spend more time together then? I'd like that. And we could have dinner again tomorrow night if you want?"

"That would be great, Laura. I'll see if I can catch us some fish."

"No eels Tim," Mary interjected. "Although if you'd like to share yours you can stay here with me tonight." Laura winced and rolled her eyes as Tim arose.

He was surprised to find two other men exiting at the same time he left as he hadn't heard much noise from the other rooms. He'd enjoyed the women's company and the supper and his head was clear. He'd definitely be back next evening.

Saturday morning dawned wet with a slight drizzle dripping off rooftops and creating small puddles in the clay streets. It didn't seem to have any effect on the populace, however, which seemed intent on heading toward the river. The reason quickly became clear as a cart heavily laden with vegetables passed him and was followed in short order by another. Farmers were busy bringing their goods to market. No wonder convicts worked on Saturday. Most of the goods were destined for the warehouses and Sydney, but a small percentage was set up on makeshift stalls for the local population to buy. Tim watched as free settler and convict women bargained over melons and cabbages, lemons and apples, eggs and fat chickens, mutton and ham, and pecks of wheat to grind into flour. One stall sold eels with a few small fish offered almost as an afterthought.

By ten a.m. the stalls were closing down, and the boats were lining up to take on produce from the warehouses. Business was orderly as everyone profited. The farmers received payment in various forms for their merchandise, the warehouses added fees for storage and bundling and exchanged chits with the river-men, who headed downstream to the merchants at Darling Harbour. The English authorities who'd prepared the First Fleet hadn't counted on the rapid development of commercial activity in the colony and had sent no money supply. Cash was effected only because administrative officials and militiamen, and some convicts, had brought coins with them which gradually entered economic circulation. If barter didn't work, then English bank writs and IOUs were the trading instruments of the day. Tim was impressed at how well the system worked. It was only fifteen years since the First Fleet had arrived, but here the ingenuity of man was very obvious.

Once the marketplace closed down Tim went back to his space in the Commissariat and retrieved his trusty fishing line and hooks. The drizzle was ending and a weak light filtered through the heavy clouds as they rose. He had no interest in eels and decided to walk upstream a couple of miles to see what freshwater fish might be available in higher reaches. The eucalypts dripped on him, and white cockatoos screeched as he disturbed their resting spots, whistling as he walked. He hadn't felt so good in ages. He figured it had something to do with seeing all the people at the marketplace. Perhaps just their togetherness, the normality of buying food, the interaction with neighbours and tradespeople alike. So different from prison life, perhaps that was it. A township in operation, doing the same things people in English towns would be doing most Saturdays. Polperro didn't have a full market like the one he'd just observed but inland towns did, and even back home merchant peddlers would often stop by on a Saturday with goods from the hinterlands.

He stopped after an hour where a giant pool formed above a small rock dam. The water was clear and he could see small fish darting to and fro in the shallows near the bank. A brightly coloured kingfisher bird sat on a bough ten feet above the dam, which he took as a good sign. It didn't move as Tim came by, obviously with no fear of the intruder into its realm. Tim dug out a fat juicy worm from the bank and baited his hook. It had hardly gone in the water when he felt a tug and pulled in one of the small four inch fish he had noticed at the outset. It was almost too easy as he managed to catch seven in a row. The kingfisher hadn't moved, so Tim tossed the last one, still alive, onto the grass by the bank about ten yards away. The orange and blue plumed bird didn't hesitate but flew down, picked it up still squirming in his bill and flew back to his old perch.   Tim wondered if he'd swallow it there and then but after a minute watching, the bird flew away, probably to a nest elsewhere in the forest. 'Glad to help you out fella', he thought.

He picked up his catch and continued on upstream. The river narrowed but ran deeper, colder, and a little faster, telling Tim the source was still a long way off. A movement on the other bank caught his attention and he stopped, patiently waiting to see what had caught his eye. A moment later he was rewarded as two emus moved out from a grove of trees, heading away from the water. 'Strange looking birds', he mused. He had learned they were flightless but had powerful legs that could let them achieve speeds up to thirty miles an hour or so. Immensely strong claws allowed them to rip attacking dingos, the wild Australian dog, to pieces, while their most successful predator was the wedge-tailed eagle which attacked an emu's neck and head from above. As far as he knew they didn't have fish in their diet so they'd probably been to the stream to drink.

Still, this seemed as good a spot as any to fish again. He put one of the small fish on a hook and threw it out as far as he could. He wasn't surprised that nothing happened immediately. Twice he reeled the line in to find his bait intact and decided to try a different tactic. In went the line but now he walked slowly along the bank so his bait moved more in the water and was closer to the shore. He stopped to let his bait sink, then started up again.   He felt a slight nibble as the line tautened and then a definitive tug. "Ah, got something bigger for sure," he muttered to himself.   Carefully he played the line, not wanting to lose his catch. Patience paid off and with a final flick of the wrist a four-pound cod flew through the air to lie twitching on the grassy verge. He dispensed it with a rock to the head, and triumphantly held it up to admire.

'Not a bad start', he thought, and readied his line for another cast.   He lost the second bait by being too anxious to set the hook, but the third and fourth efforts brought forth a pair of six pounders. 'I wonder who else knows this place', he thought. 'I can't be the only one.'

The answer came in a surprising form. As he got up to leave three shadows parted company with the surrounding woods and became natives with spears. He wondered how long they had been quietly observing. They didn't seem threatening, more curious and somewhat wary. Tim sat down cross-legged as he'd observed the natives in Sydney do, looked down, and uttered one of the few words he'd learned that sounded like *pulya*. At this the men stopped and tilted their heads, so Tim repeated the sound. One of them responded with a sound similar, but distinct, that he heard as *pully*. In Sydney the word he used was a greeting that meant something like *are you OK?*, rather than *hullo*. Dialects varied markedly from tribes living even close by so he was not surprised that his pronunciation wasn't precise enough. He next tried *magura* the best he could do for *fish*. This worked, as smiles lit up the three men's faces.

He rose and offered one of the bigger fish to the chap who had spoken. He took it, but with a couple of grunts gave it to one of his friends and pointed directly to Tim's fishing line, obviously wanting to see it up close. It was a hand line, not made for a rod and reel, but was of good-quality plaited silk with just a little horsehair woven in for strength in places. The hook of course was steel, much stronger than the shell versions the native women used in Sydney Harbour. The three men laid their spears down and pulled on the line, one testing the hook by jabbing it into the flesh of his palm. The barb at the end caught and Tim grabbed the man's hand firmly and carefully removed the hook before the man ripped his skin pulling it out. His hand bled a little but he was clearly thankful and impressed both with the hook and Tim's response. Tim picked up one of his fish and showed how the hook went inside the mouth and attached with the barb so the fish couldn't wriggle free.

Given the interest his audience exhibited he decided to show them how he'd actually caught the fish, knowing they had been watching all the time from behind the trees. He applied one of his last two bait fish to his hook and walked back down the bank, signaling one of the men to follow. He threw the line into the stream and handed the full coil to the native, showing him how to place his thumb on the line. He then walked slowly backwards with his arms reaching around the native and his own thumb resting on the native's on top of the line. Sure enough a small jerk indicated a potential catch as the unseen large fish checked out the bait. The tribesman muttered to his companions and Tim signaled as best he could to wait, and be patient. Suddenly there was a firm tug on the line, at which time Tim hauled the man's hand backward and upward, setting the hook. The line unfurled and slowed as the fish tried to escape. At its first resting point Tim showed how to start pulling it in. Out and in the process continued until at last they could all see a nice-sized cod splashing to the surface as it weakened. When close enough Tim jerked the man's wrist and the fish flew through the air actually hitting one of the other two men, who laughed out loud. Tim let the man who'd been in the flight path unhook the cod and indicated he should keep it. It was the biggest of the four caught.

Tim turned back to the bank and checked his line, anticipating using his last bait fish for the third man. But as quietly as they had arrived they suddenly left. He caught the last vestiges of their shapes among the threes where they had first emerged, and wondered what stories they would have to offer around their campfire that night. He'd saved the biggest little baitfish until last and it didn't disappoint as he landed a cod as big as the other two combined. What a day – a beautiful dazzling kingfisher, two large emus, a bunch of good-sized fish, and an encounter with natives others would probably find hard to believe.

Highly satisfied, he bundled everything together, put it in the sack which he slung over his shoulder, and set off back to the township whistling merrily again. He stopped for a minute back at the rock pool where he'd caught his bait. As he sat and rested and looked into the waters a reflection and slight movement occurred on the surface. Looking up he saw the three natives on the opposite bank. Two were standing in the one-legged classic pose with the other leg bent at the knee forming a triangle with the knee on the straight leg, their spears helping support them. The third man seemed to have lost his spear and was standing just as Tim would. He pointed downstream a little, indicating Tim should move on. Ten paces along he found the third man's spear – clearly meant as a gift. Tim waved it above his head and nodded up and down as a thank you. He smiled and clapped his hands, at which point the three men turned and vanished as easily as they had arrived. Perhaps, thought Tim, the folks back in town might just believe him now with this prized possession. What a day!

At seven p.m. he was outside the warehouse again, waiting to proudly show off his catch. Laura came bubbling out, once more with Mary attached. "Oh, Mr. Bartlett," Mary gushed. "You are positively beaming. Have you been thinking about my red parts all day?"

"Mary, do shush. Can't you see he has three fine fish we can cook for dinner. Raise your mind from under your skirt. Tim, they look so fresh. Did you catch them or have to buy them?"

"Wait till you hear my story ladies. I caught them, but what an adventure it was. Is there someone else at the house we can share dinner with? There's enough here for five people."

"Mary, I have an idea. Why don't you run ahead and see if Helen and Millie can join us for fresh fish. And maybe you can stoke up the fire so it will be ready for when we get there."

Mary ran off full of enthusiasm and energy. "You must excuse her, Tim. I'm sorry. Apparently ever since she was first paid a penny by a man for bending over and touching her toes as he raised her chemise, she's been smitten by the male touch. There's something missing in the brain. We all take turns at the house trying to look after her and see she doesn't get into trouble, but you can see her focus. This week is my week for mothering. After tonight one of the other women takes responsibility."

"Thanks for explaining. Was she like that on the ship? She's lucky to have you women care about her."

"Surprisingly, it was harder to keep track of her on the ship than it is here, and the sailors would often take her to their cabins. There were times when she was so vulgar she was an embarrassment to us all. She seemed OK at first but she clearly got worse as the voyage went on. We were so glad to see Sydney Heads which then kept the crew more occupied. One day she'll slip out of our defenses and the wrong men will take total advantage of her. We see it in the gaolers' faces when they check on us each evening. But come along, we'll enjoy your fish."

Fresh cod was a real treat for the five of them. Tim was pleased to meet two new women, somewhat older than Laura and Mary, but happy to make his acquaintance. The food was enhanced by his amazing tale, making the evening a memorable exchange. Somehow the cares of prison life left them all, if only for a fleeting few hours.

It was with great reluctance that Tim was ushered out the door at 'lights-out' time. He promised to come back for Laura at ten a.m. the next morning so they could head off for a picnic together.

21. *Upstream Fish*

Sunday dawned clear, the clouds of the previous day blown away elsewhere. Laura had put on a new dress, stitched and saved surreptitiously by one of the women in the house. As best she could she had had another woman tease back her hair and had washed her face. Combs and small feminine niceties were not encouraged by the warden of the prisoners, even though she was a woman herself.

Making clothes was a boring existence and as such, pettiness readily erupted, making mountains out of molehill disagreements. Punishments involved deprivation of food and weekend-off privileges, plus removal to locations and practices least desirable. By hard work, attention to the rules, and obsequious responses to authoritative commands, Laura had garnered one of the easiest jobs. She learned what behavior was rewarded and practiced it, even though she found it unflattering and distasteful.

Mary was a dilemma. On one hand she was simple enough that she did as she was told without complaining, not knowing any better. But she often wanted to wander away physically from whatever she was doing to find a man. Mentally her thoughts were often in another place leading to unexplainable mutterings. One day, they all knew, she'd be out the door before they realized it. Meanwhile, they did their best to protect her.

Laura had pulled together some left-over chicken and two apples along with a bottle of ale, all of which Tim added to his haversack containing his reel and line. Laura said she'd seen most of the town by walking around on her days off but would love to go where Tim had been upstream as she would never dare go there by herself or even with other women. He reached out his hand and she took it happily, as they made their way to the river. To make the day a little different they crossed the bridge and started walking upstream on the bank opposite the one Tim had travelled. Laura wore boots that had also been made secretly and was glad she had done so for the grass was long in places and would have scratched her legs had she worn her regular sandal shoes. They enjoyed the silence of the fresh morning and the various birdcalls for a while until Laura could hold back no longer.

"So tell me Tim, why did you come looking for me? We had a minimal time together on board ship when I was making clothes, but I thought you told me you were married and probably had a child already."

"I've asked myself the same question Laura, but here I am. I'm not sure I have a good answer for you. On reflection it's clear I was attracted to you more strongly than I realized at the time. I didn't deliberately turn away from spending more time with you on the boat, so please don't think that. Demands on my time and job on board changed quickly and created a different priority. Do you understand?"

"Oh yes. I was disappointed of course as I'd liked you, and I saw how things changed because you were a sailor more than a prisoner. I always thought that was a unique arrangement I didn't fully appreciate. Nor did a lot of others by the way."

"I thought I would have a chance to say goodbye to you, but along with the others like me, I was bundled back to the prisoner quarters quick smart the day before the authorities were due to come on board. And you women were first off. All we men could hear was your shouted goodbyes, but we never saw you. I wish it had been otherwise. What happened once you went ashore?"

"It was pretty terrible and demeaning actually. Sydney was a man's town, and apparently women there had set some horrible standards. We slept in big tents overnight and then were taken in boats upriver the next days. That was when things got bad. I was in the second of two boats travelling together, about ten of us in each with four guards and sailors. As soon as we were out of sight of the harbour the guards took to us. They were big and carried rifles. They hit us in the chests with the rifle butts then lifted our chemises and petticoats and skirts and fingered us, shouting obscenities and calling us whores and worse. We were scared to retaliate. Some started crying and they were picked on worse, the men groping them mercilessly. The sailors were invited to feel them up as well.

I was watching the boat ahead of us where something similar was going on. But one woman there had more gall and was braver than any of us. When they came to her at the back of the boat and lifted her skirt she reached forward, grabbed the soldier's hair, and actually pulled him over the side into the water. The other soldier hit her in the face with his rifle butt and she fell to the floor.

"The soldier in the water was quickly pulled back on board at which time he stripped the woman bare and pummeled her breasts, face and abdomen severely with his fists until she stopped making any sound. Her comrades dressed her, but when the boat reached Parramatta she was separated from the rest of us women. We heard her screaming later that night as men whipped her. They brought her bleeding to one of the houses (not ours) where the women did the best they could for her, but she died from the wounds and the shock during the night. We all applauded her bravery and learned to hate the men in charge. We also learned to obey commands and tolerate their limited abuse, although some of the women wanted to stage a mutiny then and there.

"Some of the women are still suspicious of any man they meet, and we understand. I think many of us would like to get hold of that brute alone, although we know we'd never survive any treatment we accorded him."

"I can make guesses at why the guards behaved that way Laura, as some men are just brutal in demeanor and hate women because of something in their past – a prostitute mother, or a mother who beat them or one who played games with their little bodies. But I am truly sorry. How ugly. Perhaps one day retribution will attend those men in some form just as ugly. I think that's all one can hope for."

"Well, I didn't mean to spoil the day, but you asked. Let me go back to what I asked before. And that is why did you come looking for me? I should add that I'm very happy you did by the way. Are you wanting me to be part of your life going forward

Tim, or just to be part of a playful interlude so to speak, or something else I'm not aware of? I don't mean to shock you, but it certainly was strange to suddenly see you again."

"Those are all fair questions Laura. Truthfully I don't know if I would have sought you out had I learned I was going to stay in Sydney as a fisherman or been posted to Norfolk Island or Van Diemen's Land. But I know I was incredibly happy to learn that the route across country to Green Hills would take me by Parramatta. Once I heard that, seeing you became the topmost thing in my mind. The warden in Sydney asked me if there was a woman in Sydney I wanted to take along. I said no, but that there probably was one in Parramatta. By that I meant one I might like to spend my future life with."

"That's very endearing and flattering, Tim, seriously. I thank you. But what about your wife and baby back home? Are you willing to abandon them right now? It didn't sound like that would be the case when we talked on the ship, so I deliberately didn't give myself any hope."

"That's the question I wrestle with most Laura, and I don't have a complete answer yet."

"Well, maybe I can help a little Tim. Obviously I don't know your background and early life. I hope you were head over heels in love with your wife. What's her name by the way?"

"Clarinda."

"Such a pretty name. I've said I don't know a lot about you beyond the few stories you told me on board the *Coronation*. Just as you don't know me. We're the same in that respect. What I do know from observation is that you are a sincere, compassionate, honest man of good character, with the brains and attitude to go far. I like you a lot and would love being by your side making the future happen together. Most of us women would be deliriously happy to leave early from this boring place where we are to eke out our freedom. But I have no interest in being with you if I'm to be the second woman all the time. I don't mean to hurt, but do you understand what I'm saying?"

"I do indeed Laura, and I appreciate your forthrightness. You talk directly about the same things that bother me. So here is my thought. I do not know what life will be like in Green Hills.

Even if I had no wife I couldn't ask you to accompany me at this stage until I know more about the job and opportunity there. It wouldn't be fair to either of us to make a decision without some extra knowledge. I head there tomorrow as you know.

"I wonder if you would grant me six months until I find out what's happened back home and what the future offers in Green Hills before I make any permanent decisions. I am just twenty-three and you aren't yet twenty-one. I'm aware that another man may come along in the meantime and sweep you off your feet, and that is the risk I face."

"As I've said Timothy Bartlett, I love your honesty and straightforwardness. You are right. I am young and I've only been here a month. My term is seven years. Yours is life. Yes. I can wait and live by those terms although I can't promise I won't try and influence your decision if there's any way I can do that. But I think it should be nine months, not six, given the speed and uncertainties of the length of the ships' voyages. Maybe even a year by the time letters get to destinations in both countries. I will want you to write to me from Green Hills just as you will write to your wife. Is that acceptable?"

"That's a most reasonable request, Laura. I make you that promise. Now, does this mean we are still able to go on and enjoy this fine day knowing full well we don't know what might happen in the future?"

"Yes sir, it does. And just to prove it, here's something I've wanted to do since first seeing you again."

With that she leaned up and kissed him full on the mouth, savouring the surprise and tenderness in his eyes. He hugged her in response, lifting her off her feet and joyously returning the kiss. What more could he have asked for?

Nothing. Although a small pang of doubt passed quickly through his system at the thought of leaving on the morrow.

He stopped at the rock pond and repeated the performance of the day before, catching six small baitfish. No emus were seen along the way but the brilliant kingfisher was there again in all his glory. Laura couldn't take her eyes off his dazzling coat.

He never moved the whole time Tim fished. Was he waiting for another handout? If so, they left him disappointed.

At the spot where he'd caught the cod they found two black swans paddling upstream against the current. Neither had seen one before and were entranced by their elegant carriage and contrasting red beak with white tip especially when they checked under their wings. They didn't seem to dive for fish although they inserted their necks deep under water near the banks coming up instead with weeds. Like other fauna they ignored the humans gawking at them from the bank.

Tim missed with his first line attempt, but did well with his second and third. He showed Laura what to do using the same instructions as for the natives with the clear added benefit of each other understanding the same language. Something stole her first bait but she squealed with delight as she landed a small cod at her next attempt. "OK," Tim said. "Now I want this last one to be a whopper. Steady as she goes along the bank. No, that's too fast. Come on back and try again, but at less than half the speed of that last gallop. The big chap down there needs to know he can catch that bait fish he's watching and following. Come on, that's it. Nice and slow."

The tug on the line surprised Laura and she reacted instinctively, pulling back in response. The line sped through her fingers creating a small burn and she quickly handed it to Tim.

"You've hooked the biggest one yet Laura. I can tell by his strength. This may take a while, as I sure don't want to lose him for you."

Up and down the big fish moved, anxious to get rid of the hook tight in his upper lip. Laura licked her finger burn and stood back as Tim walked back and forth along the bank. Every time his catch headed upstream Tim reeled in a little more making him use more energy against the current, all the time keeping up a constant chatter telling Laura what he was feeling and doing. After ten minutes it was clear the cod was tiring badly as his energetic bursts became more feeble. Still Tim did not dare flick him onto the bank. He hated the thought of losing him through impatience. When they finally sighted him they both cheered, for he was as long as Tim's arm. Finally, Tim reached down and gripped his line near the cod's mouth pulling him gently from the water. Compared to all the previous catches this was the daddy of them all.

"You hooked him, Laura. He's all yours. I think he should be shared tonight at the house with all your friends. He'll feed everyone. It'll be quite a celebration. I might take one along with me tomorrow but you can also have the others for the next couple of days. Ah, that was fun."

Laura basked in Tim's open generosity and unselfishness. He could have asked to take the big one along on his multi-day journey to Green Hills, but no, his thoughts were immediately for others. It was hard not to like this man. The sun had moved overhead and found a gap in the leaves of the evergreens heating up the spot where they now sat.   Tim moved the fish into the shade as Laura pulled the chicken and ale from his sack. She watched the firm movements of his hands as he pulled a leg from the chicken body and offered it to her.

"You can have that," she said, "unless you'd prefer a breast." She grinned seductively and leant forward dangling for his view two pink globes beneath her chemise.

"How could a happy red-blooded man refuse an offer like that, "Tim responded. "Maybe the chicken can wait."

And wait it did. Ages. Concealed passion and desire rose from deep within both of them. Tim removed his shirt and britches and kicked off his boots. Laura slid her chemise and dress off while Tim undid her boots for her. Their feet and bodies rejoiced in the sunlight. For a while they just looked at and stroked each other, tempting fate deliciously until they could hold back no longer.

Again and again they shared climaxes with one another until they lay exhausted and their mingling scents became stronger than that of the pines overhead.

Tim hastened to the riverbank and cautiously slid down into the water. It was surprisingly cold, but right at the bank he found he could easily touch bottom, so he let go and swam to the other side and back, then rinsed his hair and urged Laura to join him. She'd been watching the powerful muscles in his arms and legs as he swam but immediately volunteered that she couldn't swim at all and was somewhat scared of the water.

With Tim's assurances she followed his example and slid down the bank hanging on to him. She wiggled her toes in the muddy bottom and was able to stand unsupported, but was uncomfortable moving away from the bank. The water brought out goose pimples and Tim didn't try to push her to do more. Instead he helped her out before she complained how cold it was. He was dying to get out himself so his haste was for his sake as well. They jumped up and down in the sun, feeling clean and refreshed and slowly warming up. Their clothes sans boots went on before their bodies were completely dry and they tucked in to the chicken and ale ravenously.

Tim rinsed the fishes off and replacing the apples, laid them carefully inside the sack, the large one poking his mouth out. The kingfisher had disappeared from the bait pond, but they spied an eagle silhouetted against the sun and saw two baby wallabies bounding away at one point. Tim wondered if their activities had been observed by the three natives he'd met yesterday. Surely they'd understand if so.

Back at the house they showed everyone the cod they'd caught and announced it was for supper for all. The women gasped in awe and delight and scurried around to procure vegetables and make bread for a veritable feast. Since it was not yet late afternoon Tim and Laura headed for the commercial part of the river, finding it fairly quiet. Workmen were fixing the decking on one of the sloops, but the warehouses were all closed.

Tim asked if the men of the town played cricket somewhere on weekends. Laura berated herself for not thinking broadly and jumped to her feet. "Of course," she said. "How remiss of me not to think of it. The convicts play against the officials every Sunday out at what they lightheartedly call 'the oval'. It's simply an enclosed field a good fifteen minute walk from here but I'm sure the game will still be going on. Come on, I'll show you the way."

Cricket had never been a big sport in Polperro, although the boys at school would play a short hit-and-run version. Most English men, and even a number of the women, understood the game, even if they didn't play. Tim was surprised at the relatively large turnout of spectators of both sexes, and could tell that the current batsmen and bowler had clearly played for town teams back home. They were good and the spectators applauded fine shots to the ill-formed boundaries and catches behind the stumps. Laura knew the game to a minor extent, so Tim explained some of the nuances for her as they occurred. The score was written in chalk on a large slate which was held up in front of where the spectators gathered. Today the convicts were winning, to the chagrin of the officials. As the game ended it was obvious from the multitude of handshakes and clinked mugs that there was appreciation of talent and good play by members of both teams. Sort of ironic, thought Tim, as on the morrow the delineations between official and serf would be in practice again.

Dinner was a huge success with Tim having to repeatedly tell parts of his background and crime and Laura having to provide details of their fishing expedition. The women openly thanked Tim for his gifts and clearly envied Laura her relationship with this stranger who had known her on board their floating prison. Before it was lights out time, Tim and Laura escaped for a last hug and farewell kiss. Tim reiterated his promise to write. Laura reiterated her promise to wait nine to twelve months, although there was a sad twist in her tone. As if reading his thoughts Laura suddenly burst out "And no I won't be pregnant, my gallant man, although part of me wishes otherwise."

Tim laughed and kissed her. "Thank you, my sweet lady. I shall miss you in many ways. Goodbye for now." With that he dropped her hand and walked off toward the Commissariat, turning to wave until she went back inside her house.

22. *Richmond Bottoms*

The road from Parramatta to Green Hills had been forged nearly ten years earlier and was used to bring small amounts of produce from the fertile Hawkesbury Valley to Parramatta and thence to Sydney. Tim and his guard walked, their first stop being the convict camp at *Castle Hill* seven miles out, about a third of the total distance they had to travel. While his guard talked with the local militia Tim rested in the shade of a large Jacaranda tree. The first purple buds were showing and its soft foliage rendered it most attractive.   There was so much new flora and fauna to learn about, he realized, most of it highly unusual and unique.

The road alternated between strands of timber and wide open fields. They'd marched about four miles when the guard suddenly stopped and pointed off to the right, although Tim couldn't make out anything special or unusual. The guard motioned him to be quiet and wait. He unslung his rifle and undid the safety catch, raising the gun to eye level. A faint yellowish blur caught Tim's attention, and he watched as the guard rotated slightly then fired. "I think I got him," he yelled as he dropped his gun and ran across the field. Behind a small shrub they found a dead male dingo and the guard congratulated himself over his accuracy. He took out his knife and skinned the creature, planning to take it back to Parramatta on return. "They pay a bounty for these since this is sheep country and the dingo is their worst predator. Of course in the spring when the lambs come, the eagles are present as well. They are much harder to shoot but a great trophy if you get one. At least now here's one less killer to do his thing."

They spent the night at the new Government Stock Farm near *Rouse Hill.* The herds were still being mustered from Sydney and Parramatta but a few cattle already dotted the landscape and the men were allowed to sleep on the verandah of the station farmhouse. At sunrise they continued northwest for the last seven miles passing through *Mulgrave* and then crossing

South Creek via the floating Gist Bridge to enter Green Hills itself. The bridge had been built just the year before by Andrew Thompson, who had received permission to charge a toll for using it. Tim had watched his annoyed guard pass over a coin for their crossing.

When they finally arrived at the Commandant's House in Green Hills the guard handed Tim over to the officials and bid him adieu. "Good luck to you mister," he said in parting. "I think you're the type who should make it OK here." He almost sprinted away. Probably anxious to see if he could bag another dingo on the way back to his station Tim thought.

To his surprise his journey was not yet over. He'd anticipated that the two-day trek into the interior of the country would see him close to his new location. But the man he had been assigned to lived four miles further west in a small village named *Richmond Bottoms*, close to a rambling community on the river known as *Richmond Hill*. The local officials gave him directions and to his surprise indicated he would be travelling alone. They gave him all the relevant warnings about what would happen if he tried to escape into the bush and didn't turn up at the home of Mr. Jonathan Griffiths, who was to be his new master. They made it clear that if he disappeared, while it might take a while to track him down, they would surely find him, and that the penalty for re-capture would be thrashings and chain-gang work back at Castle Hill most likely.

They almost spat out the words when they talked of the convict camp, clearly having no regard for its Irish prisoners. Tim wondered why, but kept his thoughts and comments to himself. He knew he'd learn more in good time. The two men talking to him didn't seem the type you'd want to get on the wrong side of, so he didn't pursue it. With directions re-affirmed he set off alone, eager to encounter the next phase of his life.

Thinking to himself, he was more complacent over, and accepting of, his circumstances than he thought he might be. For the first time in seven months he was actually alone, and was amazed. Sure, he could bolt for the bush, but he had absolutely no inclination to do so. It took a while to realize why, but in the end he put it down to three things. In Green Hills, before striking out west, he had walked to the river front, and was pleasantly surprised to see a number of small boats on the river, most carrying produce or wool or lumber, some ferrying citizens back and forth to the opposite bank where their horses and carts were tied up. Water! That was what had unconsciously penetrated his brain and lodged there. Yes, it wasn't salt water from a nearby ocean, like the village he was raised in, and there probably weren't tides and waves, but it was water —where boats sailed, and where men respected and made use of it.

The second strange thought that registered was that finally he was about to find a fixed environment where he could hold, regroup, and take more control over his own existence. No longer would he have to endure a clammy prison, or a rotting hulk, or a fetid storage area in a ship on the high seas, or even a convict camp. He wasn't sure yet what his new environment would actually be like, but it certainly had to be better than what he'd experienced over the last nine months. His mind formed an attitude that was receptive to whatever was going to be offered.

Finally, and he had to double check that he wasn't just rationalizing, he actually was enjoying some aspects of this new land he'd been sent to. Shouldn't he be hating it and wanting to be back in England where it was more civilized and stable and mature? No, he didn't feel that way at all. Yes, when he thought about it, he missed Clarinda and his mother and Ben and Ramon and Mike and a multitude of others in the community that had been his home for over twenty years.

But there was something exciting and intangible about this land that appealed. The different fauna and flora was one aspect he'd already experienced. The clear skies, warm sun, and unpolluted fresh water were another. In Sydney his limited exposure to free citizens as they built houses or ran bakeries or managed supply shops had revealed a positive undertone of contentment, despite instances of adversity. Many of them sensed an opportunity to create and form a more rewarding existence than that possible back home. And many convicts, beneath their outspoken dislike of their treatment and the superior attitude of authorities, realized that life in the colony was probably better than the outlook which they would have faced back home, rotting in a prison, or worse, hanging from a gallows.

With an open mind, and a smile on his face, Tim pulled the entrance gate closed behind him and walked up the rutted path to the Griffiths home in Richmond Bottoms.

Richmond Bottoms was the local name for a flat triangular area of land about two and a half square miles in size. On one side it ran west-northwest to east-southeast away from the river. A second line of demarcation starting in the southeast corner ran roughly south to north to another point on the river, so that the river itself traced out a slightly curved course from southwest to northeast. Close to the river the land wasn't amenable to growing crops, as it was low and stayed wet longer than other areas.   Instead of crops, extensive boatyards lined the river banks.   The Griffiths owned a total of one hundred acres. Behind their boatyard on the riverbank was the large home. Beyond that, and a distance away, six acres were sown in wheat, two in barley and fourteen in maize. A large shed held forty bushels of stored maize from previous successful crops. Closer in to the home there were enclosures for seventeen goats and eighteen pigs, as well as stables for three horses.

Within the boatyard there were piles of different types of lumber, some sawed, some still in limbed tree form. As well, there were a number of work-sheds of different sizes. Some held a wide range of tools, some were much larger with canvas sails hanging from the roofs, drying or being cut and sewn to shape. Others held hardware to go on the boats and some provided protection for smaller dinghies, eight feet long and up, that were under construction. The big boats of course were too large to house so they were built outside. When Tim arrived there were two in various stages of construction.   One was named *Speedy*, which was nearing completion, the other in the earliest stages of construction he would later find out was to be called *Hazard*.

Tim was a fast learner with an open disposition and soon made friends with the other workers and Jonathan himself. His strength was beyond that of all the other men in the boatyard and that allowed him to bring larger loads of planks from the storage piles to the trestles holding the vessels. He could also hold the planks more securely than others, which prevented small mishaps and allowed pinning and gluing to be done more quickly. He shirked from no task, enjoying the exercise and freedom that was suddenly at hand. As he came to understand how Jonathan worked he was able to anticipate needs and be prepared with next steps in advance of being asked. It didn't take long for Jonathan to recognize Tim's talents and they started to work more closely together.

From the moment he'd first said hello to Jonathan's defacto wife, Eleanor McDonald, they'd gotten on well. She was a former convict just as Jonathan had been, and so was empathic to convicts' needs and dispositions. The fact that Tim's outlook was so positive was a pleasant surprise for her. Also, he took to her seven children immediately, picking them up and man-handling them in funny antics. Eleanor was breast-feeding the youngest, which made Tim tell her all about his wife and the child that had probably been born by now back in Polperro.

Eleanor felt comfortable enough that after checking with her mate, she had permitted him to sleep in the loft of their barn. Whenever he could he would help feed the pigs and bring in eggs from the henhouse. Two weeks after arrival he timidly asked one day if Eleanor might be able to provide him with paper and pencil so he could write some letters.

On a bleak Sunday when tools were downed for the day, he sat at a crude bench and painstakingly wrote to Clarinda and Laura. There were many false starts and crossed out words along the way. When done he re-wrote them—his vanity wanting to minimize exposure of his indecisiveness and mental wanderings. It felt strange writing to both women. He wrote first to Laura, intent on detailing his journey from Parramatta. It felt awkward, but he had fond memories and had made a promise, as had she.

August 28 1803

Dear Laura:

At last I now have regular sleeping and living
quarters and have been loaned paper and pencil to
write. While Green Hills was supposed to be my
place of assignment it turns out that I am actually
in a village five miles west of there called
Richmond Bottoms. I'm assigned to a man
named Jonathan Griffiths. He's a very decent
man, as is his defacto wife whose name is
Eleanor McDonald. They have seven children,
but have given me the loft area in the barn to
sleep in and make mine. It is cramped, but at
least it is mine. I feel fortunate to have such space
but I have to get used to being alone in it. For the
last nine months I have always been housed with
many other men convicts, so this is quite
different, and at times lonely.

Mr. Griffiths was a convict himself, having been
transported in 1790 with the Second Fleet and
sent on to Norfolk Island where he met up with
Eleanor. He came back from there in 1795 and
was granted land in this area of the country about
six years ago but has moved around a bit since
coming here. I think he is well settled now since
his house is at the back of the boatyard where he
builds both big and small boats. Apparently he
owns over one hundred acres.

I am helping him build a small sloop of about
seventeen tons which will be used to carry
produce on the Hawkesbury and Coal Rivers. He
is going to name it *Speedy* because he believes
that's what it will be, especially compared to the
smaller boats currently on the rivers.

Maybe you aren't interested in boats, but a sloop
is a type of boat we had a lot of in Polperro, so
I'm very familiar with them. This means I'm not
the novice I thought I might be working on

general boat-building. In fact I've been able to make some suggestions to Mr. Griffiths based on some of the things we learned about sailing sloops in the English Channel. I think soon he will give me some extra responsibilities. I hope so. There are all sorts of trees growing in the countryside to the northwest across the river and we use different woods for different parts of the boat. He's promised that I'll be able to go with him on one of his next expeditions to the interior to get lumber. I know I will enjoy that.

Meanwhile I am learning a lot and have met a number of the other convict workmen at the ship-yard. Most are quite a bit older than me, and have already formed their own friendships. Makes me wish you were here with me. I have written a letter back to Polperro, but who knows when I will hear back.

I hope you will write to me so I can tell you more about what I do here.

Sincerely

Timothy

He re-read it, and thought of making more changes but considered it not a bad first effort. He hadn't had to write many letters in his life, and wondered how much Laura knew about writing. As he sealed it in an envelope he hoped it wouldn't be too long before he heard back.

He knew he owed his wife Clarinda a much longer letter and a more intimate one. Tears came to his eyes as he started to write, and teardrops stained the paper. Images of Polperro, the harbour, the boats, his friends, and Clarinda swam in and out of his mind. He pictured his house and his mother and Uncle Ben so proud on their wedding day. Then the awful images of the confrontation with the revenue men and the stabbing swallowed up the loving memories and he cried again. He shook his head to banish them and gradually, with effort, conjured up loving images of Claire as he showed her his secret cave, and of cleaning up Ben's house and making love by its fireplace. At the same time as feeling close to her, he also felt wretched being so far removed. He concentrated hard and eventually rested after three separate re-writes, recognizing he wasn't able to offer anything more. What he had written would just have to do.

August 28 1803

My dearest Clarinda:

I have now been in Australia just over two months and am located in a village called Richmond Bottoms some forty miles northwest of Sydney as the eagle flies, in the middle of farm country. They grow grain of all sorts in this area and sheep farming for wool is also plentiful. The village is five miles west of an emerging township called Green Hills. It is on the banks of the Hawkesbury River which eventually flows some seventy miles north and east to the sea. Its outlet on the coast is twenty miles north of Sydney Cove.

You may wonder why on earth I am in farm country. Just beyond the farms are great forests with beautiful trees of different varieties, some soft wood, some hard wood. Convicts cut the lumber and haul it to boatyards all along the river here. This is a major river which is navigable inland to this point and so they build big boats in this area because of the timber sources nearby. I have been assigned to a Mr. Jonathan Griffiths, who is a master builder. It is a long story as to why I was moved here. It turns out there were no jobs for fishermen in Sydney but they learned I had once built my own boat – maybe it's still in the little harbour back home there, and Mr. Griffiths had asked for someone with experience to work under him in his boatyard. I've been here less than three weeks but that's what I was told.

So now I am a carpenter. I try to remember all the things Uncle Ben and others taught me, but I still have much to learn.

I think of Polperro and you often because it is so different here. Am I the father of a boy or a girl? When exactly was our baby born and what is he or she called? I'm desperate to learn as much as I can about our little one. Please tell me all the details and describe what he or she looks like so I can conjure up pictures in my head. Mr. Griffiths' wife (well they are not really married) has produced seven children, the youngest of which is still early at breast and as such is a constant reminder of what you might be doing with our baby.

The trip to Sydney took five miserable months so I imagine our baby was born before we prisoners arrived in the colony. In some ways I was lucky, as I didn't get to stay with all the other convicts on board. You will have learned that we were taken from the hulk in Plymouth Bay with no notice. Convicts are treated badly everywhere. On the ship I saved a sailor's life and the captain had me replace another tar who deserted in Plymouth. Even so the trip was long and extremely unpleasant. There were huge storms which were very scary. At times we thought we would sink and be lost forever. In the tropics it was so hot we often wore no clothes, but in the southern Indian Ocean we had ice on the mast and sails and it was bitterly cold. The food they sent was terrible but we managed to eat a lot of fresh fish we caught along the way. You would be disgusted to learn details about the quarters convicts were housed in on the ship. I was very lucky not to have to stay in them for long.

Sydney is a very primitive town, with a large number of wooden houses holding mainly

officials and militia. We worked for nearly six
weeks in gangs clearing the land, constructing
government buildings and a wharf for the big
boats. There was no paper or pencil with which I
could write to you earlier, although I kept asking.
Convicts were not treated very well, although
many other men wanted to write home as well.

The natives feel we have invaded their land and
were often a nuisance and killed many convict
men who tried to escape into the surrounding
bush. They wander around with nothing on
mostly and don't seem to have permanent homes
or caves. A few wear cloaks made of possum
skins. There are lots of little children but you
couldn't call them pretty. They are a dark brown
in colour and the men often carry a spear or
another implement they use to kill animals such
as kangaroos and wombats. They make fires
everywhere they go and are quite skilled at it as
they have no matches. I have only picked up a
few words from their language, mainly from
some of the women who fish from bark canoes,
and who I talked to.

The few female convicts in Sydney help cook
food for the soldiers and men prisoners although
one runs a pub and another owns a small bakery.
Most of the convict women were sent up the river
to Parramatta on arrival. It is fifteen miles west of
Sydney. There they were placed in houses and
made to sew work clothes for the convict men. I
met some of them from our ship, the *Coronation*
when I was being transported across country here
to Richmond Bottoms. Many of the women are
desperate or sick and the male guards treat them
horribly. One woman was beaten to death
because she pushed a soldier in the water.

The authorities are coarse, selfish and mean. In
part they remind me of barbarians from days of
old in historic England as we learned from the

story books. Because prison conditions are so bad, escaped convicts take their revenge on people who live beyond the outskirts of towns, often maiming or even killing them before stealing food and horses and riding off. It is not yet a nice place for a woman.

While I say that I must admit there are some good things here. Even though it is winter, the sun shines most days and the air is clear. There are good fish in the streams and the soil in this area is very suitable for crops and grazing. There are all sorts of colourful birds, and some strange animals. The roads are still dirt and rutted but passable, except after really serious rains. So far there are just a few stores offering goods and a very limited number of free settlers in residence. It is hard to describe because there is no equivalent place in England I can think of. Everything has to start from nothing here.

Did you get Mike to help you find my coins in the cave? You should use whatever is needed for the baby but keep the rest to buy a ticket out here in time. How are our parents doing? Polperro seems so far away, and I already find I do not remember everything there well. It's nearly a year since I left the village. I miss you badly – part of me wants to see you tomorrow, another part says you would hate it here. There are few convict wives here, and those I've met do not live nearly as well as we did in Polperro. I hope you can wait some more.

This is the first chance I've had to write, and I am anxious to hear back. I will write again once I am well into my job. Meanwhile please think of me. I love you so and miss you and wish I were home with you and our baby. I wonder when I will see him or her. I'm sure you are a wonderful mother.

A boat leaves for Sydney in the morning and I want this post to be on it so I must say farewell. To write a letter to me here you would address it to me at Richmond Bottoms, New South Wales, Australia.

Remember I love you and miss you. It is very hard living here. I feel I will always be paying unfairly for my crime. Maybe when you eventually arrive I will feel better.

My deepest love

Timothy

23. Boat Building

Speedy was nearing completion. The sloop rig was one of the simpler sailing rig configurations, typically sporting only two sails, a mainsail and a jib. A sloop also had a simple system of mast stays—a forestay, backstay, and shrouds attached to the sides. With fewer spars and control lines, sloops tended to experience less aerodynamic drag than other style boats. Sloops performed well when sailing close-hauled to windward; and offered a sound overall compromise of abilities on all points of sail. When venturing far offshore other boat styles did better since it was easier to reef small sails as the wind increased while still keeping the boat balanced. *Speedy* was built to travel up and down inland rivers and its relatively bigger sails were efficient for that purpose.

Tim talked to Jonathan about lengthening the bowsprit to increase the amount of sail carried. For downwind sailing, instead of the typical foresail he suggested a larger one overlapping a little with the mainsail to help guide the airflow and thereby make the mainsail more effective. On reflection Jonathan decided to make the change on the next boat rather than the current one since it was too far along at the current time. He was impressed with Tim's experience that led to the ideas and started to seek his input more frequently. *Speedy* was roughly thirty-five feet in length with a beam close to twelve feet, and was planned to draw about six and a half feet. Over three times the length and size of existing packet boats on the river, it was destined to change the future of water traffic on the Hawkesbury forever.

A narrow track led northwest from the opposite bank of the river to a village called *Kurrajong* on the northern flanges of the Blue Mountains. Kurrajong was the *Boorooberongal* tribe's name for a tree whose bark fibres were used to make fishing nets, ropes, and baskets. It was one of many species of trees scattered through thousands of acres. Groves of enormous turpentine, coachwood, lillypilly, scented satinwood, she-oak, swamp oak, red gum, blue gum, blackbutt, stringy bark, ironbark, box, mahogany, cedar, and lightwood trees grew in alternating climate regimes within the forest beyond. Not all species had even been discovered by Jonathan Griffiths and fellow boat builders at the time they started their boat-building businesses, and new species were to be found as late as two hundred years later, so dense and impenetrable were parts of the forest.

Gathering wood for the boats was an important task. Some of the trees grew hundreds of feet tall and had diameters measured in yards, not feet. It took a keen eye to identify one that was free of termites and straight enough for a mast, for example, or supple enough to make curved hull planks. In his first forest venture with Jonathan, Timothy stayed close, anxious to learn all he could. There were twelve men with three teams of oxen pulling large carts, ready to return with felled tree trunks. They carried large axes and saws, as well as chains and ropes for hauling purposes. Progress climbing the hills was slow and tortuous, the only reward being the time available to study local flora and fauna. Tim marveled at the luxuriant growth of the trees and the ferns and flowers. He felt like a discoverer, going where few, if any, white men had ever been before. Each day he was aware that the party was being observed by aborigines flitting behind the trees like moving shadows, but none ever ventured forth, so he presumed they were disinterested in communicating directly with these strangers in their land. They crossed small streams which presumably headed towards the Hawkesbury, now further behind each day. The smell of eucalyptus and Boronia pervaded his senses, along with an earthiness that was so distinct from the smell of the sea where he grew up.

On the fourth day out, around mid-day, the lead team halted for no observable reason and Tim hurried forward to see if some issue had cropped up with the cart or one of the beasts of burden.

"C'mon, Tim," Jonathan said. "We have something to show you." About fifty yards into the woods, they reached a small clearing and Jonathan signaled the others to stay still and be quiet. He took off on his own, and was gone nearly ten minutes before returning with a grin on his face. "Follow me, but stay quiet," he whispered. He made a path through virgin growth where twigs and burrs caught at Tim's clothes, and scratched his arms and hands. He said nothing, however, and followed the other men who didn't seem bothered at all by nature's poking and grabbing. When he finally came abreast of Jonathan he pointed upwards, saying, "There, in that gum tree, about twelve feet up in the fork to the left—a mother and baby koala." The other men had seen them before, of course, and immediately took off in all directions to find the other members of the animal group. Jonathan explained that apparently there was a good-sized family clan living in the general area but that they moved around seeking fresh food sources. A couple of the men spotted more koalas in close proximity, and rushed back to show the others their sharp-eyed findings. Koalas were relatively docile, unless perturbed, and spent most of their day sleeping. Their grey fur colour was similar to the colour of the eucalyptus trunks. Coupled with their lack of movement, that often made it difficult to find them. On one previous occasion Jonathan had seen a koala shuffling quickly across the ground, having climbed down one tree and headed for another. But it had happened only that once.

Tim was thrilled to see the furry animals, as he had heard about them but had no real understanding of what they were like. He asked Jonathan how he even knew where they were. "Well, about six years back, one of my competitors' men from down river was out foraging just as we are. He was actually looking for the source of a large mountain stream he'd seen coming down to the river. He had an aboriginal guide with him and they tracked the stream uphill for several days but never really found the source as the bush became too thick to push through. They turned and veered west seeking another way home and came upon the track we're using, but a couple of miles further inland ahead. Coming back down, his aboriginal guide said he smelled the koalas and led the chap directly to them. He thought the rest of us should know about them as they are not easy to find, so a year later a bunch of us rode out here to find them. We stop every time we go logging to check on them, and along the river we have a gentleman's agreement not to do any timber cutting in the area.

"From the little we know, their paws and legs are built for climbing and clinging. They have five digits on each front paw but the second and third digits on their hind paws are fused together to form a grooming claw. One day a female was found dead and in a pouch at her front was a tiny, tiny baby that seemed blind and without fur. The mother had teats inside so presumably the baby spent some time there growing before actually exiting into the big wide world. Other than that not much more is known. Apparently they can sleep up to eighteen hours a day. We think they are pretty finicky about which eucalyptus leaves they will eat. It's hard for us to see how the trees in that area are much different to the others nearby, but the koalas stay congregated there so there must be something special about that variety."

"Well, thanks for stopping and showing me, Jonathan. That was a treat. I've heard of some other shy animals, birds actually. Are there lyrebirds in this part of the forest, do you know?"

"I commend you on your interest in the native fauna, Timothy. There are many new things in this land we've been sent to. And I'm sure we don't even know about them all yet. I like your curiosity, and the answer is yes. Others have seen the birds whose tails fan out like a lyre, but I haven't seen them around here. I think they may dwell more in rainforest type areas, which we probably won't see on this trip.

"Now, let's get back on the trail. We have another day yet before I want to stop and cut. And by the way, let's make sure we select some hardwood just for you. I think it would make sense for you to build a slab-hut somewhere back behind the barn when we get home. You're an excellent worker and I'd like to think you'll be staying on with us for a while – at least until your pardon comes through. I think the missus likes having you around as well."

"Thank you, sir, that sounds wonderful to me. I enjoy working with you and your men. They make a good team. But more than anything at the moment I'm longing to splash *Speedy*. What do you think? Another three months and we should be ready to go?"

"Aye, lad, I want her active for the summer trade. Kable, Thompson, and Grono down the way all have similar boats under construction. As much as I'm friends with them all, I still want to beat them and get our sloop on the water first."

September flew by and Tim surprised himself at his enjoyment in boat building. He'd anticipated being unsure and uncomfortable in the job but loved every aspect, from working on the initial drawings, to gathering the wood, to cutting and planing it, to lapping and joining the hull pieces, to ensuring the wooden joints came together perfectly, to anchoring and fitting the mast in place, and beyond. Tightening the rigging, adding the hardware, to measuring and making the sails. Not that he was the leader in every department of construction, but he was happy to help out wherever it was needed. There was no task, mundane or sophisticated, that he shirked. His aim was to make the perfect boat for those who would use it.

And he'd even built his slab-hut with the help of teammates on the weekends. It still needed work but it was his alone, and he was proud of what he'd accomplished in the short time he'd been in the local lowlands. *Speedy* had been launched and met all the promises and expectations that had been made ahead of time. She was sturdy, stable, and fast, just as promised. Tim felt proud of his little part in bringing her to life, and enjoyed taking her out on the river, alone or with friends. He was looking forward to going all the way to Sydney with Jonathan in the new year and doing some real sailing down the coast of New South Wales in ocean waters, just like back in Polperro.

In mid-October as he made his way by the front door of the Griffiths home on his way to his shack, he heard his name called from within the house. Eleanor came running to the door and handed him an envelope. "Tim, you have a letter, but it's not from England, I'm sorry. Surely something should come soon from there. Here you go." He smiled as he read the address on front. 'To Mr. Tim Bartlett, C/- Mr. Griffiths, Richmond Bottoms via Green Hills'. The only person who knew that address had to be Laura in Parramatta. His letters to England would hardly have arrived yet. His pace quickened and once inside his home he threw his sack on the bed, rushed back outside, sat on the stump by the front door to catch the day's-end rays of sunlight, and carefully tore open the envelope. Two pieces of paper were filled with large writing and he slowly turned them up the right way and began reading.

> October 8 1803
>
> Dear Timothy:
>
> It was so good to get your letter. I'm glad you have found a place to stay in and a boss who is good. It's a Saturday evening here and a group of us have been playing cards, but I've left the game and found a quiet spot where I can write to you. We have no paper and pencil in this house but one of the women I work with came by at dinner time and I bought two sheets of paper from her. You'll have to excuse all my scribblings since I only have these two pages although I will write on the back too.
>
> Usually nothing very exciting happens around here as we make the same clothes every day. But there was a strange incident last month that I have to tell you about…..
>
> In Sydney late August a policeman named Joseph Luker was found murdered in a grisly fashion at the home of a wealthy Sydney woman he was supposed to be guarding. A gang of thieves was hunted down and the lady identified one, Joseph Samuel, as the main robber and murderer, although another man, Isaac Simmonds, was also suspected as a participant in the murder. Samuel was convicted and sentenced to hang by the neck until dead. Just a week ago, along with regular citizens, including a bunch from Sydney, we were all made to come and watch him and another

criminal hang in the main square, as a deterrent to our committing any crime. I never have liked watching hangings but this was weird. The nooses were tightened around their necks then they were allowed to pray with a minister, and the cart they were standing on was driven away. The secondary criminal died by strangulation but Samuel's rope snapped and he dropped to his feet, sprained an ankle, and collapsed. All of us in the crowd groaned. We were told later at the factory that the hangman's ropes were made of five cords of hemp, which enabled them to hold one thousand pounds for up to five minutes without breaking, more than sufficient to hang someone. When Samuel fell down, the executioner readied a second rope, also five-hemp, and placed it around Samuel's neck, forced him onto the same cart, and drove the cart away again. The other chap was still kicking weakly at this point. When the cart was driven off, Samuel fell again, and the noose slipped off his neck. The executioner stood Samuel up to try again, but by now the crowd was calling for Samuel to be freed. But the executioner readied a third five-hemp rope, ordered the cart driven back, forced Samuel onto it, fastened the noose around his neck, secured it very carefully and tightly as we all watched, and then ordered the cart driven away.

You wouldn't believe it but this rope actually snapped, and Samuel dropped to the ground and stumbled over, trying to avoid landing on his sprained ankle. This was just too much. He'd been hanged three times and survived them all. Now, the crowd really yelled. The governor was summoned and upon inspection of the ropes, which showed no evidence of having been cut, the governor and the entire mob watching agreed that it was a sign from God that Samuel had not committed any crime deserving of execution.

Later his sentence was commuted to life imprisonment instead. We were never told but I suspect they went after the other robber, Isaac Simmonds, as the real murderer.

It was the talk of the factory for days afterwards. We heard that Samuel was taken back to Sydney to work on a labour gang. I used to think that most of the prisoners we travelled with on the ship to Sydney had committed essentially minor crimes. What makes men do what Samuel and Simmonds did? From what we women could find out, Samuel had been a robber back in England, was transported in 1801 after five years in gaol, but escaped from the Sydney colony. He was only twenty-one on arrival in Australia, same age as you, Timothy. Why kill the policeman?

By the way, on the route to Green Hills, you must have passed the convict camp at Castle Hill. It's amazing how news filters in to our working factory, but apparently this is a bad camp. It houses three hundred Irish prisoners who are rowdy, belligerent, and unruly, in general felt to be more dangerous than most convicts. Guards do not like being posted there, fearing the men will one day break out and cause trouble, based on some of the rumours they hear. It seems the prisoners hate the hard work of clearing and de-stumping the land for a stock yard program the Governor established. I hope if they do break free that they don't come to Parramatta with evil intentions. There are times when I long to be out of here, but relative to some of the women I am still a brand new slave. I've done well in a very short time by being super obedient and subservient, which I hate.

Whenever I feel miserable I remember our picnic along the river bank, and that cheers me up.

Some days I want to know if you hear anything from people in Polperro, other days I don't want to know. But please don't stop writing.

Thinking of you

Laura

Tim was both delighted and surprised to get Laura's mail. He realized as he reread it, that in fact it was the first private letter he'd ever received in his life. He hadn't expected to hear back from her so quickly, but was glad she had responded. He thought about her for a while longer and imagined her day-in, day-out job had little variety, unlike his, and that she probably looked forward to breaking the monotony by doing something different, like writing. Her handwriting was larger than his but neater, except for a number of erasures. He wondered what Clarinda's writing would be like when she responded to the letter he had written two months ago. She wouldn't even have received it yet. Maybe, if he was lucky and it had travelled on a fast cargo boat, it would arrive in time for Christmas.

It struck him that Christmas would be very different this year. Last year at Christmas time he was on a hulk in Plymouth Bay and the family had come to visit. This year Christmas would be in summer, and from all accounts it would be hot. Back home in England it would be cold. His mind wandered back to Polperro. The winds would be pounding up the harbour and making their presence felt even through the thickest of clothes. And he wouldn't be with Claire, the baby, his mother and Ben and Claire's parents sitting around an open fire sharing tales of yesterday. What had triggered those thoughts? he wondered. The letter from Laura? Did the reminder of female companionship affect him so readily? Did he miss Claire that much? Or was it both Claire AND Laura he missed? Claire was so far away. And Laura was so close.

He carefully folded the pieces of paper with Laura's writing and stored them in a tin he had found which he replaced on the shelf at the back of the room. 'Don't get maudlin,' he said to himself. 'Take a lantern and go chop some firewood. Let exercise stop the brain from thinking.'

As Tim's relationship with Jonathan grew he became aware of business arrangements with other boat builders. Building boats required a lot of cash up front, especially in the purchase of canvas and lumber, unless one cut the latter by oneself. It could take years to build a good boat and no income was derived until she was either sold to an owner, or was in trade on the river, still owned by the builder. There were economies when the builders banded together on joint wood-gathering expeditions, and in the purchase of sail cloth, tools, and hardware. It turned out that Jonathan had several loose arrangements with the men he'd described as competitors. There were times when they actually co-operated, for there was enough opportunity and demand that selling the boats was not an issue. It wasn't an industry where one man's product was chosen over another's. It was an industry where products couldn't be built fast enough.

Jonathan had pre-sold *Speedy* to Mr. Samuel Thorley, who had arrived with the Third Fleet late in 1791. Samuel owned the Black Dog tavern down at The Rocks, and had the foresight to see how getting fresh produce quickly from the inland regions to Sydney with its growing population could be profitable. Not only had he pre-bought *Speedy*, he was also helping to finance the construction of *Hazard*, to the point of being half-owner. As Tim learned more about the business side of the industry the more he became intrigued with a desire to own his own boat. He said nothing publicly, but made sure he learned everything he could about the myriad aspects of boat building. He knew how to sail, he was learning how to build.

In late October they splashed *Speedy* for her first trials on the river. She behaved beautifully, and was a grand sight tacking back and forth while they tested the tiller and the sails under varying conditions. As Tim had suspected, she just flew downwind wing-on-wing, but even when tacking across the wind she sailed well close-in. They found a few leaks in the hull and in the roof of the small cabin, and a couple of stays loosened under high wind pressure, but she was stable, and actually drew a few inches less draft than what they had expected. It was in the sailing that Tim's mastery became evident, and Jonathan and other yard employees were appreciative of a natural skill they didn't have.

Back on shore and set up again in the land framework, the team went to work to make repairs and changes. And by the end of the month she was ready for the tougher test of worthiness on the open seas. Jonathan had spread the word locally that he would be taking the boat to Sydney on her first open water trial run. He wanted to carry goods of a less-perishable nature as he would be taking time to perform tests along the way. As a result he received several large consignments of grain, and a few smaller consignments of wool. Their size and weight provided exactly what he was looking for, forcing efficiency in loading and storing, and in appropriate weight distribution along the boat's length. He loaded up at Green Hills, two miles downstream, but headed back to the boatyard to load personal provisions.

On Thursday December 1st, Jonathan and Tim and four others pulled *Speedy* away from the bank and headed downstream. The river was full of twists and turns but easily navigable. Not much of a challenge for Tim, whom Jonathan had granted Master status. It was clear that the river and side lagoons were rich in fish, birds, and edible plants because in slow-moving water areas the aborigines were seen in abundance. From their campsite on shore they fished in their bark canoes or used their digging sticks in the soft banks, harvesting the native yam which was a staple for them. Other edible tubers and floating ferns added to the diets. At one point where the boat stopped overnight the aborigines showed them turtles that they had caught, along with fresh mussels. It was clear that the Hawkesbury was a significant source of food for the local tribes, and Tim was entranced with their ingenuity, as well as their dependence on the clear water source.

They finally joined up with some smaller boats anchored off Mount Elliott Island in Broken Bay at the head of Pittwater. Several captains rowed over to satiate their curiosity about the large sloop that had arrived and the *Speedy* crew enjoyed showing off the special features they'd built into the vessel. One of the smaller packet boats had just come north from Sydney ahead of a storm and the down-riverboats were waiting for it to clear. Conditions were just what Jonathan wanted for his tests and so the next morning they maneuvered carefully out into the rising swell. Tides weren't a big issue in the estuary due to its large size, nor was wave size or periodicity, but that changed with the high winds once out of the protection of land.

A light rain was falling as they headed east a couple of miles offshore and then turned south. The southwesterly driving the storm was running between twenty and thirty knots with waves around nine or ten feet. Conditions didn't faze Timothy in the least although the other men were apprehensive and uncomfortable. This was like a regular winter day back in Polperro even to the direction and strength of the winds. While his crew was inexperienced they were enthusiastic and trusting of his command so worked the sails as he requested with alacrity. Even heavily laden the boat rode the troughs and crests of the waves well, although Tim could see that the motion was producing the first signs of seasickness in three of the men who weren't used to the pitch, yaw, and roll of open water sailing. They were not broadside to the waves so there was little rolling, but to make their ride as least distressful as possible he worked hard to keep his direction fixed and firm, so eliminating violent yawing. There was nothing he could do about wave size and frequency so he taught them how to fix their eyes forward and to anticipate the up and down motion of each wave. The size of the waves was such that the bow often pierced the crests and water flooded across the deck. But the boat was highly stable and rode the ups and downs well.

The only distraction along the route was a pod of whales, hard to see off the port side in the rain, but close enough for the men to shout with exhilaration as the whale plumes broke in the air. No other boats were seen and after three hours the wind dropped and the waves lessened in height so Tim gladly handed the helm over to Jonathan. They moved closer in to shore and tacked back and forth, amazed at the number of large sandy beaches they could see forming the coastline. Cheers resounded across the deck as the

Heads came into view with the promise of calmer waters in Sydney Cove. Tim and Jonathan checked the cargo and found only minimal movement had occurred, and noted a couple of ideas for more partitions to help stabilize future loads.

The boat received approving stares and whistles as it pulled around Dawes Point and tied up to a wharf to unload. Sailors and warehousemen alike came and admired its size and design and kept Jonathan and Tim busy answering questions. The audience was particularly impressed by the ocean sea-worthiness the boat had exhibited coming south along the coast.

What the sailors had achieved had previously only been the purview of much larger boats several hundred feet in length. Jonathan accepted the accolades for his design but passed accolades for seamanship directly to Tim.

Celebrations at Mr. Thorley's pub at the Rocks carried on all night.

24. *What Next?*

The return trip was anti-climactic relative to the outbound journey. The load of supplies was much lighter and included various merchandise from warehouse agents, along with government supplies, including sacks of mail for residents upstream. Mr. Thorley travelled back with them, anxious to see first-hand how his boat performed. Going back up the coast Tim experimented with broadside runs to test the extent of roll that could be achieved with comfort, as well as a different jib sail of the type he had mentioned much earlier to Jonathan. It wasn't a permanent arrangement as the appropriate cleats, pulleys, and stays were not in place, but it provided Jonathan with input that seemed to validate what Tim had indicated.   With the wind generally behind them, despite time taken in new trials, they made excellent time. Even Jonathan's competitors congratulated him on arrival back at Green Hills, where they unloaded all the barrels, cases, trunks, and bags from the hold. They took the empty vessel back to the boatyard, but left her moored to the bank, there being no reason to haul her onto land. They needed to make some minor adjustments to the fittings, but that was all. Once those were complete they'd be able to pay full attention and give all their concentration to building *Hazard*, incorporating all they'd learned from their trip south.

Jonathan invited the whole team to his house for a celebratory dinner the next evening, and they all looked forward to some of Eleanor's roasts and berry pies. The weariness finally hit Tim as he trudged to his hut. The trip had been a wonderful success but he now realized, having finally stopped, just how tired he was.   Being out in the heavy seas had required deployment of all his skills and concentration, and a lot of self-reliance and effort, given that the others had had minimal exposure to open water sailing.   His head hit the horsehair pillow and it was going on noon the next day before he woke.

He was sitting in a rocker on the Griffiths' verandah when an unknown horseman sauntered up. "Hi, mister," he drawled. "Is there a Mr. Griffiths living here? "

"Sure is, "Tim responded. "This is his house. But he's out with the older kids in the back paddocks behind us if you need to talk to him. Should be back soon. Now, the missus though is inside. If you like I can go get her for you."

"No, it's actually not him I want. I need to check if there's a Timothy Bartlett here as I have a letter for him from England that came addressed to Sydney. The militia there says he's assigned to Mr. Griffiths here in Richmond Bottoms. Do you know if he's around here somewhere?"

"He sure is. You happen to be talking to him. Are you from the post office?"

"Yes sir Mr. Bartlett, sort of. Delivering for them anyway. There are many unclaimed letters in Sydney apparently because it's not known where many of the men ended up. Clearly someone knew your name and your letter and a bunch of others were sent to us in the government dispatch bags that arrived just yesterday on that new boat that came up from Sydney. Now are you sure you're Mr. Bartlett? I'd hate to give this to the wrong fella. Maybe that Mrs. Griffiths can vouch for you."

Tim could hardly wait to get the letter, which he assumed was from Clarinda. It must have been written before his letter arrived back in Polperro if it went to Sydney, not Green Hills, he thought. Did Clarinda miss him that much? Maybe it was because the baby had arrived early and she was letting him know. That would be nice.

But how many men would claim to be Tim Bartlett when they weren't?, he wondered. Damn this chap's hide for wanting to double check... I want that letter. He got up and went off to fetch Eleanor.

"Afternoon, ma'am." He lifted his hat. "I'm from the constabulary at Green Hills. Got a letter for a Mr. Bartlett. This man says that's him. Is that right?"

"Sure is, sir, I think he'll be very happy to get it. Thanks for bringing it along."

"Just part of the Governor's service, ma'am."

Reaching in his saddle bag he pulled out an envelope and handed it to Tim. "There you are, Mr. Bartlett. Happy to meet you all. I'll make sure I remember next time."

With that he pulled his hat down securely on his head, turned his horse around, and trotted off.

Tim tore at the envelope, anxious to read the contents. They were far different than what he had expected however.

July 1803

Dear Timothy:

I know Clarinda's mother wrote to you last month, but I have some extra information to share. We keep hoping to hear from you and I'm so sorry that her letter to you would have contained such horrible unexpected news. We debated whether to wait to write till we heard from you but thought you should know as soon as possible. Of course we don't even know when, or even if, you will get our letters. We pray constantly they will somehow find you.

Young Thomas is now two months old and has a fine set of lungs I can tell you. We all love him dearly. His hair is growing out. It is very thin and fine and a gold colour, as was Clarinda's when she was a baby. As you know, he was born big – his appetite matches. He's going to have your size and strength I'll warrant.

But why am I writing? I don't know if Claire's mother mentioned it but in April Mike and Betsy Anne were married. They are a lovely couple and nearly everyone in the village attended the wedding. I'm sure you weren't aware, although Clarinda may have known, that Betsy Anne cannot have children. Somewhere in her childhood days she had a disease that left her incapable of conceiving – I don't know the details, nor do I need to know.

Very recently she and Mike talked to Ben and me and to Claire's parents and have come up with an idea that I think you'll approve. There are two parts to it. First, they would like to adopt Thomas and raise him as if he were their own baby. We all think that's a wonderful idea and feel you would agree. After all, you and Mike were very close, as were Claire and Betsy.

But beyond that they had another request – that they be permitted to buy your and Claire's house. It sits vacant of course while they live with Mike's parents. There seems little other use for it and it's a shame to think that it will simply gather dust and mold if not used. Mike offered a reasonable price as he would like to have all the furniture that's in it as well since they have almost none. He would pay twenty-five percent now and the rest over ten years. In a way the sale proceeds would be yours, since the house is in your name. Ben and I would create an account and keep the money safe for you. Also, while touching on money, your stash of coins that Mike retrieved for Claire is in Claire's parents' hands, so in a way they are part of an estate in your name too. As Claire was dying she asked her mother to safeguard them. We could ask to add them to the house sale fund but for the moment they represent a sort of trust arrangement between Claire and her mother that we think should be preserved. Her parents don't need the money as the cartage business they set up with Betsy's parents is doing extremely well.

While we wait to hear from you we are allowing Mike and Betsy to rent your place for almost nothing, and Thomas already sleeps and eats there. Betsy is a wonderful mother to him. This is so hard in many ways. We have lost a lovely daughter-in-law not long after losing you. It is hard to sleep some nights. We know we cannot change anything but we keep wishing we could. It seems crass to talk about money when our loss is so painful. Please excuse me for doing so but we need to take care of things in your absence.

Oh Tim, so much has changed in such a short time. We all still find it hard to believe that you were handed the sentence you got and that you were spirited away without our knowing. Where are you now my son? My heart aches for you, for your absence, for the unfairness dealt you and most of all for the loss of your loved one. We suppose God must have a reason but he hasn't shared it with us.

I hope this finds you well. Will you ever come back here? Will your son ever know you? These are the questions that plague us daily.

We visit Clarinda's grave every day. Somehow it helps.

May God bless you in his infinite wisdom.

Your loving mother

Tim's wretchedness was palpable. Clarinda was dead? What had happened? Where was the letter from her mother? He had a son, but Clarinda had been buried? She must have died in childbirth, he thought. Oh why wasn't I there?

Tears flowed freely down his cheeks and he stood up, his head spinning.

How could this be? What happened to my lovely wife, mother of my baby? Why am I stuck here, thousands of miles away? This must be a mistake. But why would mother write so if it was? Why wasn't I told sooner? Could I have gotten special permission to go home? No, I guess not. Where is she buried? Did she nurse the baby a little or did she die as he was born?

What happened? And what is this about Michael and Betsy Anne? They can have anything they want as far as I'm concerned. Why didn't Mike tell me about Clarinda? Was she sick ahead of time? Did they know in advance but didn't tell me? What else are they not telling me? Will Mrs. Hinson's letter tell me more? How come it hasn't arrived if it was written earlier? Oh, this is miserable. I am inconsolable. Where is my Clarinda?

He sat back down on the porch and held his head in his hands, shaking it from side to side. Never would Clarinda join him now. Maybe his son would in years to come. But now he was going to be Mike and Betsy's son. Maybe he'd never know the story about his real father. Oh woe. Where was the letter he wanted from Clarinda? Maybe it was still coming, just as one was coming from her mother. Maybe she wrote way before she was due to deliver. Yes, that must be it. Her letter and that from her mother were just on slower boats. It happened. And this one had found him OK even though it was only addressed to Sydney. Or maybe the others were on the list of unclaimed letters at the Sydney Post Office. If only he'd known when they were there last week, he could have checked. Oh, misery.

A numbness was setting in as his despondency increased and the recognition that he had no recourse started to register, unwanted as it was, in his brain. There was nothing he could do except wait for the next letter and cry his eyes out meantime. He decided to take a long walk into the wilderness, wanting to see no one, to talk to no one, and to be seen by no-one. He went back to his hut, put the letter in his tin, grabbed his hat and a walking stick, and took off through the animal enclosures and the grain fields, with no clear destination in mind. It didn't matter. Nothing could change the news he'd just received, nothing could ease the heartache and emptiness he felt.

He came to the road that went back towards Green Hills one way and to Kurrajong in the opposite direction. Neither interested him, so he continued southwest knowing he'd come to the river eventually. The river was his friend. It flowed on no matter what. It didn't stop for death or birth. It just went on. Yes, it sometimes overran its banks and spread wide across the earth, but it never dried up. That's what he'd have to do now.

Let his grief take him where it would but then come back to the life he had and go on. Why should he stop? What good would that do anyone? Especially his son.

The western sun stung his red-rimmed eyes but in less than an hour he came to the bank of the Hawkesbury and sat down on the grassy bank watching the bubbles from fish beneath the surface. As his eyes re-focused he became aware that he was looking at an island in the middle of the river and immediately decided to swim to it and see if he could then swim the rest of the way to the opposite bank. The river wasn't anywhere near its full height as summer had just arrived so he knew the current wouldn't be that strong. To check, he threw a small branch in and watched as it lazily drifted downstream. He walked along the bank past the upstream end of the island, knowing that the current, possibly faster under the surface, would push him along. He waded in, testing the strength of the current, and started swimming diagonally toward the island. He made it about halfway along its fifty-yard stretch and breathed easily having enjoyed the challenge and exercise. The island wasn't very interesting and took almost no time to explore being only fifteen yards wide at the widest point. Medium-sized trees were growing on it so it clearly had been there for some time, having probably broken away from a bank years before.

Tim headed to the upstream end of the island once again, wading in until the water was chest high, then struck out diagonally for the opposite bank. The flow was a little faster this side of the island as the gap to shore was narrower. But he made it with little trouble and hauled himself out, took off his wet clothes, and hung them over a branch in full sun. His head felt better and he realized that at least for the moment he wasn't torturing himself with unanswerable questions and thoughts. He watched a kingfisher bird dive and catch a small shiny fish then sit and swallow it whole after turning it around in his beak. Guess God made his jaw muscles able to move that way for a reason, Tim thought. He seems to have a design for most things, perhaps there's one for me too. Behind him a kookaburra took up his raucous, laughing call, and it made Tim smile. That old man up there is sure trying hard to cheer me up he thought. OK, God, how about showing me a wallaby running on the wind now just to top it off...

No such moment arrived, but instead, a turtle laboriously climbed up the bank and sunned himself almost at Tim's feet. Not quite as fleet of foot as a wallaby, he thought. But nature was definitely in overt presence around him.   Was there some message here, he wondered, or was all this just coincidence? Out of the mind's logic a thought occurred that had obviously been behind some of the words in his letter to Clarinda. Maybe she was just too delicate and fragile a woman who would never have been able to make it in this tough land. Was God keeping her home for a reason? Would life have been more miserable here than in Polperro for her? Jonathan's wife seemed to have survived here OK but from the tales he told about life at Norfolk Island in the early days it was pretty clear that Eleanor was a remarkable woman with a constitution of iron.   That wasn't Clarinda for sure.

He pulled on his shirt and britches, and while still damp he knew they would dry out pretty fast as he continued his walk southwest along the bank.   He was surprised when thirty minutes later he encountered a broad stream coming down from the mountains to his right, and emptying into the Hawkesbury. No one had mentioned this to him back at the boatyard. Perhaps because the island he'd found made the river non-navigable, there was no interest in its course beyond that point.   This new stream was too wide, too deep, and too fast to wade across, so he turned and followed its course into the mountains.

The mountains now cast their shadows across his path although there was plenty of light in the sky above. He became aware of a new sound, that of rushing water, and shortly was able to see a waterfall in the distance perhaps fifty feet tall running off the ledge of a steep cliff. At its base was a giant, wide, rock pool, catching the strands of the falling water before they were channeled back into the stream he'd been following.

A movement at the far edge of the pool at the base of the cliff caught his eye and he stopped quickly to see what it was. He was surprised to see an aboriginal man sitting on a large rock with his feet dangling in the water. He seemed to be digging at something as his back moved up and down. In order to minimize surprise and any unwanted reaction Tim called out "Coo-ee, Coo-ee" several times, as he'd seen the natives do when wanting to communicate over a distance. He stood stock-still but was amazed when he realized the man was walking towards him rather quickly.

As he skirted the edge of the pool, he made a beckoning gesture with his hands, which Tim interpreted as an invitation to approach. There were no weapons in sight and when Tim could make out the chap's features he sensed a desperation in the man, who seemed to be older, with greying stubs of hair on his face and chest, and numerous scars across his body. His behavior was uncharacteristic of native strangers whom Tim had encountered before. But the closer he came the more expressive the hand and wave movements became, with Tim eventually understanding that the man was asking him to come and help with something. And clearly with a sense of urgency as well.

Back around the pool they went to the large rock Tim had observed from a distance. It didn't take much to identify the old man's concerns. For there, up to his chin in the water, was a small boy, whimpering with pain from another large rock which had pinned one of his legs against the rock bottom of the sub-pool. There must have been a cut on the leg as a fairly large stream of blood was flowing out. Tim looked quickly around and saw a couple more boulders about the size of the one on the boy's leg. He figured the boy must have been playing in the pool and reached up and toppled the stone that now pinned him. There was fear in the boy's eyes and Tim realized the old man had been bending down to try and lift the stone when he first saw him but it was too heavy. It was definitely no small rock and Tim raised a question in his own mind as to whether he was even strong enough to lift it. He nodded to the old man—perhaps the boy's grandfather?—and waded to the grassy verge of the big pool where he took off his clothes a second time. He looked around at the nearest trees hoping to find a low-hanging branch he could break off and use, but there was nothing suitable. He

looked at the old man and drew his arm back and forth in a
throwing motion pointing to his fist as he did so. The old chap
grinned and raced off about twenty yards into the bush and
came back with his spear. Good for you, old fellow, Tim thought.
Together they headed back to the sub-pool the boy was stranded
in and Tim stroked his hair in a gesture he hoped would calm the
young chap.

He now planned to demonstrate to the grandfather how he
was hoping to free the young boy. He positioned the old man
directly in front of but facing away from the boy, and straddling
the young body. He laid the spear within reach on one of the
side rocks forming the sub-pool border. He showed the old man
that he was going to want the blunt end of the spear to be used
on the rock bottom by repeatedly hitting it on the stone base of
the pool . He found a smaller rock and demonstrated how he
was going to try and pull the big rock off the boy's leg and that
the old man should wedge the throwing end of his spear
underneath the rock when it moved off to prevent it slipping
back even while Tim worked to hold it out of the way. Once the
rock pinning the boy was stationary, he should turn and lift his
grandson up onto the pool edge out of harm's way. Tim went
over the procedure three times, his eyebrows raised at the end
to see if the old man understood. He got back a strong head nod
and a toothless grin.

Tim then gestured by putting his fingers to the man's mouth
and then touching them to the boy's ears that he should tell the
boy what they were going to try and do. At first the old man
seemed puzzled but the boy said something and grandpa then let
loose a veritable lecture using his hands and the small rock to
show the boy the idea. The youngster stopped his whimpering
and indicated he was ready. The old man took up his position
with spear in hand. Tim backed away, took a deep breath, bent
over, and reached down about two and a half feet and hauled on
the stone.   But it didn't budge, and he came up sputtering,
realizing the rock was substantially heavier than he had
anticipated. He made it clear to the other two that he was going
to look more closely at the rock but wasn't going to try and pull it
off just yet. He took another deep breath and put his face down

near the bottom of the small pond, inspecting the rock on all sides. He then searched the perimeter of the rock pool looking for useful indentations. As he did so he came up with a small modification of the plan that he thought should work. The boy was whimpering again so Tim patted his head and then showed him that he needed him to pull his good leg up high and as tight as possible to his chest while Tim pulled the nasty rock in a slightly different direction than he tried the previous time.

Checking that boy and man were both ready, Tim inhaled and exhaled several times, dragging in more and more air on each repetition. Instead of standing, he now sat down on the rock bottom, back against one wall and braced his feet against the other side of the narrow pool with one leg on each side of the heavy rock. He tapped the boy's good leg and was pleased to see an immediate response as he pulled it well out of the way against his chest.

Tim reached over and around the large pinning rock and gradually tightened his grip on it. Allowing the smallest bubbles of air to escape as he slowly exhaled, he summoned up all his strength and maneuvered the rock slowly but surely off the boy's leg. He saw the end of the spear come down to form a wedge and suddenly the boy was being lifted out and Tim exhaled all the way and surfaced, his face red and his fingers raw with cuts. The lad was in a lot of pain, for the rock had caused a nasty cut deep into the bottom part of the leg, and Tim could see a fraction of bone through the opening. At least the youngster was free and they could proceed to the next stage of response. Tim carried the boy to a stretch of sand and laid him down. There were thanks evident in the boy's eyes but he was still in pain. There were thanks in the old man's eyes also and he stroked the boy's hair. Tim headed for his clothes and retrieved his knife from the scabbard hanging on his belt. Without waiting for an answer he cut two identical two-foot lengths from the spear handle and then went searching for wads of moss growing on the north side of rocks beneath the waterfall. The light was fading fairly fast now, and through a series of hand gestures Tim asked the old man to make a fire. He was worried the young boy might go into shock and wanted to make sure he could keep him warm if necessary. He then took the old man with him and indicated he was looking for vines and bark. Tim grinned as the old chap caught on quickly and soon had gathered plenty for Tim's needs.

As the light finally succumbed, Tim cut off one of the sleeves of his shirt at the shoulder, and gently pulled it over the boy's foot and up his leg to cover the wound. He washed out two of the moss pads thoroughly and inserted them into the cut upside down under the cloth sleeve, then added two heavy sheets of bark over the top of the wound area. He placed the two cut parts of the spear under the knee and behind the injury, the intent being to prevent any knee-bending of any form that might exacerbate blood loss, as well as to have something hard to tie the vines around once he had them pressing tightly on the bark over the wound. Pressure would help stop the bleeding, but he also elevated the boy's leg above his heart onto a rock so that less blood would be pumped to the wound. It wasn't bleeding enough to threaten life now but it did need attention as soon as possible.

Tim stopped and was happy to notice that the boy had drifted into a soft sleep. His grandfather nodded his head up and down in clear appreciation, his moist eyes reflecting the moonlight that had now arrived. Tim pulled his britches back on, added his one-sleeved shirt, put the knife back in its scabbard, and replaced his belt.   The old chap brought more wood for the fire then indicated for Tim to stay put while he went off somewhere. He was gone longer than Tim had expected, but he brought back his throwing stick and boomerang from wherever they had been hidden. More importantly he pulled out four large frogs from a small bag and proceeded to cook them over the fire. That's what had taken so long, Tim realized –he'd been off catching dinner.

To his amazement the frog legs were actually quite sweet and edible.

25. *Sad Acceptance*

In the morning Tim insisted the boy should come home with him to have his leg treated by a doctor. The old man protested a little but acquiesced since Tim was his grandson's rescuer. The easiest way for Tim to carry the boy was to have him sit and ride on his shoulders although that wasn't the best for blood flow. Every half hour or so they stopped and Tim made the boy lie down and elevate his leg for ten minutes. They marched down to the Hawkesbury then turned left and headed north and east. They didn't attempt to cross at the island but kept on, eventually arriving opposite the boat yard in the early afternoon.

Several small dinghies were moored at the bank for transportation back and forth across the river and it didn't take long using one of them for the three of them to be safely on the other side in the main yard. Others carried the young boy to the verandah and Eleanor and Jonathan carefully undid the splint and checked the wound. It had stopped bleeding but was still ugly and raw. Jonathan told one of the workers to take his horse and ride to Green Hills and bring back the doctor as quickly as possible. Meanwhile, Eleanor cleaned the wound as best she could with fresh towels. Two hours passed before the doctor arrived. He was highly complimentary of Tim's initial efforts and was pleased with Eleanor's further cleansing. He sprinkled some powder on the wound and indicated to the grandfather that he was going to stitch the skin across the wound and to tell the boy to be brave while he did so.

When Tim finally relaxed and turned around he was surprised to find a group of about ten aborigines sitting quietly in the boatyard watching and waiting. He wondered where had they come from and how had they heard about the boy. The old man must have somehow communicated with them during their trek along the river although he had noticed nobody on the way. The doctor applied more splints and spoke a couple of aboriginal words to reassure the boy. Hearing these, a man who had been sitting on the ground came forward and helped the boy to his feet. He signaled back to the others and two younger men rose and stopped in front of Tim. They handed him a boomerang, spear, throwing stick, and small shield, clearly as tokens of thanks, then helped support the boy as they all walked off. Tim's verbal thanks were heard but not acknowledged.

Jonathan walked up and patted Tim on the back. "That's just how they are, my son. Thankful and appreciative but not verbose in those thanks. They clearly recognized what you had done – the old man probably told them all the details. Gifts like these are not given up easily in my experience. You should treasure them. And I want to add my sincere thanks. Acts like yours do more to help the natives understand we mean them no harm than anything else we do. I'm proud of your efforts. I'm going to ask the doctor to stay and join us for our dinner tonight. He's a good man and that will be his payment since dinner will be special. Now I need to help Eleanor prepare, so we'll see you in a couple of hours, yes?"

"Ah, I guess so," Tim responded, as he suddenly realized he'd forgotten all about the celebration that was planned. His mind quickly drifted back to yesterday and he remembered the letter from his mother. All thoughts of Clarinda and his family and Polperro had disappeared on his trek and the rescue of the young boy. God did move in mysterious ways, he thought. A loss and a replacement. Would the boy have survived had he not come along? Probably, but the event was cathartic in any case. From feeling as if the world was not worth living in yesterday, he now felt a lightness and goodness in his soul, and it was comforting.

Dinner that night was wonderful. They had fresh ham, corn on the cob, homemade bread, and apple pie. The doctor and Mr. Thorley had a number of fascinating stories to tell and the time passed quickly. Jonathan led a toast to the success of *Speedy* and thanked all his workers for their extra work that helped launch the boat ahead of his competitors. Rising to the occasion, and in unprecedented fashion, Tim raised a toast to Eleanor, not only for her splendid meal, but also for her work on the young aboriginal boy, and for letting Tim be part of their lives. Tim was asked to repeat the story of what happened out in the bush and at the end Eleanor remembered that he'd gone walkabout after receiving a letter. "Was it from your wife?" she asked.

"No," Tim replied, "it was from my mother instead. She was catching me up on the news since I'd left. I'm amazed her letter found me." Hoping to cut off further conversation he added: "She says there are more letters on the way so I will look forward to those. At least now they know me at Green Hills." He decided it was not the right time to bring up his wife's death and spoil the mood of the dinner. He'd tell Jonathan in a couple of days.

It was several days before Christmas that the letter from Clarinda's mother arrived. Unlike his mother's letter, which was such a shock, Tim opened this one eagerly, anxious to learn more about Clarinda's death.

June 1803

My dear Timothy:

It is with a heavy heart that I write to you. I know your mother will write later as well. You have a fine son Thomas, born May 8 of this year. He was a very big baby and unfortunately Clarinda could not deliver him normally. I do not know how much you know about the birth process but when a baby cannot come out the normal way it has to be extracted from the mother's belly by making an incision there. This has been done several times in the history of the village but not with good results. I am so sorry to have to tell you that Thomas was brought into the world this way, but Clarinda did not survive the process. This is so hard to tell you, Timothy. Claire was able to hold Thomas, give him his name, and nurse him for two weeks but an infection of some form made her very sick and she could not survive it. She fought valiantly and we even had a doctor from Plymouth come, but it was too late.

My husband and I have lost our loving daughter, and you have lost your beautiful wife. This is so hard to even write about when you are so far away. Clarinda loved you with all her heart. She would talk about how wonderful you were in her marriage, the plans you shared with each other, and the joy you looked forward to with your unborn child. She was so happy she was pregnant and going to have your baby. Thomas indeed looks a bit like you – for that Claire was very happy. In particular he has your vibrant eyes. He coos and gurgles all the time. We have been looking after him as best we can, but he needs a father, and mother. We wish you were coming home again but know that cannot be.

We are all very sad here Timothy. There is a pall over the whole village. Few have enthusiasm for their daily business. We have lost you and Claire both. Life seems so unfair. I do not know what else to say.

We buried Claire in the cemetery on the hill next to her grandmother and not far from where your father rests. It was very hard to bury our daughter – normally parents would die before their children leave this world. There is a simple headstone marking her grave. It reads

Clarinda Hinson Bartlett

1782 – 1803

Survived by her husband Timothy

and son Thomas

Her Love Will Last Forever

Words are just not enough, Timothy but that's all we have. We will care for your son, and mourn our daughter. We hope this letter finds you in a timely manner. Please let us know your thoughts.

Again I am so sorry to have to send this news to
you.

Your loving mother-in-law

Josephine Hinson

In a way he was happy to know that Clarinda had been able
to hold and nurse Thomas. That she'd seen and loved what she
had carried so carefully for nine months. Somehow that meant
a lot to him, and while he didn't quite smile at the thought, his
mind's eye envisaged the little fellow suckling and loving his
mother. The image was satisfying and comforting.

He took out his mother's letter and read it slowly and
carefully again, coming to realize that she'd been thinking only of
him and his son with her suggestions, all of which made logical
sense. In fact he felt relieved that both she and Josephine were
so empathic, and mentally applauded their deep love. Still, it was
a tender time, and he didn't feel like exerting himself at work, so
next evening he sought out Jonathan and Eleanor together and
told them what he had learned in the two letters. Being the
mother of seven, Eleanor understood his feelings readily, and
Jonathan suggested he borrow his horse and take a couple of
days away from the boatyard. He offered him his rifle as well
and told him to go hunting as that deserved high concentration
and would distract him from unpleasant thoughts. What fine
folks these are, Tim thought, such wonderful people.

Jonathan's only suggestion was to avoid heading south to
Parramatta as he had heard there'd been internal trouble at the
Castle Hill convict camp two months back and the area was still a
little unstable. He had no more details but Tim was glad to be
forewarned. The next morning he saddled up one of Mr.
Griffiths' horses and added a rifle to the bags of goods he was
carrying, and set off east towards Green Hills along the river
bank. He stopped to talk to workmen in two of the other boatyards and moved further downstream past Green Hills to where
Mr. Grono was building a huge boat for the seal-hunting trade at
the point where the north-flowing Hawkesbury made a major

turn to the east. It turned out that John Grono was actually in the boat-yard supervising the sawing of long lengths of hardwood for the hull on the new boat. Tim tethered his horse and strolled by the huge stands holding the framework of the sealer.

A voice startled him. "Want to buy it, young man?" It was Mr. Grono himself. "Can I help you with something?"

"No thanks," Tim responded. "I was just admiring the size and shape. She reminds me of some of the bigger fishing boats we had back in Polperro. Very solid, designed for stability in heavy seas with a large load. A schooner perhaps?"

"Well, you certainly have a good eye, son. Who are you and where do you hail from locally?"

"My name is Timothy Bartlett, sir, and I'm assigned to Mr. Griffiths up the river a bit."

"I've heard of you. Helped build the *Speedy* and wasn't there something about rescuing an aboriginal boy just a few weeks back? Are you here spying on me?"

"No sir. I suspect Mr. Griffiths knows what's going on here already. I'm just passing through taking time for a 'walkabout' as the natives call it, with Mr. Griffiths' permission. And yes, I was fortunate to be in the right place at the right time to help the little fellow out."

"I heard you are pretty strong. The aborigines tell my men that none of them could have lifted the rock you moved."

"Like I said, sir, just lucky."

"Well, nice to meet someone who has compassion for fellow man, even if his skin is a different colour. Good on you. You let me know if things don't work out at Griffiths' place. I could readily use someone like you."

"Thank you, sir. I'll keep that in mind. And I'm really sorry to hear about the attack on your daughter. I hope they catch the man quickly who committed the heinous crime and that your daughter will recover. "

"Thank you, I appreciate your concern."

He had enjoyed the exchange but kept moving north and east along the river until he came to a small backwater lagoon where he decided to camp overnight. The early summer sun extended the daylight hours and he had plenty of time to go hunting. There were ducks on the lagoon but he figured they'd still be there later if he found nothing else. His real interest was to bag a kangaroo. Not for food, just for the sport. He hadn't used a rifle in years, the last time being when his father had taken him out purely for target practice, probably ten years ago. He thought of trying a little target practice again, but he'd only brought five bullets along and didn't want to waste any. At least one for a duck, two if the others didn't fly away, two shots for kangaroos, anticipating he might miss with his first shot, and one for emergencies. He headed east away from the river with the sun behind him.

He'd gone about two miles and had just crested a small undulation in an open field when he saw a mob of the animals resting two hundred yards ahead. There must have been twenty of them, a lone tree providing shade for maybe six, with the rest spread out in the grass left and right. He doubted he could get closer without them sensing his presence and moving away. From the sporting aspect he really wanted to shoot one while it was moving at speed with the high bounds that he'd seen them use during his trip north along the road from Parramatta. Such amazing creatures in flight, their power obvious, their elegance and disdain in regal perspective. For the moment he selected one of the greys sitting up under the tree. He had a profile view of its head and body, although the head kept swiveling as if it was looking for something.

Tim lay down and parted the grasses in front of him. He knew at this distance that his bullet would drop slightly from a horizontal line attempt so he aimed directly at the top of the animal's head, as if he wanted to skim it. He practiced his breathing control and snuggled the rifle into his shoulder and released the safety catch. He made sure his left elbow was on hard ground and then moved the barrel until he could see the roo's face. He breathed in and out once then held it. Moved the rifle barrel up a fraction of an inch and squeezed the trigger. The target disappeared from view and the other roos that were gathered around the tree got up and hastily moved off fifty yards then stopped. Amazing, Tim thought. It's as if they have no idea what happened, but want to both stay around and find out, and at the same time be prepared to flee if necessary. As he stood up and marched towards the group the other animals lying down arose and prepared to run off as well. The furthest away stayed rooted to their spots, however, and those from closer in moved to be with them.

He found the bullet hole in the animal's neck, so his bullet had dropped more than he expected. Either that or the barrel wasn't perfectly true. No matter, it had been a good shot, and he was pleased with his accuracy. He thought of skinning the roo but decided he'd still like to see if he could get a bigger one on the run. So he left it there and walked on. The others had all fled by now, and the fields were empty. After another two miles of seeing no other animals he turned and retraced his steps. The sun was lower and in his eyes, but the warmth felt good and he looked forward to shooting a duck for dinner back at the lagoon.

The duck made great eating and he decided to shoot another one in the morning if it was there and take it home to the Griffiths. He'd also do a little fishing and see what he could catch and take that back as well. Originally he had planned to stay out several days but he was feeling good and wanted to get back and write a Christmas note home. Perhaps it was meeting with Mr. Grono that had also helped. That, rescuing the boy, the productive trip to Sydney—perhaps all were influencing him to accept his fate and to not long for things that couldn't be changed.

Early in the morning before the birds awoke and the still waters of the lagoon were ruffled by breezes he caught two nice fish about six or seven pounds each. He sat still for an hour waiting for a duck to fly in, and was rewarded when a whole family alighted close-by. As he prepared for his shot, the word 'family' reverberated in his skull, and he put his rifle down. "No, you all go in peace," he muttered to himself. "I'll find something else."

Rather than travel back along the river's winding course he decided to go south until he came across an east-west road that he knew would eventually take him back into Green Hills. He came upon the edge of a large forest, and skirting the tree line he turned slightly southwest. It looked like fine growing soil in the area he was walking through and in the distance he was not surprised to see a farmer's hut. As he came level with the hut a group of white cockatoos burst from the forest edge, startling him with their piercing screeches. He wondered what had set them off and then saw the mob of huge red kangaroos heading his way towards the forest.

He quickly moved into the trees where he was all but hidden by the denseness of the grove. The roos were to his front and left and still heading for the forest to a point about fifty years away. He hadn't been seen. He pulled the horse deeper into cover and loaded the rifle. Rushing back to the edge of the grove he could see the roos' magnificent size as they bounded along, seemingly without a care in the world. On a slender fir he found a low branch and balanced the rifle on it. He swiveled the barrel, eventually finding the group in the sights, then isolating on one. There must have been fifteen of them, all moving in unison. It was quite a sight as he matched the movement of the barrel with the speed of the big reds. Once he felt he had their rhythm locked in, he moved the barrel a fraction forward and fired. His target fell heavily and he shouted jubilantly. The rest of the mob scattered, veering away from the trees and picking up speed to the southwest. He watched them disappear then walked calmly to check on his kill.

As much as he felt somewhat sorry about killing the animal, depriving it of the freedom it had always known, he was thrilled with its sheer size and majesty. He had no way to measure it exactly but by lying down beside it he estimated its height to be just over six feet. He tried to lift it but had no chance, even given the abnormal strength he had developed. It must be two hundred fifty pounds or more, he figured. This was a trophy he was not going to leave behind, and although he'd never skinned anything in his life he'd watched the guard work on the dingo and had some idea. Of course with the mammoth tail the roo was physically very distinct. He found his bullet hole in the chest which matched his aim at the top of the body and he was pleased it had been a sure, instantaneous kill shot.

It took him an hour to do the skinning, and well before he'd finished there were two eagles in the sky watching and waiting. He rolled the skin up, requiring two separate bundles, and tightened them with thin rope he'd brought along. He whistled a light refrain as he rode on, reaching the road he'd targeted early in the afternoon. Homeward bound, he looked forward to sharing his news with everyone back at the shipyard.

A couple of the men helped him cure the huge skin he brought back. He was glad of their experience as with the rising summer heat skins could degrade quickly. A lot of scraping, then washing in strong cold salted water, drying, re-scraping and washing, and finally hanging to dry worked well. He lost a little of the size as the hide shrank in the heat, but a week later it was hanging on the wall of his hut for all to see. They threw away the tail skin.

The day before Christmas he sat down to respond to the letters he received from home. It was hard to express himself, especially as he thought of the reversed seasons and frosted window panes and the closeness of family around blazing fires.

> December 1803
>
> Dear Mother:
>
> Your letter of July arrived four weeks ago and Mrs. Hinson's letter just two weeks ago. Yours arrived first and made me incredibly sad. I'm glad I waited for Mrs. Hinson's letter to arrive before trying to write back. Getting the letters out of order made me panic, but such are the vagaries of ship movements across the oceans between Polperro and Australia. Also, the post cannot be relied on here as conditions are very primitive. I'm glad someone in Sydney knew where I was located to arrange for me to get both letters.
>
> At least you or the Hinsons should have my letter to Clarinda any day now so you will all have

some idea of what is happening at this end of the world.

My heart is broken mother. It is so unfair that Clarinda has died. I'm happy that Thomas is there, but where is my beautiful wife? She and Thomas were supposed to come to Australia sometime, although not yet. Now she will never come. Maybe in twenty years Thomas will come. I cried every time I read your letter. I know men shouldn't cry but I miss her. I used to just sit and lean against a tree for hours wondering, remembering, disbelieving. Why, mother why? I'm better now, especially since Mrs. Hinson's letter arrived and gave me more details about Thomas' birth and Clarinda's death. I am so glad Clarinda got to see and nurse our son before she died.

I wrote to her at the end of August, nearly four months back. Now I know she will never learn what has become of me. I am at a loss with my thoughts and memories. I feel helpless and distraught so many thousands of miles away. I wish I could come home, but I will never be allowed to leave here. Some days my head spins and I wish I were dead too. I never knew how much I missed her these past months, until now.

Home seems so terribly far away. Why am I here without my Claire and baby boy? I see her in my mind, and cannot believe she is dead. Is this an extra price I am paying because they believe I stabbed a man? Is that what God thinks too? So I am to be punished twice? Maybe there is even more punishment to come. Is he going to take Thomas away too?

I'm happy to have Mike and Betsy look after him as they will be good parents. Please thank them. Thomas needs to grow up safe and replace me. And knowing he is living in our house is good because that's where he would have been raised if I were still home and Claire were still alive.

You will get some news in the letter I wrote to Claire. The colony is a miserable place in many respects, and the towns here grow very slowly. There are many more convicts than other white settlers. England with its centuries of history and seems so civilized in retrospect. Everything is new here and I wonder if it will ever be like England.

I feel fortunate that the man I work for is good to me. I like my work and am beginning to even enjoy the countryside. It is nothing like home.

Please also thank Mr. and Mrs. Hinson and show them this letter. They have lost a daughter, at least your son is still alive, if not nearby. I think this is hard for everyone, except perhaps Thomas. I hope Uncle Ben is fine. Oh yes, also thank you all for the headstone on Clarinda's grave. It is simple and I like it like that.

I will write a longer letter next time and tell you more about this place where I work and live. I am staying healthy. Oh yes, I'm sorry if my writing is confused, but I have a limited amount of stationery. You had another question about the house. I think your suggestion makes sense, mother, so please go ahead. I hope Mike and Betsy will be very happy there.

Meanwhile, I will think of you all. Christmas is coming and it will be so different here. No snow, and long days which will be very hot. Perhaps it is good that I live by a river and can keep cool in it.

Please say hello to my friends. I know this Christmas wish will be late arriving, but let them know I was thinking of them all as I wrote this note. I cannot really say 'Merry Christmas' and I hope everyone will understand.

Your lonely son

Timothy

He knew he had to write to Laura in Parramatta as well but it was so difficult to be thinking one minute about family who were so far away, and the next to switch and try to write to Laura who was so close nearby. It would have been hard to do at any time but it was doubly hard given the news of Clarinda's death. He just couldn't do it. He hoped Laura would understand when he finally summoned up the courage and ability to write.

The Griffiths had a private family Christmas so the other men in the boatyard cooked fish and a duck they had shot and drank copious amounts of grog. They tried to play cricket but no one could catch the balls and when one was hit into the river, they gave it up, crawled into the shadow of the *Hazard,* and promptly slept the afternoon away. Tim's headache on waking didn't stop him thinking about how different his first Australian Christmas was to those back home.

Traditionally, since it was holiday time, little was done between Christmas and New Year on the boats. Jonathan's sole goal for the period was to finish off all the small details *Speedy* needed after her Sydney voyage. They accomplished that two days before the New Year arrived and everyone relaxed. A couple of the men went 'walkabout', but Tim went fishing instead, and provided his friends and the Griffiths with fresh delights every day.

On the second day of 1804 he received another letter from Laura.

December 20 1803

Dear Timothy:

Christmas is just around the corner and I thought I'd send you some good cheer in this letter. We ladies, as we like to call ourselves, are anticipating having a sumptuous feast to celebrate. We know it will be very different from what we are used to since it will be hot, not cold, although we are still planning to do some of the things we used to do back home. Like caroling for example. There's a number of us who used to sing in choirs back home and we have been practicing the old Christmas songs after work each day. Even if I do say so myself I think we sound very good. We are going to go sing, not only outside the women's huts, but also at the guard shacks and the homes of the militia. We know they have a job to do but they also are far away from their homes, and probably some of their loved ones. We hope we might brighten up their memories.

Also, as you no doubt saw, there are a number of young children about. For each of them we have made a set of nice clothes and created small books they can color in with crayons we got from some of the militia men's wives who had them for their children who've now outgrown them. It's been a challenge to arrange everything but it has given most of us something extra to do and helped take our minds away from our own cares and issues.

Even the guards lately have been less strict, and when they've threatened us with punishment it often is forgotten. A nice change that we don't expect to last, but will enjoy for the moment anyway. We will do the caroling on Christmas Eve then serve our dinner next day mid-afternoon. We will be having ham, mutton, beef, chicken, duck, goose, and fish, plus all sorts of local vegetables including corn, cabbage, beans, and beets, then dessert will be apple and blackberry pie with cream. And there'll be enough tea for two cups each. Is your mouth watering?

Three of the women in my house will be getting married early in the new year, which means we'll have three new women joining us. I will dearly miss one of the women who is leaving, although not the other two. They are very young and don't pull their weight around the house. I think their husbands-to-be are attracted by their age and youthful figures. They are both very flirtatious and I'm not convinced marriage will tame them in that respect.

I keep thinking you must have heard from your family by now. I hope all is well. I doubt I will hear from anyone. I envy you that at least you know your mother. Mine didn't even come to my trial or visit me in prison. And my father is probably dead. Never was much of a father or husband.

Do let me know what you find out. I'm especially interested to know whether you have a son or a daughter and what the baby's name is. Babies are so precious. And I also want to hear about the boatyard. Did you finish building *Speedy*? What do you say about boats – did it 'ride' smoothly, or 'sail' smoothly. You'll have to teach me sometime.

Oh yes, one other piece of good news, the guard who was pushed into the water and who whipped that poor woman has been transferred to Norfolk Island. That's bad for the Norfolk Island convicts but good for us here.

Please write when you can.

Yours

Laura

Now he really did need to respond.

26. *Summer Heat*

January 15 1804

Dear Laura:

Happy New Year ! Thank you for your letter at Christmas time. I hope you and the other 'ladies' had a wonderful celebration singing and eating. I think you all have a wonderful attitude to make the best of things there.

I am sorry I did not write earlier but I'm sure you will understand when I tell you why.   In November and December I finally received mails from my family. Unfortunately they brought sad news. My wife Clarinda birthed a son Thomas in May but she died two weeks later because the baby had to be taken through her belly, and she became infected and did not survive.

Knowing I will never see her again was difficult to accept and I took off walking in the bush for several days. As God would have it, by strange circumstances I was able to rescue a little aboriginal boy whose leg was trapped under a very large stone at the base of a waterfall. It gave me a satisfying feeling to be able to help out and was the distraction I needed to stop thinking of my woes.

Before that we took *Speedy* down to Sydney and it was a wild ride along the coast, but the boat performed well. Mr. Griffiths let me be captain and I thoroughly enjoyed being out on the big water again. It was just like being home. When we got back, Mr. Griffiths threw a celebratory dinner. Not quite as elaborate as your Christmas dinner but very tasty.

Two other things have happened that have been little highlights of life here. I took two days off in December and borrowed Mr. Griffiths' horse and gun. Somewhere downstream on the river I shot a red kangaroo. It was huge. I brought the skin back with me. We cured it as best we could and it is now pinned to the wall of my hut. It helps keep some of the breezes out that come between the slabs, although with this hot weather there is little wind to talk about.

I travelled down past Green Hills through some of the other boatyards on the river, and at one I met Mr. Grono, who is very well known and respected. He is building a very large schooner that I suspect he will use for whaling or seal hunting. We talked for a while and he indicated if things didn't work out with Mr. Griffiths that he would hire me. While I have no interest at the moment to leave the Griffiths boatyard there is something about the idea of building a large boat for whaling and sealing that excites me. It has also crossed my mind that if I can get a Ticket of Leave I would possibly enjoy actually owning a boat and going seal-hunting. There are rumours that there is good money to be made, and for me it would be close to fishing in big water like we did in Polperro.

Do you know if you will be granted some latitude at Easter time? If so I thought I would try and borrow a horse and come and visit you. Please let me know.

Fond wishes

'Captain' Timothy

The heat was oppressive in January. The men worked shirtless and plunged naked into the river at the end of day to cool off. One plank at a time *Hazard* took shape. Just like her sister *Speedy* but with the benefit of learnings from the river and ocean trials her sister had been through. Small adjustments and refinements promised an even more stable and durable boat. Tim felt proud bringing her to life.

At the end of the month they went off on another wood-collecting tour. There were more men and drays this time as Mr. Griffiths had joined up with a Mr. Thompson to share the costs of the bullock teams and the extra convict labour hired for heavy work. There weren't really any roads through the forest, just tracks, wide enough for a single team. Not that there was much chance of meeting a team coming the other way, but if a wagon wheel broke everything was held up, sometimes for hours, while it was fixed, as no one could get by. Open patches of grass along the track were always a welcome sight where the bullocks and horses could rest. A couple of men scouted ahead looking for streams that would supply water to slake men's and beasts' thirst. The best circumstance was where the track actually crossed a stream which was still running. Many had dried up with the heat or simply contained small pools of stagnant water, OK for the animals, but not the men.

On finding a grove of useful trees, a branched track was hacked through the brush getting as close as possible to the selected trees. A clearing was formed and the drays carefully turned around. The convict drivers were a wretched group, with both a familiarity and dislike for the massive beasts they managed. Getting the oxen hitched to drays and then moving produced more swearing than Tim had been used to even from salty old sailors. Not a place for ladies' ears for sure.

Out came the massive crosscut saws, handed to men working in pairs. Tim's uncharacteristic strength landed him a job at one end of the two-man blade which cut horizontally into the highly resistant hardwood. The sharpener who came along with the team was constantly employed ensuring a fine edge to the teeth on the saw, but even so it was incredibly demanding work. The men sweated profusely and grunted with exertion. As the cut penetrated the trunk, iron wedges were added behind to prevent the saw from jamming. Inch by inch, foot by foot, the blade cut its way to the center and beyond. As soon as the first creaks of splitting wood were heard the saw was hastily withdrawn and nature was allowed to take its course bringing the monsters to earth.

The call of "Timbbberrrrr" as the mighty trees fell was an exhilarating time for all, even though it meant follow-on work to cut off the unwanted branches and then drag the resultant log onto the dray. In many cases the saw had to be used to cut off huge diameter branches but mainly the trimming was the purview of axe-men. Heavy chains secured around the trunk were then attached to a harness on the oxen, which dragged the tree to the wagon where it was painstakingly loaded. In many cases one huge tree was the limit for the dray and bullocks alike.

Each trip penetrated a little further into the forest. Men sent ahead had two things in mind – looking for the right trees and also determining the easiest way to get to them. The hills and valleys were steep sided and the heavy loads created enormous challenges for uphill climbs. Sometimes it required six or more bullocks just to pull one tree uphill. Flat land, scarce as it was, was revered.

After resting a bit at the end of the third day in the woods Tim decided to do a little exploring on his own. They were camped by a stream at the bottom of one of the shallower valleys, and he wondered if he went downstream a bit whether he might encounter a denser rainforest area. He'd gone about three or four hundred yards along one bank when he heard a voice close-by calling his name. "Teem, Teem." He looked across the stream and there standing by a willow was 'grandpa' along with two women. Tim smiled and waved. Amazing! Had they been shadowing the whole group for days and then deliberately approached him once he separated from the others? He waded across the stream and patted the old man on the back, receiving friendship pats in return. The women stayed back but smiled. Tim looked around then mimicked the action of searching by shading his eyes and turning his head this way and that. He muttered two of the few aboriginal words he knew, *"wungarra darra,"* which he hoped meant boy and leg. The old man listened, then conferred with the two women, and finally smiled in apparent recognition. He pointed in the distance then put his hands beside his face and tilted it, which Tim interpreted as the boy was back in camp sleeping. At least he hoped that was the case and that the gesture didn't mean he was sleeping permanently and had died. He got two words back which sounded like *"birray maraba."* The last word was close to what he used for 'boy'. The other word he could only imagine.

Since the natives seemed in no rush to head off, Tim wondered if they might help him out with his quest to find a lyrebird. He moved to a spot on the river bank where there were no grasses, and went through his search routine again. He then took a stick and first drew a bird's head with an obvious beak. He then drew his best simplistic representation of a musical lyre and stood back and repeated his search action. The women looked closely at his diagrams and started jabbering to the old man. The three conferred a bit more, then one of the women bent down and held her hand about a foot off the ground looking questioningly at Tim. He interpreted this as to a question of size and location mixed. He nodded his head up and down. Sure, a smallish bird on the ground, not in the trees. When the woman pointed to his lyre picture then bent over and waggled her backside he had to stop smirking but quickly nodded up and down again. She got it, a small bird with the lyre as its tail! Wonderful. 'Grandpa' grabbed Tim's arm and indicated he should follow them into the bush. In total trust Tim obediently followed.

It was a good thirty minutes before they slowed down and grandpa motioned Tim to be quiet. They sat still for five minutes until a warbling bird song cut through the air. One of the women nodded her head vigorously up and down. Must be the lyrebird, Tim surmised. Grandpa led them forward to a spot where they had a clear glimpse of some rotting logs and shady tree ferns. A small brown blur streaked behind some bushes and was gone. Grandpa motioned Tim to wait. Sure enough, a few minutes later a little dark female and a larger male dragging his long tail wandered into view. They stopped momentarily then moved on. Tim was now very excited but crouched and held his position as instructed. A lone male appeared. He too was dragging his tail, but as he approached the rotting tree-fern log he started to raise it. It didn't come up much, but spread just wide enough for everyone to see the intricate lacework pattern between the two outer fronds. No question why the bird had been given its name. What a thrill it was to observe. Like the others, the male didn't stay long and as he disappeared Tim rose up and extended his hand to grandpa. Handshakes were not in the natives' set of standard gestures but grandpa and others had observed that this was often how white men greeted each other and sometimes said 'thank-you'. Grandpa reciprocated in kind, but the two women didn't respond when Tim held out his hand towards them. He was sure they understood his gratitude however.

As the late afternoon shadows lengthened, Tim was led back to the place where the three aborigines had found him. He hurried back to camp, where he pulled in a good-sized audience as he repeated his story over the dinner fire. No one seemed surprised nor concerned to hear that blacks were monitoring their progress, as relationships with the *Boorooberongal* tribe were generally good. The settlers generally understood it was the tribe's land and that the tribesmen just wanted to know what the white man wanted with it.   Tim slept without a concern in the world.

It took far longer to bring the logs back to the boatyards than it had taken to lead the empty drays on the outbound journey. It sometimes took a combination of both men's and beasts' strength to move some of the drays uphill or across small creeks, where getting from one bank to another meant managing a two-foot drop on one side and a two=foot rise on the other.

The men in both yards were spent, and were given a day off to recover. Both owners relaxed as well. The extra convict labourers were paid off and the oxen taken away to their storage retreat. The yards had enough wood for several small boats and even a large one if they wanted.

At Jonathan's yard the men set to work first cutting the massive logs into working sections, then cutting smaller sections, and from those creating the appropriate boards and beams to the select shape and size as needed. February slipped by, and as

March rolled in, the first cooler signs of autumn declared their presence.

Laura had responded with a very sensitive note. Tim was noting a decided empathy in her makeup that reminded him of his mother, and which he found most appealing.

February 18 1804

Dear Timothy:

I am so sorry to hear about your wife. I don't think I can even imagine what you must have felt getting those letters from home. I'm very sad that she died in childbirth, but at least you have a son and she got to hold him before she died. I am sure one day you and Thomas will find each other here.

Some of the women here had to leave children behind, and have no idea whether they will ever see them again. Some children were left with relatives, some with the parish church. A few have heard from their kin who tell them about the children, but it seems to many that now they are out of sight they are also out of mind. It's also probably the case that for many families back home, having to look after another child thrust into the family unexpectedly is not always the easiest thing to accommodate. Some relatives probably even feel resentful, and that worries some mothers here.

There are others who carry a different form of grief. I speak of the ones who were pregnant and gave birth on board ship only to lose their baby to disease or other reasons. Remember, there was one on our ship. That woman is in a different house from mine. Perhaps men can't really understand how devastating that really is for a woman. She carries the baby for nine months and it becomes a part of her everyday life. She can't see it, just feel it, but it's a living part of her. It grows in her and with her. They are one but two at the same time, and when the baby is born she finally sees what she has nurtured and loved unconditionally for so long. Her heart overflows with love and care for this vulnerable little child she has brought into the world and which now commands her attention twenty four hours a day. To be aware of all that and to experience the associated joy is inimitable. To have it taken away through death so quickly afterwards is absolutely overwhelming. I am not surprised that some women are never the same mentally afterwards. The loss itself is one thing. The sudden emptiness after being locked in an embrace for so many months is a cruelty of the worst form. But it is compounded even further when the child is committed to the deep and there is no marker of its burial location to re-visit and weep over. In that instance the loss is not just relative, it is absolute. Those are the women I expect to be totally inconsolable. I know I would be.

But it sounds as though you have done some things, distractions as you call them, that are helping to minimize your grief. For that I am most thankful. You are a good man Timothy Bartlett, and there is plenty of life still ahead of you. I understand your despair and hope the grieving period is short.

I have checked with the authorities here and we are to be unfettered so to speak on Easter Saturday and Easter Sunday both, so it would be wonderful to see you here. Thank you for wanting to visit. Could we please go fishing again?

Yours

Laura

27. *Convict Madness*

Jonathan rang the bell on the verandah vehemently. The men downed their tools and hurried to the homestead, where Jonathan was striding up and down, clearly upset. "I've just returned from Green Hills," he declared. "There's been a riot at the prisoner stockade at Castle Hill and we must all be truly diligent. Here's what I learned.

"Two nights ago on Sunday the fourth, hundreds of those damned Irish vermin in the prison there rose up in rebellion with cries of 'Death or Liberty!' No one seems to know what their real intentions were but they were noisy and scary. Many think they simply wanted to escape from the colony itself and that they thought convicts from all over would join them. Anyway, they started marching as a group towards Green Hills but were confronted by the New South Wales Corps at Vinegar Hill. The soldiers fired on the rebels and captured the two ringleaders, men named Philip Cunningham and William Johnston, and hung them right there and then. Some of the rebels had taken guns from the guards at the camp and fired back but when they saw Cunningham and Phillips arrested so quickly and hung, they ran away in panic and confusion. The militia is now out searching for all the rebels that went bush, and that's what we have to be aware of in case some of them head for the boatyard here. So keep your eyes peeled for strangers. Watch for shadows under the boats and behind the huts. I'm going to stay up all night tonight keeping watch on the house, so if you want to join me that would be good."

"How many rebels were killed, do you know, Jonathan?" a voice asked.

"No idea, and the constables at Green Hills didn't know much more than what I've told you. They had their muskets loaded and were prepared for trouble, that's all I can tell you."

Tim spoke up. "I heard on my trip from Parramatta to here that those prisoners were not the best behaved. One reason was that they'd been moved from Sydney where they were housed in separate huts into the one big barracks building. A lot of their individual freedom had been taken away and security was much tighter. There were also small cells used to intimidate any who had seditious ideas. Not a nice place, I gathered."

"Well, I don't care what the reasons were. It would be a good example to any more prisoners with the wrong idea to hang many of the rebels. I know you are all convicts, as was I. If I thought any of you had escapist or overthrow ideas, you wouldn't be here, so I hope you agree. We all have to make our future here, not anywhere else. There's plenty of opportunity as you can see by the business we are in."

Talking among themselves, the men dispersed in small groups, some shaken, some portraying fake bravado, but all disturbed and not fully comprehending what had really happened so relatively close by. This wasn't a story from Sydney or Norfolk Island or Van Diemen's Land, but south of Green Hills, maybe fifteen miles away. Too close for comfort. They all wondered if the camp at Castle Hill would be closed down. Meanwhile, they all agreed to stay up at night and patrol the premises. No problems were wanted in this yard.

Tim reflected on Jonathan's message and was a little surprised at the strong dislike of the Irish, something he'd never been conscious of by Englishmen back in Polperro. But he'd heard others in the colony who despised them as malingerers, and trouble makers. The Irish convicts that had been sent to the colony seemed to have a stronger criminal streak in them. They were viewed in general as blatant liars, full of con-man blarney, who took advantage of their fellow man readily. The irony was that some of them entered the police force, which then completely distrusted by the general populace. Corruption and interpretation of the laws to personal advantage was seen as a way of life. And they weren't reluctant to hand out heavy punishment to convicts of a different background. As convicts, they hated authority. As policemen they could in fact be the authorities and act out their vengeance.

For the next few days the men adopted extra vigilance in all corners of the yard. A poor hen couldn't cross the yard without being checked that it wasn't running away from, or to, a stranger.

Bartlett 217

Elsewhere, a couple of the rebels were caught as fellow convicts turned them in. As much as the rebels were despised, there was condemnation of those who turned them in as well. They were labeled 'dobbers' associated with the phrase 'to dob someone in'. Public hangings of the rebels were carried out in various towns to spread the message of intolerance of insurrection. It seemed to work, as the colony soon settled down again to its everyday functions.

Timothy asked Jonathan about borrowing a horse to go to Parramatta at Easter and inquired about the cost of buying one from a nearby trader or farm. He had money back home, held by Clarinda's parents, but he thought if some of it could be placed in a bank and he could be sent letters of credit he might be able not only to buy a horse but also a small house nearby. Next time he heard from his mother he'd ask her in return mail.

On the last Friday evening of the month he set out on Dottie, one of Jonathan's mares, for Parramatta. The roads were deemed safe again and with a horse this time it wouldn't take but two or three hours depending how hard he pushed to make the trip. He passed Castle Hill camp but it looked quiet in the distance so he couldn't tell whether it was populated or not. He'd heard that the convicts were to be transferred to Newcastle but couldn't determine if that had already happened or was still to take place. Only one cart had come the other way towards Green Hills but it was loaded with furniture, presumably for someone moving house. The road south was amazingly empty although it was the end of the day. Perhaps more people would be traveling for the holiday tomorrow.

He hitched the horse to the railing in front of the house Laura lived in and knocked on the door. A young girl answered and admitted him in to the large downstairs kitchen while she went off to fetch Laura. The women had clearly been baking bread because it smelled so homey, and made him hungry. Laura found him peeking in one of the ovens looking for left-overs.

"Ha, caught in the act, young man. There's nothing in there. The loaves are all on a rack outside cooling down."

"Well, they smell delicious, and you look great. I can tell you were one of the chefs by the flour in your hair. The ovens make it warm in here. Can we step outside for a minute?"

"Out back to smell the bread, or out front to smell your horse?" Laura cheekily replied. And before he could answer she grabbed his arm and led him through the back door to the racks of buns and loaves being watched over by two of the women he'd met before and the young girl he'd met at the door. His face flushed and he volunteered "They smell wonderful ladies. Let me know if someone has to taste test them all."

The women smiled and laughed, and one said, "Take him away, Laura, before we all want to jump his bones. And feed him good. He looks like he could do with a little fattening." As Laura walked him by the side of the house and out to the road they could hear the women guffawing. It was a warm, happy sound which made Laura say: "I guess they like you, Timothy. They remember the fish you brought. Welcome by the way, it is definitely good to see you again."

They stood and nattered for a while, avoiding the subject of Clarinda's death, until it was time for lights out. Tim jumped up on Dottie's back and looked down. "I'll sleep down by the river and come by two hours after sunup. I hope we'll be able to take some of that bread with us tomorrow. I can tell my stomach is craving it already.

Good night Laura. It's good to be back."

As he trotted off it started to rain, and Tim made a quick decision. For some inexplicable reason he suddenly didn't want to sleep out in the rain, although he'd done it many times before. He didn't even want to sleep under a bridge protected from the elements. Something about the women's domesticity had softened him momentarily, so he turned Dottie around and headed for the Freemasons Arms Inn, one of the first ten hotels licensed in the new land, and which had been opened almost six years earlier. He led Dottie around back to the stables where an eager stable lad quickly moved her under shelter and started to brush her down. Tim gave him two pennies for his effort. He had borrowed some cash forward from Jonathan against his due wages, and asked for actual coins for just such an occasion.

Inside, he approached the French publican, James Larra, and organized a room for the night. He slid a coin in payment across the counter. "Well, traveler, you also get a pint with that, so here you are."

As he climbed the stairs to his room the rain and hail started to come down in buckets, bouncing off the tin roof and creating an incredible din. Somehow, however, he didn't mind the noise, and strangely satisfied, he sank into the softest mattress he'd felt in ages. In his last thoughts before sleep took over he hoped the women had brought their bread indoors and not left it out all night.

In the morning, feeling mightily refreshed, he enjoyed eggs and tea with toast, a breakfast the likes of which he'd last had somewhere in Polperro. The rain had stopped hours before but the streets were full of mud with rivulets running through the ruts towards the river. Thank heavens he'd brought a horse. He checked with the stable lad, who told him the storm hadn't bothered Dottie in the least. "I brushed her real good, mister, and gave her an apple. I have two more if you'd like to take them with you." There were no apples in sight, but admiring the little fella's approach, Tim handed over a penny and soon had them in his pocket. The clouds and mist were rising, and he had no doubt it would fine up later in the day and that by tomorrow the sun would be out fully and the ladies of society would be able to wear their Easter bonnets to church without any problem.

Rain still dripped off roofs, but the commercial buildings looked like they were appreciating the wash they'd been given overnight. A few hailstones still littered the streets but they were disappearing quickly. A stray dog drank at one of the puddles and a crow pecked at the remains of a small bird that had been knocked out of its nest. One cycle of life ends, he thought, while another is sustained. Does that apply to me too? It was still a little early to pick up Laura, so he headed down to the river, the life-blood of the town. The first passenger boat for Sydney was leaving as he arrived and he was surprised to see at least six or seven passengers on it. He figured they must be going off to spend the weekend with friends in Sydney. Good for them he reflected, and then quickly dismissed the subsequent thought that there was no family he could be going to visit, had he wanted.

Even though the thought had disappeared quickly, it had pricked his conscience, and he turned and led Dottie to St. John's Anglican Church, its building having been completed just the previous year. The front door was shut against the overnight rain but it was not locked, and taking off his muddy boots, he walked in woolen socks to the altar. He was not a very religious man, but since there was no one else inside, he knelt, bowed his head, and offered a short, awkward prayer.

"Dear Lord, in your compassion you have taken my loving wife from me. Please be merciful with her soul for she was a wonderful woman who was loved by everyone. I miss her terribly, but I thank you for letting her know her son before she died. In her and my absence I ask you to protect him from harm, and to look after all the good people in my village back home. I pray for forgiveness for all my sins."

Two big teardrops filled his eyes and he slowly stood and wiped them away with the back of his hand. It felt strange alone in this quiet, reverent place. At home the church was always filled with others when he went on Sundays. Perhaps he should have thought more about it being Easter and said something in his prayer. But no, it was done, and he hastened to leave.

It was still early and he rode back to the river. Always the water, he thought. Even though this water is just a river, rivers flow to the sea and that is my destiny. I was raised by the sea, I am one with it, it is my comfort. I must work to make it happen again. A veil lifted off his mind, and clarity and purpose replaced it. He wanted to share his feelings with others and was glad he would be seeing Laura shortly. When he got home he would write to mother and tell her his ideas. He would make his life work in this new country. No point in regretting the past. The future was in his hands and no one else's. It was time to move things along.

It was a happy and determined young man who lifted Laura into the saddle and jumped up behind her. "My, you are fresh and happy this muddy morning," she remarked. "I expected you to feel damp and chilled from sleeping under a bridge somewhere given the storm last night."

"Well, I sort of cheated, because I went and stayed at the Freemasons Arms Inn instead. I hadn't planned that until the rains came, but I had a few coins in my pocket and they just wanted me to use them, so I did. I'm glad because I checked under the bridge this morning and the rain had clearly blown in there. The whole place was very wet. I think I would be in a bad mood now had I stayed there. But I also realized this morning that I probably could have slept on the floor of the new church had I thought about it. I went there earlier today and prayed for my family. I was all alone but there was a rolled up horse bag behind the last pew that someone had probably used as a pillow and forgotten to take with them."

"That was very enterprising of you. The hail was so noisy – I hadn't seen ice in that size before – it was little golf balls. As soon as we heard that coming down we rushed out back and pulled all the bread in. No damage at all and the ladies made sure I had a big hunk ready for you this morning. I put it in the sack along with some biscuits we also made."

"Do you have somewhere in particular you would like to go, Laura? We have an advantage in that Dottie can take us further away than just up the river where we went last time."

"I've heard of a place northwest of here called Toongabbie. I believe you get there by taking the road towards Green Hills then turning west along the creek. You must have crossed it on your trips up and down."

"I know where the creek is and I like that idea. We can do some more fishing along the creek and then see what is in the town as well. Toongabbie sounds familiar. It must be an aboriginal word. I wonder what it means. Let's go."

Across the Parramatta River and northwest along the road to Green Hills they let Dottie set the pace picking her way carefully between the ruts as the mud started to dry. A few farmers were coming from the north to late market and they exchanged pleasantries with ones where families members were travelling together.

"Have you heard anything more from home since December?" Laura asked.

"No, I suspect there are letters on the way. It is so frustrating that it takes so long. Maybe in years to come faster boats will speed up the process. I think I will have to start writing longer letters, but frankly I'd rather be building boats. I use a hammer and saw better than a pencil."

"You do fine, Tim. I'm sure the folks back home dwell on every word you pen, and I imagine they read your letters over and over. In fact, I bet your mother can recite them word for word without looking again. Mothers are like that."

"Which reminds me of something I was going to ask you, Laura. You don't talk about your family in any detail. How about filing me in a little bit? I know you were born in Edinburgh about two years after I was born, but I don't know exactly when, and then you moved to York when you were very young. Do you remember anything of either city? You have a northern accent that isn't very strong so I suspect Manchester was the place where you lived longest. Were your relatives all Scottish, and what exactly happened to your mother and father? If you told me before I forgot. And, while I think of it, where's your friend Mary? I didn't see her last night or this morning. There that's a whole bunch of questions for you... Sorry."

"Well, let me tell you about Mary first. It's a sad tale. You saw how she was, totally interested in her body, especially what was under her skirt, more than anything else. She went out the backdoor one night, ostensibly taking the garbage out, but didn't come back. The kitchen was busy and no one had kept good track of her, just one of those unfortunate oversights. At lights out and we realized she was missing. Next morning we found her asleep on the step at the back door. At least we thought she was just asleep and had been locked out, but it turned out she'd been with a bunch of the guards all night, and they'd had their way with her. Her clothes were torn and she was bleeding and exhausted. The men had dumped her back there sometime in the early morning. We took her to the hospital where all the pregnant women and those with other injuries are. That was a week ago and I'm almost ashamed to say I haven't been to see her since. Some of the other women have. We hope the doctors and nurses will keep her there for a long time because they are much more disciplined in where and when the women are allowed to roam. Longer term when she's physically healthy she'll still have the mental issues and I don't know what can be done about those. It's very sad."

"I'm so sorry to hear that. I feel I should apologize for the behavior of the guards. Some of them are animals of the worst form."

"No question about that. I'm sure Mary didn't help herself, but some of their behaviour is totally inexcusable.

"But let me respond to all those family questions. The Stewart clan goes back hundreds of years, Tim. We had a proud heritage, as did many of the clans, and when our relatives gathered once a year at the games, I was part of something grand. My father was a drunkard basically and at times he would beat my mother. Why she stayed with him I don't know, but I've learned that's a common problem. Many of the women in our camp can relate easily. I was born in April 1782. I don't know the exact date. My father certainly didn't know and my mother told me different dates at different times. It must have been in the first week and a half of the month as her dates never went later than the tenth. So it could be my birthday tomorrow or anywhere in the next ten days. When I'm forced to pick a date I choose the fourth because that was a Sunday in 1782. When I finally learned about calendars I worked backwards to find out the days of the week in April that year. Sundays were always special. They were quiet because the pubs were shut, and Father went down to the Firth and sat there most of the day just looking into the water. Mother and I would explore the city or just go play in the park. Sometimes we'd meet up with other mothers and their children.

"We moved to York when I was ten years old. I loved that city with all its history. Edinburgh had history too, but in York I was old enough to start understanding it. York Minster to me is still the most beautiful church I have ever been inside. I think of the thousands of persons who have seen it or visited it over the centuries. Its presence alone is like a mighty force rising and protecting the city, reaching out to touch the walls and encompassing all things underneath the cloak it extends. We moved there because an uncle that Father trusted had said good work was available. I'm sure it was, but not for drunkards.

"We didn't stay long, maybe six years, before trying Manchester. Compared to York, well really it just didn't compare. Some say the Industrial Revolution started in that city because it was full of factories. The charm of York didn't exist, and it was polluted, and I grew to hate it. As I told you before my father found a job working in a pigsty on the edge of town, and mother washed dirty clothes in the River Medlock, which was like a giant sewer. I started pickpocketing at age seventeen to bring in some coins. We lived in a one-room hut closer to the outskirts than the center of town.

"One day Father didn't go to work. He pretended to be ill. Mother went off to do her washing. I knew Father was faking illness. He accused me of keeping some of the coins I stole to myself, which wasn't true. At least not then it wasn't. Before I knew it he grabbed me and tore at my clothes saying I probably hid them in a girl's special place. He was crude and rude, and I know he just wanted to touch me and that was his excuse. He tripped and fell and hit his head on the side of the fireplace which was made of brick. He was unconscious but still very much alive. I got up and ran to where mother was doing the washing and told her the story. Remember I said how Father used to beat her. That had continued all this time, all those years. His assault on me was somehow beyond her ability to accept and tolerate. I remember her talking to me very slowly and deliberately. When Father started to come around she hit him hard with the poker and he went out again. It gave him a cut and a nasty bump but Mother no longer cared.

"We waited till dark then loaded him into the cart Mother used to collect and deliver the clothes she washed. We scrunched him down and then put a thin layer of dirty sheets over him so that it looked like a full load. It was much heavier than usual of course and the two of us wheeled it through the streets till we got to the Medlock River. Then we tipped him into the water and pushed him out into the stream. The cold water woke him up fast and he started to wave his arms about and flounder. We had no idea if he could swim or not. No one was about so no one heard his pathetic yells. We went home and cried in each other's arms in the big bed that night. Next day we moved to a new neighbourhood, and we never saw him again.

"Mother soon found more washing to manage in areas closer to the Irwell River, and I went out pickpocketing. It didn't take long to identify others doing what I did and after several liaisons I found a partner who thought and worked just like me. Her name was Kendra and she came from somewhere in Africa, so she was attractive to men because of her skin colour and accent. She also had bigger breasts than me and enjoyed flaunting them to male victims. I was more deft with my fingers and hands in actually pulling wallets, coins, handkerchiefs, and even timepieces out of pockets. We made quite a team, and would use a number of different pawnshops to sell our prizes. More money started flowing home and I managed to conceal some for myself because I knew at some point I'd have to leave mother behind. After two years or so at our new location she was growing more feeble, and it appeared to me she probably had consumption.

"In the end Kendra and I simply got too cocky. We thought we could pull off any heist, but right at the end of 1801 we got caught. I was nineteen, going on twenty. Kendra was eighteen and a half. Somehow a parish priest got involved in our case. I think his church did missionary work in Africa and had helped bring Kendra's family to England some years before. I never saw her mother or father and she never, ever talked about them. My mother never once came to visit me and when I asked the priest if he talked to her he said no. I suspect she died shortly after I was caught as she was very sick.

"Kendra and I were taken to a house which the Church used to 'reform' girls like us. In December of 1802 it burnt down when one of the other girls there deliberately started a fire. No one was hurt but we were all placed in gaol. The men gaolers all lusted after us and touched and felt us up whenever they could, but the priest had some sort of influence and we were never actually assaulted. I think we were an unexpected burden on the gaol system so when the opportunity came to send some of us away the authorities took it. We were split up. I got sent to Plymouth and I know Kendra was headed for London. We cried and hugged good-bye, but I have no idea if she made it here or not. None of the other girls have turned up here yet which makes me wonder if the Church helped out again in London. Maybe they are all on Norfolk Island or some are in Sydney and some in Van Diemens Land. I keep hoping to see one of them, but so far, nothing.

"So there you are. A long story and now I'm thirsty. Can we stop and have some of that ale I saw you had brought along?"

"My gosh, that is some story, Laura. Here, I'll get down and lead Dottie to that willow tree and tie her up then help you get off. It's probably too wet to sit down here but we can lean against the tree for a bit.

"There you are, now let me get that bottle of ale."

"Ooh, Tim, I can hardly walk. My backside hurts. How can you sit and ride Dottie all day?"

"Hmm, I didn't think about that. I'll add the blanket over the saddle for you – we'll just have to watch it doesn't slip. We'll ride to the creek then I think it will be easier to walk anyway. We probably only have thirty more minutes to ride. Think you can suffer that long?"

"I'll try, although I may complain the rest of the day. I must be too soft and flabby. So what did you think of my life history?"

"I think you are a very special person, is what I think. To have put up with all you did. I feel rotten for how you were treated along the way. Your father was a louse. And I am sorry your mother never came to see you in gaol or at the church house. That is very sad to me. I hope you are right and that she didn't come because she couldn't, and not because she didn't want to. I think she must have loved you, because of the way she responded when your father went after you, and how she moved you so quickly to another neighbourhood. She was a smart thinker in her way, just never able to use her brain to full advantage. You have done well, Laura, to be what you are today and not to have followed in your mother's or father's ways. I'm proud to know you. You make my life seem like a bed of roses compared to what you have been through.

"One part that was very special was your love for York and especially York Minster. I've heard of the cathedral, of course, but I envy your having actually been there and been inside. What an incredible thrill that must have been. All that history beneath your feet, all that beauty around you, surrounded by all that amazing craftsmanship that is only found in the spires and domes of churches from ages past. I doubt future generations will ever see anything like that in this country."

"As I said, I loved York. If I were to go back to England at any time that is where I would go. It was the place which I feel closest to calling home."

"Would you like to go back Laura?"

"I don't know, Tim. At the moment I just want to get out of our virtual gaol in Parramatta. In six more years would I want to stay here or go back? I can't tell at this point. There are no relatives in York dragging me there, and there are none here either. You've hinted at opportunity in this land. In York I'd have to find some menial job and I doubt that even frequent visits to York Minster would bring happiness. I'll just have to wait and see."

"Well, do you feel ready to move on again or do I need to go hire a dray you can sit on for Dottie to pull?"

"You are a funny man sometimes, Timothy Bartlett. Don't laugh at my sore bottom, you rotter. What if I sat behind you this time and clung on instead of sitting in front? Maybe a slightly different position would help."

"That's fine. I'll have to get on first so it might be a little awkward getting you up but I'm sure we will manage. Let's try it.

"There we go. Well done. OK, Dottie, next stop Toongabbie Creek and please be gentle on Laura's behind. Try and avoid large potholes and don't spray mud up her back." A hearty slap across the shoulder blades told Tim his voice penetrated rearwards without any trouble. He grinned happily.

While Laura tried to mitigate the new bow-legged shape she'd inherited, Tim led Dottie for a well-deserved drink in the creek. She wasn't used to carrying two people and he gave her an apple as reward. She nuzzled his chest. "The best way to get rid of that soreness is actually to keep walking," Tim told Laura. "Come on, let's take the south bank and see how we do."

In and out of the trees they wound, keeping as close to the bank as possible. It wasn't a large stream, which is why it had been called a creek, Tim guessed. But it was pretty with moss on the banks in dense shady areas. Laura was picking out the way ahead with Tim following and leading Dottie. "You are right," Laura called. "I'm already feeling like my legs will be normal again at some point. Do you think there's open fields up ahead? This forest seems to be going on forever."

"I don't think it is actually a forest, just a very wide line of trees enjoying water at their roots. Every now and then I glimpse open land to our left through the branches. It's a fair way off but definitely there. The same on the other side of the stream."

"When do we stop and fish, Tim? I see a good-sized fish in this pond I'm standing at."

"Really? Let me catch up. I thought the stream was too narrow yet to see big fish."

Tim was lagging behind but hastened forward at Laura's call. He tied Dottie's reins to a low-hanging branch and found the creek had widened a bit where she was now staring intently into the water. "See there to the left a bit. It looks somewhat different but that little ray of sunshine filtering through the leaves is making the reflections on the surface distort things."

Tim slithered forward on his stomach to the edge and leaned out as far as he could. He watched silently for a few minutes then turned face up to Laura with a huge grin. He surprised her by whispering: "Well, my lady, I believe you have made a truly remarkable discovery. For that is not a fish down there. I believe it is something that's being called a 'platypus'. Copy what I am doing so you can see better but let's be as quiet as possible. This is amazing.

"If you look closely you'll see this 'thing' looks a lot like a fat fish in parts, except it is covered in fur, not scales, and it has four stubby little legs. Wow. Even more amazing, it has a bill like a duck in front. And in fact the legs are webbed like a duck's as well. And there's a tail, almost like a beaver's. The men at the yard told me about it, but I didn't believe them. Now I do. Just look at it. Is there any way it could be more unusual?

"It looks like it is digging out weeds at the bottom of the creek with that bill thing. It eats some but then heads back to the bank and disappears in a hole not far under the surface. I bet that's its home, and that there's a tunnel that heads upward, but doesn't come through the grasses on top. I wonder if there are young ones in a nest. And how do you tell the male from the female? I can't wait to tell the men back at the yard."

Totally fascinated, Laura whispered back: "It makes you wonder if God assembled parts from different animals and experimented to see how odd an animal he could make. And then he threw it into the water so it would have to swim all the time. Although when I think about it, since it has four legs you'd think it could walk. Ducks and geese walk on their webbed feet. Maybe it does come out of the water at times.

"I think you'll have to be there to support me when I tell the ladies at the house about this creature. Do we want to catch it and take it home?"

"No. I think we should let it be. It's so unique, and we can tell others where to find it if they really want to come and see it for themselves. I'm sure we'll find some fish further along."

They continued on and where the trees started thinning into open pastures they found the stream tumbling over a series of rocks into a large pool. Tim dug for worms, and hooked a couple of smelt quickly. Using these for bait on lines for Laura and himself, they patiently waited for a strike. Laura's line twitched first and she played her catch well, using the tips she'd learned last time. A nice bass dangled from her hook as she reeled him in. Tim wondered if it was the sport or the food aspect that she liked most.

With six bass caught in an hour they decided to move on. A small creek entered from the left which they managed to wade through twenty yards upstream, and when they checked back, the new section of their Toongabbie creek had narrowed down substantially. The stream they had waded across turned southwest and they decided to follow that. They crossed back to the bank they'd been on, but after three hundred yards the stream split again, with yet another one entering almost directly from the south. Tim was starting to feel a little uncomfortable in that they'd seen no signs of civilization along their route, and he decided to travel only a little further south before turning east and looking for a way home. In the distance they'd seen a small mob of kangaroos, but they'd come across no grazing cattle or sheep and no huts indicating people living in the area.

A quarter of a mile on they finally came across a rough track traversing east and west. They turned left. The ruins of a slab hut appeared and Tim showed Laura how it had been made and how similar his own hut was. The biggest problem, he said, with these huts was that, as the vertical boards dried, they shrank and left gaps between them through which the wind constantly whistled. He'd been working on his own hut adding more slabs across each gap and had nearly finished. It was also much warmer with the breeze no longer swirling inside.

As they walked on, the ring of axes and saws working against trees became faintly discernible and Tim started to feel better. He wasn't worried for himself but didn't want to feel lost while being responsible for Laura. He vowed next time they set out to get a little more information first about the country he intended to investigate. They never saw men cutting the trees down, just heard them in the distance. But it finally dawned on Tim where they were and what was going on. They must be coming up to the western end of the new Government Farm that he'd stopped at with his guard when traveling to Green Hills originally. It was planned to be a huge farm and this was definitely in the right vicinity. It also meant that at least some convicts were still behind at the Castle Hill camp, because they were the ones engaged to clear the land. Now he knew if they kept going in the current direction they'd hit the main road they'd set out on in the morning.

And a memory bell was suddenly triggered. Now he realized why the name Toongabbie had sounded familiar. The guard had said the farm would extend inland as far as the old town of Toongabbie which hadn't worked out about six years before. And he remembered the name was an aboriginal name meaning something to do with the meeting of waters. Right, they'd seen three creeks come together once past the fishing hole. Maybe there were even more they hadn't encountered. It all made sense now. He happily explained his recollection and thinking to Laura.

"Let me get this straight, Mr. Timothy Bartlett. You admit now that for a while back there you were feeling somewhat lost but didn't say anything. And that you now feel better because we are close to where those three hundred Irish convicts who started a rebellion are working with murderous axes in their hands? You're happy about that? Do you think you could hold all those men off if they came after me?"

Tim just loved her sense of humour and responded in kind. "No, Miss Laura Stewart. I just pretended to be lost. I knew where that platypus was all the time. I just wanted you to discover it before I had to point it out to your dim eyesight. But you are probably right. If those men saw your beauty I'm sure they would chase you. But that's why I brought a horse along so we could escape easily and leave them behind running their legs off after you."

They looked at each other and burst out laughing. It felt good to get on so well together. Tim let Laura ride while he walked Dottie back to the Green Hills road and then south into Parramatta. Laura and the women grilled the six fish and fed those who had gathered around the big table. Laura held their rapt attention with her tale about finding the platypus, and, as expected, had to have Tim back up her description. Even so, some of the women figured the two of them had concocted the story, and no matter how hard the pair protested, just wouldn't believe them.

Night had fallen and Tim suggested they take a walk down by the river together. He waited outside while Laura went to her room and came back with a bag slung over her shoulder. Tim looked at it inquiringly and she said, "Just in case we are still hungry later."

They'd gone about a block when Laura stopped and said: "You know what, Tim? That dinner was so good, I'd actually enjoy an ale. Not what we have back at the house, but what they can pull for us at the pub. What do you say?"

"You are speaking my language, lady. Let's see how the festivities are and how a good drop tastes."

The pub was rowdy. Songs in Scottish dialects were being sung, and when they were over, a Welsh contingent stepped forward. One of them had an accordion, another a fiddle, and the third a mouth organ. The fourth sat down at the piano and was the lead singer, belting out verses first in English then Gaelic, to the delight of all. Tim and Laura found a table in a corner and enjoyed the showmanship, applauding enthusiastically when the exhausted quartet finally stopped. The publican offered them free drinks as payment. For a few seconds low talk took over the room as everyone quenched their thirst or waited for refills. Tim stood up to join the throng at the bar, but Laura reached out and touched his arm, gently indicating he should wait.

She then stood and started to sing a capella. With only two notes escaped, the room instantly hushed as she broke into the charming popular English ballad "Scarborough Fair". In a pause after the first verse, a gentleman stepped forward and sang the next three verses asking for a linen shirt without seam, washed without water, and dried on a blossomless thorn tree. Laura raised her head and rendered the next six verses asking for an acre of land, in an impossible location to be cleared, sown and reaped with a feather, when only then would she give him his shirt as his lover. Her beautiful voice captivated everyone present, bringing forth vivid memories of their homeland. The applause went on and on as she bowed to the gentleman who helped her.

The publican spoke for all of them when he asked, "And what else may you offer us, lassie? You do our hearts good." Laura replied, "There are three more I'd be happy to sing for you kind sir. One from England, one from my home country Scotland, and then one I think you'd all know well."

"Well, give me a minute to fill some glasses girl then you go for it."

Laura smiled down at Tim, who seemed to be pleasantly dazed. While the publican was filling mugs Laura walked over to the Welshman who'd been playing the piano and whispered in his ear. He nodded up and down and moved back to the piano. Laura moved next to him and tapped him on the shoulder, at which point he started to play 'Drink to Me Only with Thine Eyes'. The crowd 'oohed' and 'aahed' then settled back to listen. Once again they applauded with gusto, a couple of the other women wiping their eyes surreptitiously. Laura pointed down to her accompanist and as he stood they gave him a round of applause also. Cries of 'more' made Laura hold up her arms for silence, and when she felt she could be heard, she said gently, "This next one's for all of you who can understand me when I say 'Mony a mickle maks a muckle!'" Shouts from around the room identified many nationals. She pointed to several of them and said, "In which case 'Lang may yer lum reek'"

One yelled back plainly: "Aye, ye be a bonnie lassie. Sing your heart out for us."

As soon as she started on Robbie Burns' 'Ye Banks and Braes O'Bonnie Doon', the same piano player rushed to the piano and accompanied her again. It took a little extra talent to know that melody, as it was played only on the black keys. Laura nodded her head in appreciation and he matched her speed perfectly. At the end she moved over and hugged him and the cheers this time were for them as a duo.

Laura sat down for a bit and finished her drink. "You are incredible," Tim whispered. "Where did you learn to sing like that?"

"In the choir at York Minster. Sometimes we sang for pure pleasure."

"You never told me that part of your story this morning."

"Aye, you are right. And there's plenty more you don't know either, my man. Telling everything in a life of twenty-one years takes more than a few hours, I'm afraid. Would you like to know more?"

"You know I would, you amazing woman. But for now I think you'd best do your last one as they're all looking at you here."

Laura leaned against the piano and spoke to the whole room. "This final song is one I absolutely love. It has helped to keep me going through dark times, and it has enhanced the light in good times. I know you all will relate."

There were few dry eyes left by the time she finished 'Amazing Grace', a popularized English folk hymn with its positive message of forgiveness and redemption. But afterwards she was mobbed, with multiple offers of drinks. When she couldn't take them up men pressed coins into her hands, and she had to hurry back to the table and empty them.   Tim was speechless. How little one knew about one's companions, he thought. I was on a ship with her for five months and never heard that she was a singer. I've spent several days with her here in this new land, but no one at the house told me she sang. We've talked about all sorts of things together and yet still I'm learning about some basic attributes. So much talent. I wonder what else I don't know. More than I'll probably ever learn, I imagine.

The tavern was abuzz for ages. People hummed the tunes and walked around talking to strangers about the new voice in their midst. Laura clearly was enjoying the attention and Tim felt sorry for whatever group planned to entertain next. At length she wandered back to her chair, but even then others came back to congratulate her or wish her well or to register their enjoyment of her songs. Tim enjoyed watching the flush in her cheeks and the gentle pride in her eyes as she graciously responded to all the comments.

Finally the piano player started up a polka, which got some limited foot-thumping going and started the transition back to normality. "I'm so happy, Tim. That was a lot of fun. I haven't sung like that since leaving England. The people here have been so nice to me."

"Deservedly so, Laura. You were a sensation. I think you are wonderful. Your voice is superb. The world needs to hear it more often. Shall we take you home and get you a good night's rest? I'm going to make you sing all day when we ride tomorrow."

"Well, I had a different thought. In fact, I had it before we left the house and now all these coins are just reinforcing it. I think the publican wouldn't mind trading some of them for a room upstairs. What do you think?"

"I think, Laura Stewart, that you are incorrigible. Let's go. Oh no. Wait a minute – what about the checks at 'lights out' back at the house?"

"I've taken care of that. I asked one of the girls to cover for me if I didn't return. I've done it for her before. And that's my night robe in the bag if you are wondering." She grinned, certain he had been.

And Tim smiled. This lady was miles ahead of him. Full of mirth and fun and mischief. What a delight she was. He wanted to hold and kiss her right there and then. But he had no chance. As the publican handed her a key and as she headed for the swing door, spontaneous clapping broke out, and she waved as she exited. "I gotta go pee," she whispered. "Me too," he replied.

The mattress was as soft as Tim had told her that morning. Luxurious compared to what she slept in every other night. She stretched out as Tim took off his boots and britches and sat on the one chair in the corner. "I'm glad I know you, Laura. You are very special. It was so good to see and hear you in your full Scottish person. You'll have to tell me what you said for the benefit of the clansmen."

"Well, you know the saying about how frugal Scots are. I just told them that 'saving a small amount soon builds up to a large amount' so they knew I was truly one of them. They got the message. And for those that understood I just wished that they would 'live long and stay healthy'. It's a common greeting."

"Well, it was nice to see you owning up so publicly to your Scottish heritage. I'm proud of you. And I think the crowd was too, no matter where they came from."

"You didn't know but at first I thought of singing an Irish song as well, but given the Castle Hill break-out I wasn't sure how well that would be received, so I substituted."

"Smart move, I think. But what made you want to sing in the first place?"

Laura sat up and in an indignant tone pointedly asked: "Are you going to keep sitting over there asking me a thousand questions, Tim? Can't you see this gal's a-waiting? We gals have needs too in case you didn't know. So get over here and help me. I need attention."

Needing no second bidding, he quickly finished undressing and jumped on the bed.   Their coupling was fierce and passionate, responding to the euphoria and positive mood emanating from the events downstairs and a mutual need to rekindle the fires within.

They both woke during the night and enjoyed extensive coupling again, finally getting back to sleep as the dawn broke outside. It was mid-morning before they made it downstairs and the innkeeper's wife fixed them a plentiful breakfast of fresh eggs and ham, washed down with English black tea. "Happy Easter," she wished them as the church bells rang out calling the faithful to service.

"Would you like to sing your hymn in the church this morning?" Tim asked. "I'm sure the reverend would be happy to allow it. And we know the congregation would love to hear it. Those that were here last night will tell others about your voice."

"That certainly is a nice idea. And it is Easter, an appropriate occasion.   If you want to skip out and talk to the minister I'll wait here."

It wasn't York Minster, but Laura acted as if it was and the little church building reverberated to her beautiful rendition of the hymn. Totally unprecedented, and against all custom, the stunned audience rose as one and clapped in appreciation, something never seen before. The minister was extremely gracious in his thanks and invited Laura to come and sing the hymn of her choice at any future Sunday service. Tim knew people would talk about 'the lady with the voice' for years to come.

In the afternoon during time together by the river bank Tim unfurled his dreams for getting into the whaling and seal-hunting business in the future. He mentioned his discussions with Jonathan and Mr. Grono. He impressed Laura with his creativity, vision, and drive. Inside, she secretly applauded what she heard, loving his business acumen wrapped up with sailing experience. She listened and empathised but was just a tad reserved in her enthusiasm. Her assessment was that they were brazen thoughts for a soon-to-be twenty-four-year-old in a new land. But she wondered about the practicality of his ideas given that he was a convict not even resident one year in the Colony. She knew he'd push and was the sort of person who by dint of hard work and perseverance would use every approach possible to pursue his dreams.

A random thought struck her. "Tim, did you say 'Grono' just a minute ago? Was that the name?"

"Yes I did, why?"

"Well, once in a while we see a Sydney newspaper, called the *Gazette,* here when a guard leaves one behind. I remember reading last month that a chap had been convicted for his third assault upon a child, the last being a Mr. Grono's daughter. The name sounded Italian to me which is why I remembered it. So different than other surnames here. Whatever the chap's name was he was sentenced to three years hard labour and to appear in the stocks every Sunday for two hours. How can men be so evil – hurting children like that? I despise his crimes. Do you know how Grono's daughter is? "

"No, but I will ask when I return."

They reveled in their evolving companionship, going over the adventure of yesterday and the fun they'd had together both upstairs and downstairs in the Inn. Tim couldn't resist asking Laura where she had learned to be so enthusiastic in the bedroom. "Another part of my life you didn't hear about yesterday," she replied. "In my last year in York when I was sixteen there was a chap in the choir whom I had a crush on. It was reciprocated. When my father talked of moving on, we were both sad. It was then that we got together. I gave him my virginity in exchange for some lessons. We were both young and full-blooded and made the most of it.

"And what about you, Tim? Was Clarinda your first?"

"Well there was a girl in Guernsey who approached me on one of our trips. She was very seductive and I fell under her charms for two days. She was my first. Clarinda had had no one before I came along."

"So now we know more about each other's past. I thank you for sharing things with me."

From bedroom to church their discussion continued. Including her gift of song to the church, it had been a wonderful weekend together and they both cherished the feelings it had evoked. They cared for one another, more than each probably realized. Yet Laura was still strongly cognizant of Tim's wife's death and wondered if she'd overstepped her relationship with him. Was he rebounding in some sense in seeking her company? Was it just loneliness that made him want to be with her, or was there genuine interest? She thought it was the latter since he had visited before he knew Clarinda had died. But men could be weird in dealing with emotions so she wasn't sure. And like other men it wasn't his nature to be totally revealing over his vulnerability.

Tim was having analogous thoughts. Why did he enjoy Laura so much? Did it stem from her unselfishness way back on the ship? Why had he sought her out even though he was married at the time? Had he intended to abandon Clarinda anyway being so far away? No, definitely not. Had her death made Laura more desirable? Did she fulfill a companionship he now knew he'd never have with Clarinda? Or was she attractive in her own right? If Clarinda were still alive would he be as intimate with Laura as he had been or would they just be friends in some fashion? His mind told him Laura was very real and could be part of his life now that Clarinda could not fill the part of his life they had planned. It was his heart and his soul that needed to tell him what his mind concluded was right.

He thought about the letter he would write to his mother as soon as he was back in Richmond Bottoms. Would he mention

Laura? Probably not. Which meant he really wasn't yet fully ready for a new commitment. It would have to wait a bit.

But as he said goodbye he couldn't help saying, "You are an absolute treasure, Laura. You mean so much to me. I thank you for being so close but there's some pain I have to heal from yet. You will be in my mind constantly till next time."

Laura thought for a moment then decided to declare her interest. She had nothing to lose. "My dear Tim. I truly care for you. If ever the time arises that you feel you might want feminine companionship along the road ahead, I would welcome the chance to join you. You are an honest man of fine character with strong principles, compassion for others, and a love of life. It would be my pleasure to travel with you wherever you might go."

They hugged and kissed. He mounted Dottie, turned north, and waved once more till she was out of sight.

Part Four

28. Paths Ahead

April 1804

Dear Mother:

I imagine we will have to get used to letters crossing in the mail since they take so long to travel between us. I didn't want to wait until I heard from you again to tell you some of my news. We had a very successful launch of Mr. Griffiths' boat, taking it all the way to Sydney and back. I even got to captain it out on the Pacific Ocean as we travelled down the New South Wales coast. It was stormy so it was a good test, and it made me remember all the things I had learned sailing out of Polperro. It felt wonderful to be out on the open big water again. I like working in the boatyard although sailing on the river is not as challenging as I would like. But I am learning a lot and now know more about boats and their construction than I ever did before. We have to go into the forest and cut down huge trees, then saw the beams and planks to the right size. On my last trip cutting wood I got to see a strange bird that doesn't fly but runs across the ground and has a tail that looks just like a lyre. It's amazing. I also got to see kangaroos and wallabies, which are small kangaroos. I managed to shoot a big red kangaroo and its skin is now spread across one of the walls in my hut.

On the ship coming out to Sydney we were told how the natives here are like savages, but the ones I've met, while reserved, seem really harmless. In fact it is some of the convicts I worry more about. Just a month ago hundreds of Irish prisoners broke out of their work camp nearby and terrified all of us. But the ringleaders were quickly captured and hung, and things have calmed down since. I will admit that in some of the camps prisoners are treated awfully. I am so glad I didn't have to work long on a gang but was assigned to Mr. Griffiths. He was a convict at one time so I think he knows how to treat other convicts. He also has seven children. Over ninety percent of the convicts here are single, and eighty percent of those are men, and have no one but themselves to care for. Sometimes that makes them mean. Those that escape have little place to go. When recaptured they are whipped hard.

I have only been to the village of Green Hills a few times but each time I go there is a new building there. No church or school yet. I imagine they will come in time. Meanwhile, Parramatta, twenty five miles away, grows much faster. An Anglican church was opened last year, there is a market down by the river every Saturday, and there has been a hotel there for the past six years. It seems very progressive compared to Green Hills.

Of course it is spring here now and I have to tell you that after the heat of summer the current weather is much more enjoyable. There is a tree here they call 'wattle'. The aborigines call it *Meruko*. It has vibrant tiny yellow balls for its flowers and in the forest they can be seen from a long way away. There is also a beautiful red flower called a 'waratah'. Waratah and kangaroo are aboriginal names. There are also incredible parrots and cockatoos here. I have seen small parrots that have all the colours of the rainbow on them. There are white cockatoos which screech, and giant black ones which crack nuts in their big beaks. I love seeing all the new things this country has to offer.

By the time you get this, young Thomas will be nearly seventeen or eighteen months old, I imagine. That means he will be walking around, probably pulling things off the low shelves in the house. Has Mike taken him out on a boat yet? He needs to develop those sea-legs early like Father did for me. I hope you share all my letters with others, Mother, as writing is not something that comes easily for me. I can draw boat plans and plans for the sails and show the course of a river. I will have to learn to do more in the future as I have a business idea I want to pursue.

From many stories I have heard there is a lot of money to be made from seal and whale hunting south and east of the Australian mainland. A man at another boatyard has invited me to help him build a large boat for the purpose, and I am thinking of going to work with him. But the way to make money is not through building but to be an owner so I am going to ask him if I could be a part owner with him. That's a common way of doing business here, just as it is back home, spreading the risk by sharing the costs, and sharing in the profits. Since Mike and Betsy are raising Thomas I would like you to please take my money that the Hinsons are holding and put it in a bank and send me several letters of credit to its full value that I might use here.

I hope you approve and will respond as quickly as is feasible as I think there is great opportunity if I act now.

I hope you and Uncle Ben are well and that the Pilchard catch this coming season is the best ever.

Thank you for looking after my interests,

Your loving son

Timothy

Tim was torn. He'd discussed some of his ideas with Jonathan, avoiding explicit mention of working with Mr. Grono. Jonathan had indicated that the next boat he planned to build after *Hazard* would be a schooner designed specifically for whaling and seal hunting. It would be done probably three years later than the one Mr. Grono was already building, and Tim's impatient streak didn't want to wait longer than was necessary. Jonathan was also very direct in emphasizing that generally speaking, convicts were unable to own property until they had earned a Ticket of Leave, and for convicts on life sentences, like Tim, those could take fourteen years to be forthcoming. He agreed that ownership of the boat was the way to make money, but thought Tim had absolutely no chance of getting any exception made, given his lifetime conviction.

The Colony was an authoritarian state as Tim well knew, but he figured that rules were rules until they were challenged and that there were always exceptions made to rules, if not in general, then sometimes for the selective use by officials when an exception worked to their advantage. He figured the government office in Parramatta would be a good place to try and learn more. In May he ended work one Friday early after lunch and rode Dottie fast down to the township.

He came back with hope in his heart, for he learned there was no set of established guidelines to grant exceptions, and that Governor Phillip King, currently in office since late 1800, had been known to grant them, even on a couple of occasions as soon as the convict had arrived. It was an issue to be taken up at some future point but clearly exceptions had occurred. Officials in the Parramatta office suggested that at a minimum Tim would need four things to support an early Ticket of Leave. The first would be to be married, as convicts with wives were considered more stable than single convicts. Second, the longer he had already served the better. Third, a high-level recommendation from home, meaning England, would definitely help generate a favourable consideration. Having money would also help. Convicts without the ability to self-sustain themselves would not be considered. And while not necessary, any relationship with the Governor, or a high official reporting to him, would also go a long way.

Tim felt positively elated on learning this information and nearly ran poor Dottie into the ground by galloping most of the way home. He knew he could have stopped and caught up with Laura, but he didn't want to create any inappropriate expectations from his findings so he didn't tarry. Back home he borrowed more paper from Eleanor and put together a list of thoughts and actions.

1. Write to the lawyer at his trial and Captain James Clavell (how do I find him?) of his transport ship. Ask the lawyer to see if he could find a well-respected gentleman who, perhaps for a fee, would sign a glowing recommendation of Tim that the lawyer had created. The captain needed to write and verify that Tim had been treated as a free citizen for nearly five months on board, and paid accordingly, and this was because of his exceptional character. Mention saving the sailor and capturing two murderers. Could the lawyer help here again to find the captain?

2. Obviously get his savings from home, but also arrange some validated letter or contract from Mike or his lawyer showing that Tim also had a substantial amount coming from the sale of his house over time.

3. Ask the lawyer to procure an affidavit showing he had been married and so was stable, as well as explaining the unfairness of the decision to transport him and revealing it for what it was—an accident where he valiantly supported a fellow member of his community.

4. Ask Laura to marry him, satisfying that condition.

5. Get Jonathan to appeal directly to Governor King on his behalf. Jonathan had been an exemplary convict at Norfolk Island under then Lieutenant-Governor King there. As well, he had since become successful as a businessman, with value in dramatically opening up trade on the waterway to Sydney with fast distribution of goods to citizens there.

Writing this one down created a headache and pangs of conscience, for he knew if he were granted a Ticket of Leave early, he would immediately want to go work for Mr. Grono. No doubt this whole process would take at least a year, maybe two. It depended heavily on the willingness of his lawyer to act. And on the ability to find Captain Clavell quickly.

That night he dreamt uneasily, tossing back and forth the likelihood of success. In the morning, he wondered if it were all too much to hope for, and a black mood hung over him. By Sunday morning, however, it had dispersed and he was back to a 'what have I got to lose?' feeling. He spent most of the day writing long letters to his lawyer and to his mother. She'd be amazed to get two letters from him so close together. It was in writing the letter to the lawyer that he inadvertently identified why he'd felt so bad the previous day.

It had to do with Laura. Had he unwittingly revealed that his interest in her was totally selfish? That he would only be marrying her in order to meet his goal of owning a boat, adventuring, and becoming rich? Or, if he was to be content being a boat builder for the rest of his life, would she not matter?

No. He rejected both thoughts. That was being unfair to both himself and Laura. He cared for her no matter what. He had started caring before he had even thought about whaling or seal hunting. And he was starting to realize that her companionship was something he definitely could enjoy forever. If that was so he should approach her shortly. She'd indicated her willingness to join him. But now he'd have to be careful, for he'd hate her to think he was in fact marrying her to solve his exception plea. He quickly reread both letters and felt relieved. He hadn't said anything in either one about marriage being viewed as a favourable input.

He started calculating. It was early April. If he were lucky and there was a ship leaving Sydney next week the letters would arrive probably late August or early September. He was sure the lawyer would take at least three months, so that meant nothing ready before December, but it could be a lot more if the captain was on the seas somewhere. That was the worst part, not knowing. At the very earliest he might expect something useful in return around this time next year. My gosh, a whole year to wait.

When would he see Laura again? he wondered. And another thought came wandering into his mind. Was there a way to get copies of that newspaper, *The Sydney Gazette and New South Wales Advertiser* at Green Hills? Maybe he could learn more about which boats were coming and going and what was happening in other towns. He hadn't known the newspaper even existed until Laura mentioned it and gave him its name. How could that be? I guess we really are out in the bush here, he thought. We need to fix that.

As soon as he could get away, which was two months hence, he rode to Parramatta and arranged a subscription to the newspaper. He also paid in advance for a delivery boy to bring the paper to him at Richmond Bottoms. It was an official publication of the government of New South Wales, authorised by Governor King and printed by a Mr. George Howe. Once a week on Sundays, consisting of four pages, with a variety of news, including government proclamations, letters from citizens, High and Low water readings, temperatures at Sydney and Parramatta, news from English newspapers, notices of ships arriving and leaving and debt notices as well as auction sales and commercial advertisements. It had started just a couple of months before his arrival, but convicts were never informed about it.

On July 8th he found an advertisement from Captain Clavell looking for persons, property, and goods to take to England and Europe. The advertisement indicated the captain was leaving very shortly, so Tim arranged for time off, rode to Parramatta very early one morning, left his horse at the public stables, and took a boat down to Sydney. The boat was moored against the newly constructed wharves west and south of Dawes Point. He found Mr. Clavell in a nearby wharf pub finishing an ale and reading the previous Sunday's newspaper. On introducing himself, the captain quickly remembered – he'd made another round trip between London and Sydney in the year gone by, but had forgotten nothing. He listened to Tim's plea, and indicated if

Tim would pick up his drink tab, he'd go with him to his cabin on board and write exactly what was needed.

On the way back Tim stopped in to report his activities to the nilitia commandant at Green Hills. He was sad to learn that further downriver at Portland Head, in the previous month natives had killed a settler, and that the commandant and his men had shot two aboriginal people when other angry settlers confronted the natives, who had stolen some of their goods. Apparently the natives were upset that the white man was stealing their land along the river which they depended on for fishing and river vegetables. Two aborigines named *Yaragowhy* from the Branch tribe and *Yaramandy* from the *Boorooberongal* tribe had helped avoid a nasty uprising. Tim took it as a bad sign that discontent was on the upswing and determined to warn the boatyards in Richmond Bottoms to be alert for possible trouble. There was a group of aborigines from *Yaragowhy*'s Branch tribe living across the river from Richmond Hill that had always been less friendly than others and he worried that they might become active.

Mr. Grono launched his schooner named *Speedwell*, in clear competition to Mr. Griffith's *Speedy*. It really was a magnificent sight on the river with its two masts and attendant sails, taking the one-upmanship game to a new level.   Unfortunately, and perhaps because of poor captaincy, it ran aground in October in a backwater near Mount Elliot and Lion Island at the exit of the Hawkesbury into Broken Bay. Another boat builder, Andrew Thompson, bought it cheaply, but its loss sent John Grono heading for financial ruin. Tim felt bad, and realized he could no longer consider going into any partnership down the road with Mr. Grono. He needed to learn more about Mr. Thompson, for sure.

As the year headed for a close his sense of loneliness grew. He hadn't even stopped to check on Laura in his two trips to Parramatta and now he was feeling not only guilty, but missing her companionship as well. He had big plans, the first small part of which he had luckily executed. He'd dashed off a letter to the lawyer as soon as he had arrived home with Captain Clavell's document. One less thing for the lawyer to pursue.

By late November, as spring faded and the sun climbed higher, one of the things in his mind was what to do about a Christmas gift for Laura. An idea formed slowly over time.   He found a ten-inch block of soft wood in the boatyard discard pile, and started whittling away whenever he could.   Slowly and carefully he worked up the shape of a big skeleton key.   It wouldn't fit any lock but it matched the brass keys some folks in nice homes had for their doors.   He painstakingly smoothed it down and brought out the natural colours of the wood.   It felt soft and almost sensuous in his hands with the grain revealing long yellowish-brown sinews along the main shank, the tooth at the end a light brown on one side, a dull gold on the other.   He was immensely proud of his work and looked forward to showing it off after the final steps.

Christmas Day was on a Tuesday in 1804 so he sent a very short note to Laura saying he was planning to come and visit late that morning.   Unfortunately, he couldn't come the night before because Mr. Griffiths had generously invited all his workers to a Christmas evening dinner.   He was sure she would understand.

He already knew what wrapping he would use for the gift, for one of the yard men had passed on a small kangaroo's skin he didn't want, and Tim had worked it into a lovely supple leather. The big challenge was the note to go inside the present.   He wrote numerous drafts and was finally happy just four days before the celebration was due to take place.   It was the simplest version.

> This key is really two keys
> One is the key to my heart
> The other is the key to my home
> I hope you will accept both
> With affection and devotion
> Timothy Bartlett

In tiny capitals on one side of the bit he engraved HEART. On the other side he engraved HOME. He brought it along to the dinner, declaring his intentions to invite Laura to live with him.

Eleanor was totally overcome with emotion. She cried on Tim's shoulder, called him the most romantic man she'd ever met, and wished him well. "Do you expect Laura to actually accompany you when you return?" she asked. "If so I'll add a little feminine touch in your abode if that's OK, like a posy of flowers, and a new mug and a fresh pillowcase. They'll be Jonathan's and my gift to you both. Ooh, I'm looking forward to meeting her."

"I don't know what the rules are about her leaving camp, Eleanor. She must have to give notice to the local authorities and I think their offices will be shut on Christmas Day. I may have to go back later in the week to collect her. But thank you for the offer anyway. You are very kind."

Jonathan spoke up: "Well, the lads and I wondered what you were whittling away at back at your dwelling. You do nice work I must say. Maybe we need to think about polishing some decorative chair railings in the main cabin of our boats. Mr. Grono won't have thought of that, I'll warrant. But forget that for the moment. We all hope your lady-love is as smart as you tell us, Tim and that she thinks the key is the best present she's ever going to get. Good luck to you."

Christmas Day that year dawned cloudy and was decidedly cooler than previous days, with the eight a.m. morning temperature in Sydney being only fifty-five degrees and the barometer at 29.93 millibars. Laura was uncharacteristically nervous waiting for Tim's arrival. Not since Easter had she seen him, and his note that indicated he was coming today had been enthusiastically welcomed. She'd missed him, and for the first time in a year the presence and company of the other women in the house and the factory had not fulfilled the void his departure had created. She'd had a little scare after he'd gone when her bleeding time was three days late, but it was his warmth, his consideration, and his gentle support that the other women were no longer able to replace. The married women in the house had all complained that one thing they missed was the simple physical presence of their husbands, and for the first time she started to understand what they meant.

She'd gone and opened the front door and looked out three times before the woman she was working with making peach pies said, "Laura, for heaven's sake, he'll be here, and he knows how to knock. He's done it before. Concentrate now. I don't want you adding salt instead of sugar or messing up some other way. And didn't you tell me he said it would be late this morning before he would arrive? It's not even ten a.m.. So relax. Come on, girl."

She'd spent more time than usual brushing her hair this morning, and had made sure she wore her prettiest dress. She'd asked three women how she looked and they all smiled and told she looked perfect. A couple of others were also planning on their beaus turning up. One was a local guardsman, the other an older carpenter who lived alone on the edge of town and who made furniture for people. In any event there was to be a Christmas dinner mid-afternoon for all the women in the house and a few select friends they had invited or whom they knew would drop by. The kitchen was a war zone as the first of two large turkeys was already roasting, bread was nearly ready to bake, stuffing was being made, and vegetables were being washed and sliced. The chatter was loud and Laura wondered if she'd even hear a knock on the door above the din they were all creating.

Tim tied Dottie to the hitching post by the river landing and strolled along the shore watching the second boat for the day getting ready to head to Sydney. He reckoned the passengers were all going to spend Christmas Day with relatives in the big town. They were dressed up, some carrying large hampers with either food or gifts or both inside. The mood was upbeat and he exchanged 'Merry Christmas' greetings with several of the men and women as they boarded. He waited till the boat departed, and then unhurriedly headed for Laura's house.

She jumped into his arms and hugged him tightly, wishing him a Merry Christmas, lights dancing in her eyes from affection. Oh my, she had missed him. By now he knew several of her house-mates well enough to be greeted enthusiastically. He offered up a flagon of ale he'd purchased at the inn, and it was immediately taken outside and placed on a trestle table.

Laura still had some chores to perform so he left her and wandered outside, where he struck up a conversation with the old carpenter who had also arrived early. His name was Jacob. They swapped tales on their backgrounds. The carpenter had owned a little shop in west London from which he sold furniture items he made. There was a workshop in the back where he did all the work. He was two doors away from a lumber yard on the Thames so he didn't have to store his own wood, for which he was very thankful as wood was an attractive item to steal. The lumber yard held enough that it employed special guards to watch over the inventory. Usually Jacob made chairs and tables and dressers and beds to order but he had a couple of stools and a kitchen cupboard and a hat stand just inside the front door so people could peer in through the glass and see his wares.

One day while working in the back he thought he heard the front door open, but no-one called for him from the shop so he kept planing a backboard. A movement caught his eye and he realized a youth was stealing one of his show chairs and heading out the door. Being older, he didn't move fast and by the time he got to the front the young kid was a few yards away, dragging the chair behind him as it was heavier than he had anticipated. Jacob yelled to him to stop and at the same time hurled the iron planer. His aim was true and struck the kid heavily just behind the right ear and sent him crashing to the ground. He quickly ran up and sat on the chap and asked a bystander to fetch a constable. The boy never moved or struggled, and when the constable finally arrived and they turned the lad face-up it was clear he was dead. Why the heavy sander had had such an effect was a surprise to all.

There were witnesses to the theft and everyone felt Jacob was justified in chasing his robber and trying to stop him. His death was an accident as the carpenter certainly hadn't intended to kill the boy. But, as circumstance would have it, the boy was the son of one of the King's cooks. He arranged for Jacob to be charged with the boy's death, and at his trial the judge bowed to pressure from the King's advocates and Jacob was sentenced to transportation for life.

Tim felt an immediate kinship. Both of them had been unfair victims of an overtaxed system. Both were gaoled based on an accident, both were sentenced by a less than impartial judge. The fortunate part for Jacob was that he had plenty of money put away and with skills in demand the rules were bent and he was allowed to set up a shop making furniture for the authorities as well as free citizens. He was excited about today because just two weeks ago he had been granted an early Ticket of Leave and he and his bride to be were going to go off and live together in his home. This was to be her last day at the convict house.

Tim became intensely interested and plied Jacob for more information about the granting of his Ticket of Leave. He explained his own dreams, and Jacob thought he would have a harder time getting a Ticket since he didn't have goods and services to offer as Jacob did. In any event, he offered to introduce Tim to the guardsman who was also coming to the Christmas dinner as he had been very helpful in forwarding letters and forms to the authorities in Sydney on Jacob's behalf. Tim couldn't believe his good fortune. This could end up being one of the most rewarding days of his life, he thought.

The afternoon dinner turned out to be a gala event. The women had done an outstanding job preparing the feast and had even hung paper decoration chains across the backyard. They were all dressed in their best and there were multiple toasts to friendship, families back in England, and good wishes for the future. They took turns going around the table so each person had a chance to say something. Maybe a prayer, a toast, or a thanks to a friend. One read a letter she'd received from her daughter back home. Another handed a knitted cardigan present to a friend. And so it went on until Tim and Laura's turn. Tim reached behind him and explained to the crowd that he was a man of few words and that he just had a little present for Laura. He handed her the kangaroo skin package and watched her puzzled smile as she ran her hands around the soft leather and untied the leather straps.

Tim had told no one about the present so it was a total surprise to all. She held up the key for everyone to see, and then passed it around. The woman next to Laura picked up the piece of paper that had floated out of the package and handed it over. Laura read it quickly then turned to Tim with a look of amazement on her face. "Do you mean it?" she asked. "You bet I do," he responded, and she leapt into his arms, kissing his face and hugging him. She handed the paper back to the woman who had picked it up and asked her if she would read it out loud as tears streamed down her face and she choked up.

Needless to say Tim was the hero of the afternoon. Jacob introduced him to the guardsman and the three couples were toasted repeatedly so that by the end of the dinner Tim and Laura were feeling slightly drunk from all the liquor they'd absorbed. Jacob was impressed with Tim's carving and engraving abilities, and said: "If ever boat building doesn't work out, I think I could make a spot for you easily.That's fine work." While Laura received continued congratulations and well wishes from her friends Tim chatted with Graham Portman, the guardsman. He discussed his interest in getting an exception to the standard procedure for Tickets of Leave, and was encouraged when Graham told him to seek him out as soon as he heard back from his lawyer. Almost as an afterthought he added, "By the way, you seem like a very sincere sort of chap. If you would like to take Laura home with you today I'll make sure her leave is registered and approved when we are back at work on Thursday. I'll need you both to come back before the end of the week to sign the paperwork but given the occasion I don't see any problem. What's her last name? I was in church at Easter when she sang and I know the reverend introduced her but I forget her last name."

"It's Stewart, and I thank you so much. I'll make sure we come back Friday or Saturday. You've been very helpful." He told Laura the good news and she took leave of her friends to pack up a few things for Richmond Bottoms. Oh my, her new life started today. Yippee….

Even Dottie seemed affected by the happiness in the air and was perfectly behaved with both of them on her back. Tim let her walk, so the pace was slow, but he savored the warmth of the sun on his back since it had finally come out. Once they passed Toongabbie Creek, Laura was in new territory and he pointed out some of the land's features as they travelled along, noting particularly the house at the front of the Government Stock Farm. There was no guard on duty at the Gist bridge and they spent time wandering around the small village of Green Hills. He proudly introduced her to the grand Hawkesbury River running past.

Then on to Richmond Bottoms, and the boatyard, Dottie picking up speed as she recognized the trail to her stable. The first thing that struck Laura was the quiet and the remoteness. Of course it was now evening on a holiday so few folks were outside. Tim showed her his hut and she immediately noticed the flowers and the fresh pillows. "So, someone else cares for you too?" she asked with a smile. "Just one of many," he replied impishly. "Come on. Before they put the children to bed I want you to meet Jonathan and Eleanor. She wanted to make you feel welcome and have a gift waiting in case you were in fact able to come here tonight. She's a lovely person."

Back in the main house, Laura said, "Delighted to meet you Eleanor. Thanks so much for the flowers and the pillows. You made it feel like a home already. That's very gracious of you. And Jonathan, Tim has mentioned you so many times I feel like I already know you."

"Well, welcome to Richmond Bottoms, Laura. Tim has been talking about you for months so Jonathan and I are delighted to finally meet you. It will be nice to have another woman close by. If there's anything you need don't hesitate to come and ask. I look forward to getting to know you and showing you the ladies' view of the place."

It was bath time for some of the youngsters, so Tim and Laura didn't stay long. He was proud to introduce her to established emancipists—folks who'd been convicts but had earned their Tickets of Leave and Pardons. Such people held a special form of respect, for they had conquered the odds and were making a life for themselves without complaint in this new land.

Just what he wanted to do with Laura now by his side.

29. Time Passing

The new year arrived with temperatures in the seventies and cloudy skies. The temperature stayed constant throughout February but the skies cleared. It was great boat-building weather, far less hot than previous summers and the December just past. The newspaper that Tim and Laura received every Sunday kept them abreast of widespread happenings in the colony, and with time on her hands Laura would go into Green Hills every few days and catch up with local information from the store owners and militia there.

A new drink was being produced illicitly down near Sydney. Ten gallons of cider from abundant peach trees could be distilled into one gallon of brandy, a great conversion ratio. And each gallon of brandy commanded two pounds ten shillings, an extraordinary price for the times.

Nearer to home a William Roberts started up a covered wagon service between Green Hills and Sydney three times a week. The fare from Green Hills to Parramatta was five shillings with an extra two shillings and sixpence to continue on to Sydney. It was definitely faster than taking a boat but still took a slow sixteen hours crossing two days.

Even closer to Richmond Bottoms John Grono had been threatened with legal action by the Provost Marshal, Mr. George Blaxcell, if he didn't meet the claims of creditors by the end of January. His assets would be seized and sold. Thankfully he managed to meet their needs but stopped boat-building for the time being. Tim was highly upset at the legal issue but glad Mr. Grono was able to overcome it.

Laura became aware of some of the risks of boat ownership and became more apprehensive of Tim's scheme to use an exceptional Ticket of Leave to get into the business. Living in the real remote bush world of country New South Wales, she no longer enjoyed the sheltered protection that she'd had under military administration in the Parramatta colony. And in March another aboriginal uprising further down the Hawkesbury scared her badly. This time things were more serious… as the killings and burnings of settlers and their homes increased.

The garrison at Green Hills was enlarged and armed boats were sent out from there to patrol the river banks.   The Branch tribe was suspected, especially when houses in Sackville were burnt down. The previous aboriginal ally named *Yaragowhy* betrayed his agreement with the authorities and warned his fellow tribe members that they were to be hunted down. Two unnamed men from the *Boorooberongal* tribe helped the soldiers avoid ambushes and led them to the Branch camp. There several natives were killed, including *Yaragowhy*. It was an anxious period.

In June and July messages from Tim's mother and lawyer arrived. The lawyer had been able to do everything Tim asked, although he wished he could have found someone closer to the King's court to sign a recommendation of Tim. He had found a sympathetic magistrate in Plymouth but wished he could have done more. Other than that he had sent a bunch of papers and letters of credit in a package that arrived perfectly intact. The lawyer had deducted his fee from the substantial amount in Tim's bank deposit. His mother's letter was a mixture of sadness and support. She understood his desire to push his business interests but worried about the risks. She also was a little uncomfortable that he wanted all his money moved to a bank in Plymouth.   In so doing was he abandoning Polperro and his family? She hoped not. Thomas was a little charmer. He'd gone through a couple of baby sicknesses and now was teething and driving Betsy to distraction, but generally was still a loving little youngster. She intimated that Michael would be writing soon.

Given all the relevant material he had gathered, Tim talked to Jonathan about a reference to Governor King, and with that added to the others went off to Parramatta to visit with Jacob and Graham again. He took fresh fish he'd caught as gifts, although he knew the men could also buy the same locally. These, however, were large and free. Graham promised to make sure the material would be safely delivered to the right contact in Sydney and told Tim the hardest part now was ahead, in trying to be patient. There was no guarantee when the Governor would consider his petition, nor what his response would be. One could only wait and hope.

A letter from Mike and Betsy in September brought a nice touch of home and a tale of a memorable event.

May 1805

Dear Timothy:

It is two years since Thomas was born. Mike is bouncing him on his knee as he tells me what to write to you. My handwriting is much better than his which looks like he wrote with a thumbnail dipped in whale oil. We read the early letters you wrote to your mother and to my mother, and they made us feel sad for you. We know we can't undo the past, but it's still hard to forget all the unfairness. Of course your son is a constant reminder. Thank you for agreeing to let us raise him and to buy and live in your old house. Your later letters about establishing a business made us feel much better. It's so strange to have the letters take so long back and forth.

Mike is obviously very busy – in fact this is one of the rare days he is home – I haven't seen him much this past month, nor do I expect to over the coming summer. He wants me to tell you that that big ugly Lieutenant of the guards who took you away came by, alone, one day a month ago, we think to gloat. It's just as well that Mike and the other men of the village are peace-lovers else he might not have gone away unharmed. He tied up his horse and paraded up and down along the wharf, waving his arms, cursing, and spitting over the wall on the boats below. Do you remember Ruth, the wife of the informant who was banished? She surprised us all by taking a bucket of grain to the horse and feeding it. We thought she was trying to show the Lieutenant that we were all peaceful and that she was now a part of the village, and no longer had anything to do with her evil husband.

But when the Redcoat left she told us that the bucket of grain had mixed in it a bunch of poisonous mushrooms that she'd seen the day before and had gone out and picked the minute the guard had arrived. She anticipated that within a couple of hours his horse would be very sick indeed, and that if it had eaten enough of the mushrooms would lay down and might even die. She hated to kill any animal but the arrogance, imperialism, and brutality the guard commanded reminded her too much of her ex-husband and the circumstances of the guardsman's last visit, so she thought he needed a lesson. Even if he thought of poisoning she felt it would be hard to prove she had made the horse sick because after he left she had quickly washed out the bucket with sea water and thrown in a few dead pilchards so there'd be no smell of mushrooms should he ever come back. She was viewed as a heroine in the village after she told her story. Mike felt you'd enjoy hearing it.

We love the house that you and Claire lived in for three years. We haven't changed it much at all frankly as it suits us perfectly. Thomas has his own room with a little crib, and he's a good baby for us, hardly crying except when his new teeth coming in hurt. There's one thing we wanted to talk about however as we think of him as our own baby Tim. He's just starting to walk after crawling around for some time and we're waiting for his first words. As much as he will always be your son we want him to call us mother and father. When he's old enough, and when it makes sense we'll tell him he's adopted. We hope you will be OK with that. You know now I can't have children so he is like a gift from God for me and I love him dearly. We thank you for sharing him this way and promise to raise him well.

There's not much news to add really. Oh yes, Mike says we still trade with Guernsey, and that a more reliable form of signaling has been set up along the coast, so the men feel more sure that they won't be caught inadvertently coming back to port. There is still trade with big boats that have stopped in the Channel, although much less is done now since at Falmouth there was an instance of the sailor rowing ashore from the freighter and having been bought off by the Redcoats. His traitorous position was discovered before anyone bought illicit merchandise, but everyone up and down the coast has been very wary since.

Mike took me to your cave and showed me how incredible it is. One day we'll show Thomas. But no one knows outside our families. Perhaps one day it may become useful if someone has to hide for a period. It is so well naturally camouflaged that we wonder how you ever found it initially. Mike helped Clarinda retrieve your small treasure chest and Mrs. Hinson has it in safe-keeping until you need it. She is a lovely lady but misses Claire terribly. She is a great grandma to Thomas, always willing to look after him for a couple of hours if I need to get supplies and so forth.

I think everyone is sad that Claire died and that you are not here with your son. We know you will never be allowed to return but maybe, just maybe, one day Thomas will come and visit you. That's a dream we all keep to ourselves.

Meanwhile, we are glad you have what sounds like an interesting job and a new opportunity. Please stay safe and write when you can. We miss you.

Mike and Betsy Anne

The letter brought tears to Tim's eyes and Laura comforted him with hugs. It was time to write back to Mother, and he wondered how she would react to the news that Laura now shared his life. He'd have to remember it would arrive around Christmas-time. It was odd to have to think so far ahead.

September 1805

Dear Mother:

There is so much news to tell you I don't quite know where to start. Oh yes, letters from you and the lawyer arrived in July. Thank you for helping organize things for me at your end. I've now submitted all the forms and paperwork to try and get an exception for my Ticket of Leave and there's nothing more I can do but wait. I've made friends with a guardsman in Parramatta who is making sure the papers get to the right officials in Government house down in Sydney, but no one knows when Governor King will act on them. I just hope the day his aides talk to him that he's in a good mood.

The biggest and most important news to share with you, however, is that a lovely lady has taken up with me. I'm sure this will be a little hard to understand and accept as you have the memories of Claire close at hand. I am not forgetful of Clarinda and am thankful that Thomas carries our bloodstream, but I cannot bring her back, Mother, and her loss has deprived me of a hope that can never be fulfilled now, that one day she might join me. Betsy Anne's letter of May just arrived and I'm so happy to hear about their love for Thomas. They should indeed treat him as their flesh and blood and one day, when it makes sense, tell him about Claire and me.

Laura Stewart is a Scot born in Edinburgh in 1782, who moved later to York and then Manchester. Her parents abandoned her, and to survive she turned to pickpocketing but was caught and sent here to Botany Bay. She has values that I know you would appreciate – honesty, courage, realism, sacrifice, and care for others. And she has the finest voice you can imagine as she used to sing in the choir at York Minster. She has been invited by the minister at the Anglican church in Parramatta to come sing there any Sunday she would like. At Easter the congregation there was stunned when she sang "Amazing Grace' for them. She has no brothers or sisters or relatives to correspond with and it was at Christmas time that I asked her to live with me. She'd been in a house for women in Parramatta sewing clothes for convicts on work gangs.

Speaking of which we've had several unhappy incidents in recent times with both convicts and natives. I mentioned the Irish convicts in my last letter I think. As more settlers take up land along the rivers where the land is fertile and the farming is productive the natives feel they are losing not only sacred ground, but places where they used to fish and hunt. They become angry and burn down settlers cottages and sometimes kill them. It's their form of retaliation. In a way I feel for them for it is true, we take what we want thinking we have a divine right to this land, which is really theirs and we should act as visitors. But as one man I am powerless to do anything and the Governor hands out instructions to the militia to make sure no settler employs any natives or encourages them. I find it inconsistent behavior because the authorities try to make friends with select aborigines and use then as trackers to hunt down native killers or white convicts who have escaped and become 'bushrangers'.

One good thing is that we now have a newspaper published every Sunday here. It gives us news of the world as well as of other parts of the Colony, and makes us aware of what is happening in government policy and on economic issues. This town where we live is remote and it is nice that we now get worldly news more regularly. To illustrate progress, a covered wagon service was established earlier this year to run between Green Hills and Sydney.

One thing I am thinking of is building a better house for Laura and me to live in. At the moment we have a shack that you would not be proud of, Mother, as it is very primitive. I'm hoping if I get my Ticket of Leave I will be able to buy thirty acres in the area and build a house I've already designed. In late winter and early spring when the rains come the river here swells enormously and I think we are destined for a flood sometime. So I want to build a house on stilts that will sit above any rising waters that cover the land. There's a place nearby called Richmond Hill and I've been looking at land there. Again, it all depends on getting a Ticket of Leave because convicts can't own and hold property unless they've been granted one. Please pray for me that it comes through.

I wish there was a way for you to meet Laura as I know you would love her. We care for one another and she is wonderfully supportive of me. I am sure you will want to know about children. So far there are none in sight and if they come that will be fine by both of us.

Please also thank our lawyer for me. Everything he sent has been well received and is most useful according to my guardsman friend. And tell Betsy and Mike I did get a chuckle out of Ruth's actions in feeding the Lieutenant's horse. I hope the redcoat had to walk miles to get aid.

And to dear Uncle Ben, I have been thinking of taking up a pipe as I remember the smell of his that I used to love. I imagine it's now a constant aroma in your house.

I will be taking this letter down to Parramatta in the morning to make sure it gets to Sydney faster so that it will definitely get to you by Christmas. I hope the season isn't too cold – please wish all my friends the best of the holiday. May you and Ben have a Merry Christmas and please give Thomas an extra hug for me.

Thank you for caring.

Your loving son

Timothy

Laura looked over his finished note. "Nicely done, my man, but what's this about taking up a pipe? First I've heard you mention it."

"Don't worry, my love. It's not true. I just wanted to say something nice to Uncle Ben as he has been good to me and Mother through the years, and as a youngster I truly did love the smell of his pipe. When Clarinda and I inherited his house, though, we spent weeks getting rid of the smell. I'm not sure it ever went completely away."

"Well, you are a bit of a rogue then with your pretense, but I imagine it can't hurt. I'll let it go this once Mr. Timothy, but please don't tell me any stories like that. I don't like blatant lies."

In the last week of October Tim was busy inside one of the large sheds sanding a plank for Jonathan's next boat when he heard his name being called loudly and urgently from the yard. He emerged to find Graham getting off a horse waving a package in the air and smiling broadly. "You got it," he yelled. "Your Ticket of Leave.

"All the official mail comes through our office and as soon as I saw this I intercepted it and decided it couldn't wait for the next mail courier so brought it up myself. Congratulations, Tim, you did it. I'm so pleased for you."

Tim thought for a moment. What an amazing sentiment. Here was a guard who was employed by the militia to look over and manage convicts, but rejoicing at a convict's version of semi-freedom. Graham was obviously one of those men with principles higher than what his job commanded. They shook hands as Graham explained what the Ticket meant. An extra copy was available for Jonathan since Tim was assigned to him. What a marvelous document Tim held in his hands. He felt privileged to have it as he knew others waited for years to get theirs. He could now proceed with his business and personal interests. He showed the document off to his fellow workers, noticing a little jealousy on the part of a few, and invited Graham to head home with him to show Laura and stay for a celebratory supper. Jonathan was down in Sydney and he'd share the news with him later.

It was a great day, no doubt.

The first thing he and Laura did with his new capabilities was find some acreage for sale. They settled on property at Richmond Hill where they cleverly bought elevated ground. Tim was able to build something he and Laura designed together. He modified his previous idea with Laura's extra input, giving up on the stilts since they were no longer building in the flood plain. The thirty acres he bought were on the north side of the river, outside the vulnerable 'S' bends surrounding the lowlands. During the summer months Tim hired convicts to help him build the new home and they moved in in February 1806. Their timing was propitious as just a month later a giant flood devastated the countryside. The Hawkesbury overflowed its normal height by over forty feet and water inundated properties and fields for weeks afterwards. The militia were kept busy rescuing people using boats.

Richmond Hill rose two hundred feet above the surrounding countryside and Tim and Laura's house was well over eighty feet above the flood line, although water rose to several of the lagoons on the hillsides. Other families in the area had to abandon their properties and when they returned, many of their homes were full of mud. For some, the best recourse was to build again. The Bartletts were able to repay some of the kindness the Griffiths had provided over time and the parents and children slept on the veranda for weeks. It was a difficult time for all, but at least they had access to boats to move across the countryside to buy produce from areas unaffected, and help people move goods from one place to another. For most residents their homestead livestock of goats and pigs had to be moved to higher ground, but still needed checking frequently until the waters started to recede. The wood in the boatyards stayed confined in sheds but was waterlogged for months. Tim had prophesized potential flooding in a letter back home to England, but was not happy to see his predictions come true. Once again his insight had been rewarded, but there was no rejoicing.

Laura loved her new home, although she hadn't finished decorating before the floods came. They hadn't gotten around to buying any laying hens or pigs but were offered some at good prices when the floods came, when others found it hard to move them. The rains didn't last long but the floods did as the waters ran down the Blue Mountain creeks and slopes with force. Farmers lost wheat fields and had to move their herds of cattle and flocks of sheep miles to find large enough vacant fields on higher ground. Tim and Laura had planned to buy a horse and cart but that also was put on hold for the period.

The flood spread across the land, ruining everything in its path. Many of the wild animals suffered. Not the winged birds and koalas, nor the kangaroos or wallabies or emus, but the snakes and echidnas and wombats and other ground animals perished, being unable to move fast enough. Aborigines were nowhere to be seen, retreating to high ground in the mountains. Tim and Laura had seen minor floods in England but nothing like what they experienced here. It was a frustrating time, as inability to control nature and desperation at finding no solutions became constant companions. Close forced proximity between strangers didn't help, although in the end run, as with most calamities of major proportion, bonding between select individuals grew. Eleanor and Laura became the firmest of friends and Jonathan and Tim talked through some new business strategies and options.

By August, life was on an almost even keel again although for some the despair and losses would never really ever be reconciled. It wasn't just the local community that was affected as the floods had spread way down river as well, inundating communities for tens of miles. Once the waters went back to normal levels, more construction of houses took place where they were raised a little off the ground.

And just as the land became usable again, and crops were re-planted, a second flood hit, almost as bad as the first one. The residents despaired. There'd been no river water problems for years, but now floods had occurred twice in six months. God must be vengeful for some reason, they all thought. Once again everyone had to go through the move and rescue process again. Life was decidedly a challenge, to say the least. Some moved away for good, unable to come to grips with the losses they had experienced. It was a bewildering, sobering time.

With the increased agitation of aborigines all along the river, the rebellion at Castle Hill, and more bushrangers being apprehended by authorities, the number of convicts being killed in the area had increased dramatically over the past three years. Officials decided there needed to be a place where dead convicts could be buried and before the year was out had established a special burial ground just for convicts at Green Hills. It served communities from Parramatta to the Hawkesbury region and parts of the Blue Mountains.

As 1807 dawned Timothy made his move. Mr. Grono had overcome his immediate financial problems and had taken up seal hunting, captaining boats for others. Tim joined Jonathan and Andrew Thompson in investing in a large two-masted schooner that Thompson was building for the explicit purpose of seal and whale hunting. For the last six years seal hunting had been concentrated on the islands in Bass Strait between the Australian mainland and Van Diemen's Land and around Van Diemen's Land itself. Thousands of mature and pup seals had been bludgeoned or stabbed to death for their skins and oil.

There were three types of seals in Australian waters— Australian fur seals, New Zealand fur seals, and Australian sea lions, the latter sometimes called 'sea elephants', providing the most oil. In the fur seals, a dense, short underfur occurred beneath the outer hairs. Initial demand for skins came from China, where the fur was used in the manufacture of men's hats, and the skins were used for shoes. But as imports there from North America increased in volume, Australian traders found better prices in London. There, skins could fetch anywhere from six shillings to fourteen shillings each. Oil sold between thirty-five pounds and forty-two pounds per ton.

Seal hunting was an unpleasant business. 'Hunting' was a really a euphemism as men simply strode through unsuspecting colonies of sleeping seals and clubbed them to death. As beaches and rocky shores where the colonies roosted were cleared, men did have to 'hunt' for rocky islands where smaller colonies existed. In the early days, six to eight men were dropped from a boat at some remote island outpost with rations of rum, hard biscuits and water, to be augmented by seal meat and fish, calculated to last up to six months or more. As well, they were often provided with timber in order to construct a small boat to explore nearby islands. Their job was simple – collect as many skins and as much seal oil as possible before the big boat returned.

The men who took on these tasks were uncouth, unkempt, and uncivilized. They led a very tough, lonely life, living in caves or under boats, and were always cold and wet. The work was dangerous, mainly taking place at night, quickly killing all the seals in a group, then going back later to skin them and hang the skins to dry. Many men slipped on the rocks and drowned. Their only motivation was money – paid by the number of skins and the number of full barrels of oil. The clear, scentless oil was used to lubricate machines, or be burned in street lamps, or incorporated into commercially produced foodstuffs. Over time the value of skins and oil fluctuated mightily so that in some cases it was the oil that made the returning crews rich, in other times it was the skins.

The toll on 'seal-rats', as the hunters on the islands were called, and the impact on their families while they were away for extended periods, became the subject of an official inquiry, for seal hunting was an important industry. Seal products earned the greatest export income for the colonial state in the early years. Between 1800 and 1806, officially over 112,000 skins found their way back to England. More found their way unofficially. In September 1805 a Government and General Order was issued which forbade men with families to go hunting unless their employers entered into a bond to maintain their wives and children until such time as the man returned from sealing or there was appropriate proof that he had died. Employers were obligated to return sealers to the port where they had departed.

This order, which raised costs to those sealing and the annihilation of seal communities in Australia, encouraged all Australian sealers, including Tim and his new-found companions, to look further afield for very large seal communities to gather skins and oil. Their target was New Zealand, which required even stronger boats to manage crossing the Tasman Sea and to sail the rugged coasts of the island of 'the long white cloud'.

30. Boat Innovation

Tim's experience from years of sailing the English Channel plus his apprenticeship on the *Coronation* coming to Australia qualified him to suggest appropriate structural adjustments to the boat that they were in the process of completing. Reinforced hulls below the waterline, large sails of new wind-catching shapes, duplicate rigging, masts with larger bases, a mix of fixed and movable partitions for the hold, and a small false keel for whatever purposes, should any arise.

Back in the days of the Second Fleet, a couple of the ships had been used for seal hunting and had headed for the southern extremities of the South Island of New Zealand based on Captain Cook's observations back in 1770 of seeing myriad seals there. But once Bass Strait had been discovered and its islands charted, it was a much quicker trip to hunt there than in New Zealand.

Now the tides were reversing and the hunters had New Zealand in their sights again. The standard plan had a boat taking out a crew of hunters, depositing them at a select location, picking up a few supplies at a New Zealand port and returning home, then going back out again in six months or so to pick up the sealers, skins, and oil. Boats had to be very sturdy and seaworthy as they faced risky, turbulent waters beset by storms along the New Zealand coast

Tim and the others were pleased with the structural refinements they'd made to their boat, but Tim had urther ideas, more about the business side of things than the boat per se. He approached his partners with several trade-related suggestions. His logic was simple. Money was only made when seal-rats were in place killing seals. The wider an area they could cover the more likely they would bring home extra skins. Which led to two things. First, why take just one band of seal-rats along, why not two to be deposited at different places? Second, make the smaller rowboats in the shipyard before they left. That had several advantages. First, it would give the sealers confidence, save them from expending energy on building instead of hunting at the seal grounds, and give them a much more robust and secure boat than what they could build themselves in a wet climate. Plus there was another intangible. It would give the partners an edge in attracting men to the kill-gangs since they would be offering something their competitors didn't.

There were of course two associated problems. One, the more trivial, was how to transport the ready-made boats, as they would take up more room compared to simply taking lumber along. Second, far more important, was whether they had enough storage space to bring back two hauls of skin and oil, instead of one. Tim had thought about both. He'd already devised building a heightened stern and essentially hanging the rowboats behind vertically, fastening them tightly so they would ride as if they were simply an incorporated design part of the main vessel. She might look a bit funny but he didn't think the addition would impede their speed.

The second problem required a bit more ingenuity. At the first pickup point on the return trip they would take smooth skins only, no furs, and lay them tightly in the false keel. If it didn't fill they'd add more at the second stop until the false keel was filled. The barrels of oil would go into the hold next, but fur skins would be stuffed between them to both fill vacant space and minimize movement. Once an area of barrels was established they'd place horizontal boards across them leaving no airspace, further confining them. Regular skins would be piled on top. This would be done in both holds, enforcing tight packing and guaranteeing stability. That still wouldn't be enough space and Tim had an outrageous suggestion to build multiple storage sheds on deck between the masts. They'd be raised off the deck so that water coming over the bow or under the side railing could still escape. They had to build a bigger cabin anyway to carry sixteen seal-rats instead of eight, which was what had generated the idea. The downside was some slight impediment to the vision of the captain at the helm, and the need to ensure that they didn't raise the boat's center of gravity too much. As a last resort they could load up the dinghies hanging behind the stern.

Finally Tim came up with two more ideas of a marketing nature. He suggested adding barrels of flour to the seal-rats' provisions and supplying them with large boards and a few tools from which a primitive shelter could be made in case there were no caves to be used. The partners agreed that both ideas would make their boat more attractive to seal-rat prospects down in Sydney.

English companies would charter local boats and hire skippers, such as Grono. Tim and his friends owned their own boats, and to avoid conflict with the East India Company in particular, planned to sell their goods to independent freight forwarders in Sydney, breaking the monopolistic chain of ownership from source to landed goods. Jonathan's friend Samuel Thorley was to be their agent in Sydney, hiring the seal-rats, procuring provisions and arranging sales of the seal products.

While Tim kept busy at Thompson's boatyard, making the refinements he'd suggested to the schooner, Laura was busy converting their house into a home. Finally, at age twenty-four she felt she was in charge of her life. As much as Tim was her partner, she was free to decide what furniture they needed and the implements and accessories that would make life more comfortable. Last December after the floods had receded Tim bought her a horse and taught her to ride. He had one for himself now as well. She took the time to ride and meet their neighbours, albeit several hills and pastures away. But Tim forbade her to ride past Green Hills or to take the road to Kurrajong. There were areas where a woman alone would be an obvious target for bushrangers, and Tim felt very protective of his mate. In self-defence he also taught her how to shoot both rifle and pistol, both of which she carried when she rode off the property.

Sometime between the two floods of the previous year Laura had decided what furniture they needed so she and Tim rode to Parramatta on a Sunday to meet up with Jacob again. They commissioned him to make them a bed, a kitchen table, and two chairs, plus a swing rocker for the front verandah. At the time they were sleeping on a mattress on the bedroom floor and eating off two large crates, so the promise of having new hand-made furniture in three months thrilled them.

Jacob and the furniture arrived once the roads were passable as the second flood receded. He stayed overnight before heading back with the empty dray. Laura had plied him with fresh eggs, plus a chicken they had killed in his honor. He was one of those men who was the salt of the earth, dependable, caring, giving unconditionally, and they both enjoyed his fellowship. At Christmastime they had gone to Parramatta again to see Laura's friends at the old house and so she could sing her hymn in the little church again. They talked about making it an annual pilgrimage and a tradition. They'd survived two floods and were thankful to be safe together.

Tim's mother had written back in response to his announcement of taking up with Laura. The letter had been delayed getting delivered due to the first flood, finally arriving early July.

February 1806

Dear Tim:

Your letter of September 1805 didn't quite make it by Christmas last but we all appreciated the thoughts and wishes you sent. I admit we were a little surprised to hear about Laura, although when we sat down and chatted we all realized that none of us had been that conscious of how much time had slipped by since Claire's death. When you wrote in September it was nearly two and half years, and while she is still very much in our minds with Thomas around, we can understand how that is not the case for you, and that loneliness, and the longing for a mate, would be important to you.

So we welcome Laura to our family now. May she love you for the man you are, and not pity you because you lost someone before or were sent away under unfair circumstances.

There is little new in the village. And perhaps that's the way we all like it. Thomas took his first sea-ride last month in some of the coldest weather. Mike said he did really well. Brought up his breakfast once but didn't really complain and in fact was in good spirits when they returned. They'd had to fix the tiller on Ramon's boat and had simply been out testing it. Since they were not going far it seemed like a good chance to start Thomas' sea-life indoctrination. He'll be three this coming May – just three months away. He's a sturdy little chap, reminds me in part of you when you were a youngster. Curious, energetic and sometimes a little defiant. Definitely knows what he wants to do and doesn't want to do at times. Betsy is a good mother and exercises good discipline with him but is also flexible in letting him be the little boy that he is.

Ruth's little girl, who has always been very shy and clingy, has become Thomas' best friend even though she is two or three years older. Having Thomas to play with has brought her out of her shell a bit, which is so nice to see. She often goes over to Mike and Betsy's to play with him, and I think, as well, that Mike is a bit like a pseudo father to her, so different from the one we sent away.

We all get a little older. Ben and I both notice a few more creaks in some of our joints – especially in the colder weather. But we are very happy together, and that is good. I told Ben you might take up a pipe and he beamed from ear to ear. Somehow though I can't picture you with a pipe. It seems pipes are for older men who have more time to think about things. From what you tell me I would think you are dashing off into new ventures and don't have much time to sit and ponder.

Whatever you do, do not forget your new partner Laura. I'm sure she's a wonderful supportive mate. You will have your boat building and your new 'hunting' business to keep you occupied. Perhaps Laura will be left at home for extended periods just as most of the women in the village here are. Never forget to come home to her smiling, and if there's a chance for even the smallest gift showing your appreciation of her don't hesitate to bring it with you.

See, here I am still handing out advice. It's a mother and son thing that will probably never go away. Please accept it as just one of my many foibles.

I love you son. That will never change. And I wish you great happiness in your life with Laura.

   Your loving mother

Laura reread the letter over and over. How hard it must be she realized, for a mother to embrace her son's actions thousands of miles away with no hope of ever being face to face and sharing a hug with him again. How hard must it be to accept news of a total stranger entering his life when you were used to the ways of a village where everyone knew everyone else and there were no strangers. If only my mother had been as loving and trusting. Did she ever miss me when I moved away? Had I been a burden to her all my life? Perhaps I was never wanted, but an accident that happened and had to be lived with. What a contrast. My mother couldn't even take to my choir friend at York Minster, yet here's Tim's mother welcoming me into the family and wishing us great happiness in our life together. She must be a very special lady.

September 1806

Dear Mrs. Bartlett:

It does seem strange writing to someone I don't know and whom I may never meet, but your letter of this February to Tim touched my heart and I wanted to write back.

Thank you for welcoming me into your and Tim's life. I'm sure it is very difficult for you knowing that you will never see Tim again and wondering what I am really like. We've been living together nearly a year now, and Tim has proved to be a wonderful provider. With the money he had, he built this house which is on a hillside rising up from the west bank of the Hawkesbury River where it runs north before turning more easterly along the boatyards. We have a commanding view of the area, being about one hundred fifty feet high and well out of the flood zones. We had a mighty flood this past March but the farmers and other residents seem to have finally recovered, although it has been a very trying and unpleasant period. Although we were quite safe, Tim helped many people move their belongings to places on higher ground. He used some of the small boats he had built and of course his strength allowed him to do far more than many others could. I remember him carrying two large sheep that he had found up to their necks in water into our yard then brushing them down and feeding them fresh grass. He was exhausted from rowing others from their homes all day but he still couldn't stand by and see those two sheep suffer. Many native animals died, which distressed us both. It was horrible to see carcasses of bandicoots and echidnas floating by, but presumably God had some reason for the flood. Most of the aborigines in the area disappeared into the nearby Blue Mountains, but we've had a few come by asking for food. Tim can't fish of course, so we sometimes kill a chicken for them as we really have more than enough for our own needs.

The local aborigines like Tim because he rescued one of their little boys whose leg was trapped under a huge rock in a pool by a waterfall. He then carried him for miles back to the boatyard where a doctor sewed the ugly gash up. Some white men would have walked away and never tried to help but not Tim. Obviously you knew all about him in the first twenty years of his life so it will be hard to tell you anything new but perhaps I can illustrate how loving he is by describing the present he surprised me with last Christmas and why we have come together.

From one of the wood offcuts at the boatyard he carved and fashioned a large skeleton key nearly nine inches long. He rubbed it so smooth that the wood feels soft to the touch and it has gorgeous coloured veins running through it. But there was a little note attached with the following words on it.

This key is really two keys
One is the key to my heart
The other is the key to my home
I hope you will accept both
With affection and devotion
Timothy Bartlett

I think you'll agree he is a romantic of the first order. Who couldn't love him?

Your son is a man with ingenious business ideas, compassion for his fellow man, and a love of life. I'm proud to be alongside him and intend to look after him for as long as I live.

At the moment our house is a little sparse inside. We have ordered some furniture to be made by a carpenter named Jacob down in Parramatta. We want a bed, a kitchen table and two chairs, plus a swing rocker for the front verandah. He should be able to deliver them shortly. We need curtains and linen and many small accessories to make our house into a real home and I'm slowly working on acquiring those. At the moment our main decorations are a large kangaroo skin plus a spear, a shield, and a throwing stick that the aborigines gave Tim as gifts. Having been at the Female Factory I have learned to sew all kinds of garments so we are OK for clothes, and when the right cloth is available to buy I will make us a tablecloth and a bedspread etc.

At some stage we hope to make you a grandma again – but that will happen only when God sees fit. For now we'll just hope that Thomas will be able to visit us one day in the future. I know his father would love that.

Thank you again for all your thoughts.

With warmest feelings

Laura Stewart

At least she'd gotten the letter on its way before the second flood hit in October. Now, as autumn headed for winter more than six months later she anticipated it shouldn't be long before she heard back from Mrs. Bartlett. Tim and the workers were within a month of launching their schooner. They'd just named her *Hawkesbury Spirit* in honour of where she was built and the sense of adventure she was to undertake. Tim anticipated he'd be gone for up to two months as they had to get to Sydney, load provisions and men, and sail across the Tasman Sea, which alone could take between six and ten days depending on winds and current. Their destination was the southwestern tip of New Zealand's South Island which was characterized by both fresh and sea water fjords. It was the myriad islands at the outer edge of the sea water bays in Dusky Sound and Preservation Inlet, however, that were the specific targets. There were sealing grounds further north on the West Coast but their studies and discussions convinced them there was more opportunity for large colonies where they were headed. Plus potentially no problems with the cannibalistic Maori natives of the country since the climate and rocky islands were far less habitable than elsewhere.

The Maoris were known to be a fiercer race than the Australian aborigines, hailing from Tahiti some six hundred years earlier. Experience of sealers and whalers off the east coast of the country was mixed, but there were enough stories of killing and eating white visitors that Tim and his partners vowed to stay as far away as possible from known ports of conflict.

Once in the area the schooner would explore the nearby islands to determine where best to disembark the sea-rat gangs who also would have a better idea of places to move to once a specific colony was depleted, if that happened. Supplies, shelter boards, empty barrels for oil, and crates for skins would be unloaded and then the *Hawkesbury Spirit* would return directly to Green Hills. Coming back would be a good test of the boat's ability to be managed through the violent westerly winds and turbulent seas. The next trip back with the skins on board would have the boat loaded much more heavily and Tim wanted the practice. He wanted to try an idea of taking a more northerly route on return before heading west in order to avoid the strongest westerly winds tearing through Bass Strait, and to use the southerly busters to advantage.

In the last week of May, Tim and his partners untied the lines holding *Hawkesbury Spirit* to shore and let her drift out to midstream before running up small sails to control her downstream movement. Eleanor and Laura clung to each other and waved bravely, but there were tears in their eyes from hoping and praying that nothing would go wrong. They had faith in their men's abilities, but there were always unknown factors and unexpected turns of events that could change life in an instant. They would be each other's best company in the period ahead. Eleanor had her children to keep her busy and preoccupied. Laura just had memories and plans.

Back at Richmond, a letter from Tim's mother arrived and brightened Laura's day. Tim had only been gone one week, and she regretted that he'd missed its arrival by such a short period.

31. *Southern Islands*

The first day out of Sydney Heads was smooth sailing with a northerly breeze allowing fifteen knots, giving them one hundred miles under their belts by nightfall. The night was clear and the second day started out the same way. By late afternoon, however, the wind was up to thirty-five knots and the swells were coming straight off the beam, nearly breaking on the boat. By that time many of the seal-rats were decidedly seasick, with repeated trips to the rail to void whatever food they had ingested. The three experienced partners and the five crewmen they'd hired had no problems. As the wind picked up they reefed and furled some of the sails to cut down on over-power.

As nightfall approached, lightning flared in the distance, and despite their hopes that it would pass them by, it surrounded them for a full hour before passing on. The winds behind abated somewhat, and they were thankful for the extra support they'd applied to the masts in their design. The sheds on the deck picked up a lot of wind, augmenting that collected by the sails. Since they couldn't be flattened, the crew soon realized that reefing and furling the sails had to happen at an accelerated pace or as soon as an indication of increasing wind strength was felt. They travelled less distance that second day, but doubled their progress on the third day when a solid twenty-five-knot northerly blew all day and they ran before it calmly and evenly. Similar results were achieved on the fourth day, but out of the northwest in the middle of the night a fierce storm broke and drove them forward even with all sails furled. The rain was cold and piercing and the crew kept a close watch for any increase in storm behavior until dawn, when the rain stopped and the winds lessened. Once gain the masts had stood up to the tempest well and Tim was proud of the crew, who had been aroused from deep sleeps and worked hard together without complaint. As the next day was clear again he happily handed out extra rations of grog to both crew and those seal-rats who had found their sea-legs OK.

On the eighth day out they sighted the coast in the distance, and by the following morning were making good headway southwards to Dusky Sound. Nearly all the seal-rats had gotten over their seasickness and were excited to be nearing their destination. They had formed the appropriate alliances and two distinct teams whose members seemed to get on well together had materialized. The area had been charted by Captain Cook, yet Tim was still wary and kept the lookouts busy watching for uncharted reefs and rock outcrops, as he stayed within one hundred yards of the shoreline, deliberately making slow progress. The temperature was dropping, and the seas rising, along the coast of Resolution Island with its long peninsula connected to the main body by a tiny piece of land no longer than five hundred feet north to south and no wider than two hundred feet east to west. They rounded the rocky southwestern tip and sailed east to Anchor Island, then around the northern side to a protected harbour where they happily anchored, sheltered from the wild wind and spray. Dusky Sound at last!

With the next morning dawning clear they decided to circumnavigate the island clockwise, observing through telescopes the seal populations at all the small islands they passed—Petrel, Passage, Prove, Stop, Nomans, Many and Seal and other numerous unnamed outcrops. New Zealand fur seals were everywhere, clearly having bred rapidly in the absence of sealers over the past five years or more.

Discussing options back in the sheltered harbour, the first team elected to set up an initial camp on Seal Island, since the weather seemed steady, albeit cold. It was living up to its name and as the closest island to the wide open Tasman Sea. Working there first then moving to islands further inside the Sound seemed a logical way to proceed. Even Passage Island to the northwest was no more than four miles away – not a hard row in the longboat they were inheriting.

Once landing had been completed the *Hawkesbury Spirit* headed twelve miles south to Preservation Inlet. Past Chalky Island and the eastern passage, around the southern tip of the mainland they pulled into Welcombe Bay, sheltered especially from the chilling westerly winds. With only the second team on board they circumnavigated Coal Island then explored the islands to the northwest, Steep-To, Round, Weka, and Cording. Captain Cook had even marked Whale Rock between Coal and Round Islands and it stood out as a reminder of the hazards of proceeding without charts, or in closed sounds at night. Depositing the second seal-rat team on Steep-To island on its only accessible shoreline, they wished the men well and promised to be back in four months or so to pick them up.

With sixteen men no longer on board, plus the two longboats, provisions, and all the extra timber for huts gone, the boat had an eerie feel to it. The partners and crew didn't reminisce for long, however as they had no sooner reached the latitude of Doubtful Sound than an incredible gale fell upon them. Thick, low, dark grey clouds scuddered before them, driven by furious winds that whistled through the rigging and seemed bent on destruction. Angry thunder surrounded them and filled the air with incredible crashes and rumbles, as flashes of wild lightning lit up the clouds from below emphasizing their threatening features. The waves increased in height and frequency and the only positive aspect that anyone could think about was that they were being driven roughly in the direction they wanted to go. The ship was tossed like a cork, riding almost helplessly up the swells and plunging to their depths. Water cascaded over the bow and Tim struggled to hold direction and not turn broadside. Hour after hour he stood at the helm with the rain pelting down. His hands nearly froze and the rain gear held no real protection after the first thirty minutes.

But they came through well and the partners were all pleased. The storm provided a major test of the structural integrity of the boat. No leaks were found. A few loosened boards above deck were quickly refastened, and the main discussion centered on how well the *Spirit* would have performed had she been full of skins, oil, and sixteen more men. The conclusion was that the extra weight would have added stability and helped dampen the vicious yaw movements but that the up and down pitch would still have depended on the height of the waves. The larger they were the more water would come over the bow and threaten the sheds on deck. They resolved to strengthen the front of the sheds before returning for the skins and oil.

February 1807

Dearest Tim and Laura:

What a delight it was to hear from you, Laura, and thank you for providing so much detail about your corner of the new world. I couldn't believe Tim's note to you accompanying your Christmas present. It is clear that you must be very special for him to have been able to pen such beautiful lines. As I read his words I could almost imagine hearing his voice saying them. Thank you so much for sharing them. They were more comfort than I would have thought. I think mothers always worry about their sons no matter what age we both get to be. And if we're honest we think no other woman is good enough for them. You've dispelled that notion readily, just as sweet Clarinda did. Thank you for that, for I am at peace with my feelings now.

By now your furniture will have arrived and I hope you have had the chance to make some curtains and a bedspread. Tim mentioned you have a fine voice. Did you sing 'Amazing Grace' at the church in Parramatta again this Christmas? And this will seem like a funny question, but do you sing when you are working around the farm animals? I hear they can be quite docile in the presence of song.

Your flood sounds awful. Once a year we have 'spring' tides which are very high and fill the harbour right up to the cobblestone walk-arounds. They have nothing to do with the season so I don't know where the name came from. High tides are extremely high and low tides are extremely low. Which is the opposite of 'neap' tides when the difference between low and high tide is minimal. I only remember one time when the spring tides actually flooded the streets and swept across the floors of the merchant stores and taverns by the docks. It caused an awful mess with the fishermen's nets which took days to unravel as they had been washed together and re-tangled. I remember my husband being in one of the darkest moods I'd ever seen on him. And this was a man who loved the sea. I think he felt it had gone just one step too far that time.

Young Thomas will be four years old this coming May. He has a little swagger to his walk and has the most endearing cheeky-type of smile. He seems to have no fear and Mike has started teaching him to swim. He calls me 'granny' which I like.

I wonder if you are a painter at all. You and Tim mention the animals there but we have no idea what they look like. Can either of you send some drawings, even if they are crude? We'd love to see them.

Meanwhile, thank you again for writing Laura. We all feel we know you a little better. I hope your business ventures are working out Tim. Do let us know what happens.

Warm wishes

Your loving mother and perhaps mother-in-law to be?

PS. What is an echidna?

Three rifle shots and the vigorous ringing of the captain's bell heralded the *Hawkesbury Spirit's* arrival back at the boatyard. Eleanor sent her eldest son on horseback to fetch Laura since her house was way out of earshot. By the time she got to the boatyard the men were already unloading but Tim dropped his pile of goods and lifted her off her feet as she came running up. He twirled her around and around and hugged her tightly, happy to be back home again.

They hadn't stopped in Sydney on the way back, just headed north for Broken Bay and the river. They dropped the crewmen onto another boat at Pittwater that was headed to Sydney Cove and paid them handsomely as they had done a good job. The men were offered positions on the return trip starting out in two and a half months at the end of September if they cared to make their way to Richmond. All promised to do so, anticipating bonuses if the collected seal products were plentiful.

Tim's enthusiasm at arriving home safely and in shorter time than anticipated was contagious and the boatyard rang with laughter and cheers as they had a quick celebratory ale at Jonathan's new house built after the floods. Laura had brought Tim's horse with her and finally had to drag him away in order to catch up privately. There was nothing meek and mild about the lady and the minute they were inside she was relieving Tim of his shirt and britches and leading him to the bed. He didn't even notice the new bedspread as they crashed on the mattress together and deep kissing led quickly to copulation and release. Laura lay in Tim's arms and quietly whispered: "Will you be away that long next time? If so I'm going to make sure I get extra loving before you go. I missed you, my man."

"Even longer next time, my love, as we'll have to unload the boat in Sydney. Maybe we should start preparing in advance again now. What do you say?"

"Only that you are the best man around, Timothy Bartlett. OK, one more round, then I have some things to show you. Come on mister, share yourself again."

Happy to oblige, Tim responded heartily but to Laura's dismay fell asleep afterwards. Guess it really was a long journey she thought, and he's back in real comfort now. I'll make him a hearty stew for dinner.

Satiated from loving and good food, Tim retrieved his knapsack and reached inside. He pulled out a small parcel and handed it to Laura. "A gift from the land of the Maoris," he exclaimed. She carefully unwrapped the skin around a fist-sized rock which fell apart into two halves. Inside, a beautiful green jewel-like stone glowed in one half, clearer and more subdued in the other half. "It's beautiful, Tim, but what is it?"

"It's what the Maoris call 'greenstone', or 'god-stone', a form of jade found only on New Zealand's South Island. I was very lucky to find it. One of the crewmen had seen examples of it years earlier in a jewelry shop in Sydney, brought back by sailors before 1800 and fashioned into a pendant. I'd never heard of it before but on one of the islands we explored, this chap saw a hint of green between two large boulders and we found a few small rocks around the base like this one. We split them open and a couple of them had insides like this. We didn't see any Maoris as I think they stay further inland at the top ends of the sounds. Probably just as well as we'd probably be accused of stealing their property. From what I hear I really don't want any encounters with them. They seem naturally predisposed to be war-like."

"I'm going to put it on the mantle above the fireplace so we can always see it there. Thank you for thinking of me— such an unusual gift. Now I think you owe me a long story about your voyage. I want to learn as much as I can."

Two months flew by and too soon it was time to say goodbye again. Laura had tried her hand at drawing some of the wild animals, hoping to respond to Tim's mother's request. Tim thought she had a natural talent, just like her singing, and took some of her early attempts with him on the *Hawkesbury Spirit* when it departed. Once again they ran into nasty storms crossing southeast across the Tasman, and the partners hoped the weather might be more stable on the return voyage, knowing full well that nature would offer whatever was on her mind, and they could do nothing about it. They were excited, looking forward to learn what the seal-rats had accomplished. Approaching Seal Island they shot the rifle and clanged the captain's bell but could soon see the men were not there although there were crates and barrels lined up on shore. There were also many rotting carcasses and skeletons stretched along the rocks, so clearly the colony there had been depleted. Sailing further up the sound one of the crew with a telescope spotted a crude hut on Passage Island. They shot the rifle off again and even with the naked eye they all could see men waving back at them. Cheers went up and they steered the boat into close quarters as the seal-rats rowed the longboat out to meet them.

The first order of business was to cook up a hot meal for the men as they told their story about their hunting experience. They'd been hit with the same mighty storm Tim and crew had survived shortly after they'd started killing the seals back on Seal Island. The winds and rain that followed were too fierce to work in and they spent two days in their shelter as a consequence. Some of the seals slipped away and didn't return so they completed the killing and skinning process, leaving the crates and barrels as the crew had seen. They took everything to the next island northwest and soon depleted the colony there as well. Barrels and crates were better hidden so they had not been observed as the boat sailed past. Finally they'd ended up on Passage Island as they'd been able to create a shelter in an overhang that was fully protected from the elements. It had been incredibly cold and all of the 'rats' clothes were filthy. Their beards and head hair sported luxuriant growth. Tim had secured new clothes for a reasonable price made clandestinely by Laura's friends back at Parramatta. The seal-rats were pleasantly surprised and grateful and happily threw their old clothes overboard. They then set to the task of loading the skins and oil, which took the better part of a day and a half, including the supplies left on Seal Island. The count was well over eight thousand skins, more than anyone had anticipated.

Based on the count, expectations were high as the boat headed for Preservation Inlet. Once again at the sound of the rifle the seal-rats dropped their knives and clubs and waved as the *Hawkesbury Spirit* anchored at the thirty-foot depth level.

"Something's wrong," Tim observed. "I count only seven men. I wonder where the eighth is." They soon found out as the men fed. It was a sad tale. The youngest team member, a lad named Jason, became despondent after two weeks, gradually sinking lower and lower in depression, becoming severely wearying to the other men. He hardly worked, despairing at the killing, the blood, the skinning and the cruelty.   He apparently decided one night he could take no more and when the men awoke in the morning he was gone.   It had been wet enough that they found his tracks leading across the island to the other side.   They stopped at the top of steep cliffs with surf smashing on the rocks below.   There was no trace of him and they assumed he had jumped to his death and been dashed to pieces on the jagged rocks then washed away.   As far as anyone knew he had no kin and had been simply hoping to make a pile of money in order to buy a passage back to England. The partners realized they'd have to report the death to authorities back home and check with Thorley on the chap's background.   It was a sad experience, but after he'd gone, the men were at least spared his constant whining and complaining and in fact their own productivity picked up.   They'd spent time on two of the other islands but there were several colonies where they were and they'd worked hard to get as many skins as possible from them.

Tim and the crew were amazed to find almost as many skins as the first team had collected – some seven thousand five hundred plus, and that from seven, instead of eight, men. They put it down to the fact that the first team had had to move around a lot more. Loading took a little longer than it did for the first load as they undid crates, added skins to the false keel, stacked the oil barrels tightly, packed fur skins between them, and pressed skins in the crates more tightly, keeping hundreds out to fill the lower hold to the boards that were the floor of the upper hold.   The partners were happy with the efficiency achieved and while the ship sat lower in the water, the plimsoll line was as planned and the optimal level of buoyancy preserved. Still she was much heavier than outward bound and Tim knew he'd have his hands full were any storms of the type experienced three months ago to hit them.

Once back west of the entrance to Dusky Sound, they turned north northwest and headed for home. The westerlies coming out of Bass Strait wanted to push them off course, but the further north they sailed the more the southerly winds took over. Thankfully, they encountered no serious storms this time – just one small tempest that slowed progress for three hours then dissipated as quickly as it had arrived. With confidence in continued reasonable weather Tim turned and set a more direct course for Sydney. Crew, partners, and seal-rats all heaved welcome sighs of relief as the Heads came into view and they sailed majestically up the cove and around Dawes Point into the commercial harbour. They commanded curious and widespread attention with the magnificent haul, worth a small fortune at the current market prices.

Wanting to capitalize on their success they planned to head back in three months, wanting to beat other sealers who no doubt would also now be attracted to the high yielding islands, and to take advantage of favorable world prices. Each partner became rich overnight, bank loans being satisfied quickly with plenty of funds left over. They knew future runs may not be quite as successful but with a paid-for boat and money in the bank there was no point in not following up quickly.

It was a joyous trip back up the river to Richmond.

32. Life Progresses

Three more successful trips in the next two years solidified the men's fortunes, and tiring of the strain of captaincy, Tim turned the physical sailing aspect over to one of the crew who'd been with him since the first voyage. He bought out Andrew Thompson's share of their business venture and set up a second boatyard with Jonathan on the less flood-prone northern bank of the river, a few miles further downstream and opposite Pitt Town Bottoms. By then Mr. Grono was building a huge cargo and passenger boat and had re-entered the sealing business by captaining the *Governor Bligh* to the southern isles of New Zealand. One of his trips rekindled how dangerous the business was when the *Governor Bligh* struck an uncharted rock in 1809 in the nineteen-mile-wide Foveaux Strait that separated the large South Island from the third main isle called Stewart Island. *Governor Bligh* limped home after temporary repairs on the country's west coast. As the seal populations dwindled, the returns from expensive trips were more marginal and while others turned to whaling, Tim decided to minimize his risks and stay home.

Laura had become the letter writer back to family in Polperro and Tim was proud of how well her capabilities as an artist had become. He decided future vessels would honor in some way the unique Australian fauna. In the master's cabin of the next boat, a plaque on the wall held an appropriate engraving of Laura's kangaroo drawing, sculpted by Jacob down in Parramatta.

Despite good old-fashioned regular night-time activity Laura still had not conceived and she started to wonder if she was never meant to do so. Tim was clearly capable of breeding as his son was now six years old, and by all accounts a charmer in the community.

One evening when Tim was reading the newspaper after dinner, he suddenly laid it down and reached over to lift Laura's chin and look deeply into her eyes. "I have a wonderful idea, my love. We've been together nearly four full years and life is good. But there's one thing missing that I'd love to rectify. Would you marry me and become a true Mrs. Bartlett?"

Taken aback, Laura asked, "What prompted this proposal, my man? I love it and can think of nothing else I'd rather have. You are such a romantic, always coming up with something different when I least expect it. Of course I'll be your wife. What a wonderful offering. But tell me, just how do you plan to make this happen?"

"Well, it's been on my mind for some time, I will admit, but an article in today's newspaper is the real catalyst for my question. See here, a group of Scots who settled in Ebenezer, further down the river, have built, by themselves, a small Presbyterian church there.   Since you were baptized Presbyterian in Edinburgh I thought it would be nice to get married there. What do you say?"

"You make me cry, Tim. I have always wondered whether you might want to stay unmarried so that your marriage to Clarinda would always be sacrosanct in your memory. I'm glad that's not the case. Thank you, thank you." She rushed around the table and hugged and kissed her man, cradling his head against her bosom, delirious with happiness.

"Do you have some timing in mind or is this too much of the moment to have thought that far ahead?"

"I think we should check when the Reverend Robert Bishop, who is mentioned here, will be available. But it could be nice to be married at a Christmas service where you could sing your hymn as a return thank you gift to the church. "

"Tim, as I said before, you constantly amaze me with your creativity. I love the idea. It's a truly beautiful notion."

"In that case, next week I will sail to Portland Head and see what can be arranged."

"You make my heart pound, Timothy Bartlett. I must ride off and tell Eleanor this afternoon. I hope she won't be jealous but I just have to share this with another woman. You stay here, my man, and keep thinking new things. I do love you."

Tim decided to forego a sailing boat and instead, for the exercise, rowed down the river to Portland Head then trekked to the newly built church. It was made of sandstone, cedar, and hardwood, and had been built by the local group of Scots without help from the government or church officials per se. Several families cultivated farms in the vicinity, having chosen the spot in 1803. Across from the chapel was an old gum tree where they'd previously conducted Sunday services. While the reverend admonished Tim slightly for having lived in sin for the previous five years he said he would be happy to offer up the marriage vows and would sincerely appreciate Laura's hymn singing.

And so it came to pass that on Christmas Day 1809 Laura Stewart and Timothy Bartlett were wed in the simple chapel at Ebenezer by the Reverend Robert Bishop. The congregation consisted of the fourteen local Scottish families along with Eleanor and Jonathan, the Grono and Thompson families, and Jacob and his wife, who'd come all the way from Parramatta. It was the first marriage in the church for a family outside the group that had built it. As such it set a precedent that was followed hundreds of times in the years that followed, still in vogue over two hundred years later.

Laura immediately wrote to her now mother-in-law, confirming a hope that had been expressed in a signature on a letter nearly three years back. Three months later, before any note had come back, she wrote again, excited to say she was pregnant at last. She wondered, was it the fact that she was married that had allowed her to conceive? God's hand at work? She remembered they'd made love on return from the church, passionate, sensual, thankful and fulfilling. She hadn't felt so happy since singing in the York Minster choir one Christmas. Perhaps that was it – remembering one of the best times of her life that had allowed nature to finally grant a long-held silent wish.

Eliza Bartlett was born on 24th September 1810, bringing joy to her parents, and ultimately to her grandmother in Polperro. Tim named his next boat *Thomas and Eliza* after his two children, and following a pattern set down just three months prior when Jonathan named the eighty-ton schooner he'd just built with

Samuel Thorley after his twin daughters, Elizabeth and Mary. Both men were proud fathers, Tim's fervent wish being that one day Thomas would indeed walk the land with him.

It was an historic half year, culminating in December with Governor Macquarie's visit to the region when he renamed Green Hills as 'Windsor' after Windsor-on-Thames. Windsor was declared one of the five *Macquarie Towns*, the others being Castlereagh, Wilberforce, Richmond, where the Bartletts lived, and Pitt Town, where Tim had his boatyard. The region defined around the five towns supplied the fledgling colony with half its annual grain requirements and was vitally important to its health and growth.

From that time on, progress in the area became more rapid as free settlers moved in and merchants saw new trade possibilities. Unfortunately, Tim's friend Andrew Thompson, who had been appointed as a magistrate in the new Windsor, died at the early age of twenty-seven, his granary and ships sold off, and his brewery converted to a hospital. A square in Windsor town centre was named after him in 1811.

By 1815 Laura had produced two more children; Charles in 1812, and Mary in 1814, the same year that a major wharf was built in Windsor. Tim had ceased hunting for seals when his friend Andrew died, buying a portion of Andrew's grain estate and still concentrating otherwise on boat building, which was becoming an even more lucrative business as trade on the river grew dramatically.

He and Laura celebrated their fifth wedding anniversary at the new Macquarie Arms Hotel in Windsor. It was a time for celebration and reflection, but also thanks, as Tim had received his Conditional Pardon just the month before due to an impassioned plea by his partner Jonathan to the authorities. It was two years earlier than normally would have been the case but it recognized his service to the crown on the convict ship, his contributions to the export seal products business, and his pioneering boat-building efforts.

Laura had received her Absolute Pardon shortly after she married, as her seven years were up and the marriage further enhanced her forgiveness and perceived stability by the state.

This meant that had she wanted, she could have returned to England, taking the children with her. It was a topic of discussion at the anniversary dinner as she checked with Tim whether he'd like his children to be seen by his mother. If so she'd happily take them back to Polperro.

"That's a wonderful thought dear wife, but I don't think it would be fair. I don't mean to sound selfish, but first, it would be a major passage for you alone even if we waited five years until Mary was six. Travel would be a tremendous hardship on you, and I think in a way it would be difficult for everyone in Polperro without me appearing alongside you. Probably hardest on my son Thomas, who would be seventeen by then and surely aware of the story of his birth.

"You are kind to think of the idea and it's very unselfish of you. You are such a loving, considerate woman, which is just one of the many reasons I love you."

With a twinkle in her eye she poked her chin forward and asked, "And what are all the other reasons, my lover?"

"Finish your apple pie, and I'll take you home and show you some, you pretty lady."

Every now and then there were still uprisings among the natives as the five grain towns grew, and farmers cleared new fields and encroached on the lands the natives thought of as rightly theirs. There were no easy solutions to the quandary that arose. Some natives started to live on the outskirts of the towns instead of retreating to the dense forests of the Blue Mountains as others did. That raised different problems as grog became a favorite libation and select tribal women, or 'gins', engaged in prostitution. In Windsor, a local chief named Nurragingy helped maintain peace in several instances, and as reward, in 1816 Governor Macquarie presented him with a brass breastplate, whereon his name was inscribed as chief of the South Creek tribe. Even so, a state of unease remained between white and black man, with the former constantly aware that earned trust was too easily destroyed by unknown and misunderstood native values. Those had been inherited since their dream time in a totally alien culture, and didn't readily transfer to the new processes thrust into their lives.

Tim and Laura seemed to have turned off the baby tap, although not for lack of trying, both sporting strong libidos, An Anglican church, St. Matthews, designed by the noted Mr. Francis Greenway was built in 1817 in Windsor and became the Bartlett's place of worship. Next to the commandant's house a new barracks guard house appeared in 1818, and the hospital was enlarged in 1820. When she had a spare moment, which wasn't often, Laura continued to write and send drawings of the children to Tim's mother and Mike and Betsy. Polperro, on the other side of the world, seemed never to change, and the only news centered around the growth of Thomas. In 1822 another building, the Windsor Court House, designed by Sir Francis Greenway, was opened. But for Tim there was a sad twist to the year as his long-time partner and former master, Jonathan, left the Hawkesbury to start a new business in Launceston, Tasmania, taking with him his two sons John and William. Eleanor, along with seven other family members, remained in Richmond.

Laura noticed a change in her man. He was no longer quite as outgoing and enthusiastic about projects and dreams. Of course he had turned forty-two and while healthy and busy, he no longer whistled with the tea kettle in the morning, and discharged a lot of his duties with the farm animals in a semi-automated way, avoiding the care and close involvement he once exhibited with them. They'd added on to the house to accommodate the children they'd brought into the world and Tim still played with them, read to them, and was patient and encouraging when teaching them to ride, shoot, and swim, happily laughing at their antics and the little tests they threw at their parents. But something was definitely missing. His ardor in the bedroom had diminished naturally with age, as had Laura's, but nothing there seemed amiss. She failed to believe there was anything wrong in their emotional relationship, so she decided to tackle things head on, as she found herself worrying continually, and distracting herself from her own chores and needs. Which wasn't good.

One Sunday morning, instead of getting ready for church she suggested the pair of them go for a ride together. Tim looked at her quizzically. "It's a gorgeous morning and we haven't had much time together lately," she said. "Let's head along the Kurrajong Road, climb up into the mountains a bit, and find a fishing hole in some stream. Like we used to do years ago. The kids will be fine here at home. And fresh fish for supper wouldn't go astray."

"Well, when you put it that way, who could refuse? I'll go saddle up the horses and get the fishing lines and our guns. Maybe you can put some ham and bread and ale and a couple of boiled eggs in a hamper for us."

The sun felt good on their backs as they trotted westwards. It had been a while since they'd spent time in the Mountains and the scent of eucalyptus wafting through the glens set the mood for an enjoyable ride. They travelled without talking, the only sounds being the clip clop of their horses' hooves and the call of the early rising birds. At the second creek crossing they dismounted and led the horses along one of its banks penetrating alternating pine and eucalyptus groves. They passed several ponds until they came to one beside a clearing where a few droplets of dew remained on ferns still in the shadows but elsewhere the sun warmed the grass and the earth. Tim dug out some worms and baited their hooks and they sat side by side watching the shadows flit back and forth underwater.

"This reminds me of the days we were courting down Parramatta way when you first taught me to fish," Laura offered. "Although I remember walking along the bank and your telling me to slow down as I was pulling the bait along too fast. And here we are sitting instead of walking. I still like rubbing against you. It makes me feel warm all over. Remember back then?"

"Oh yes. What a lot of fun that was. Especially seeing the delight on the faces of your friends back at the house when we returned with a fresh catch for dinner. I wonder whatever happened to Mary and others over the years. Did you ever hear about them?"

"No, and there are times when I feel bad for not checking back. I guess I was more interested in my new heartthrob than keeping up with other friends. I especially wonder what happened to Mary. Perhaps she found a man who cared for all of her, not just her red-parts, as she would say."

"At least Eleanor was here and became a replacement friend when you moved up here. You and she have become very close over the intervening years. I must admit I don't understand why Jonathan's leaving her behind."

"Neither do I and I'm going to make sure I spend as much time with her as I can, even though she has older children still around. I'm sure they will be supportive, but it's just not the same as having another mother and adult friend like me to talk to."

"No. You are right, dear. I've been feeling quite miserable with Jonathan now gone. I didn't realize just how close we'd become over the years. Not just from building boats, but we've stood shoulder to shoulder at the helm in the height of storms holding on for our lives as the boat followed nature's forces more than our commands. There's a bond that forms then—taking risks together and coming through, willing to face the dangers again if needed. Hard to explain, but I guess I'd taken our relationship and its permanence for granted. Never thought it would get challenged the way I feel now."

Laura held her breath waiting for more. Here was the crux of her man's mood swing. He was missing his friend badly. She'd wondered if that had indeed been the cause of his semi-depressed state. Clearly so, but affecting him far more than he realized. She was desperate for him to continue talking about the issue, knowing it would be therapeutic. She ignored a tug on her line, not wanting to disturb his train of thought. "Do you think Jonathan feels similarly?" she asked.

"I'm not sure. Possibly. He didn't say much before leaving and maybe he's like me, feeling the loss more once apart. We men don't tend to talk to each other about such things. But his departure made me think back to my leaving Polperro so many many years ago. Although it was forced I suspect it had a heavy impact on a number of people. I probably underestimated the true effect it really had on Clarinda and my mother especially. While I was more worried about myself I didn't think enough about those I'd be leaving behind. There's no way now I can undo things, of course, but the thoughts have saddened me.

"Do you remember that Christmas dinner on our fifth anniversary when you offered to go to Polperro in my place and take the children? On reflection I think you were more aware of the possible feelings of people back home than I was. I still wouldn't have wanted you to go – for the same reasons as I gave then, but thinking back just reinforced how important certain relationships can be.

"But enough of being maudlin. I see you had a small tug a while ago. Let's re-bait your hook and see what we can do."

"Before we do that, Tim, I'd like to suggest something. We've talked about it in letters to your mother and Ben. It's time to put words into action. Your son Thomas is now nineteen, and from all accounts is a strapping, well-adjusted lad. Let's send money for a ticket for his twentieth birthday. You'd have something new to focus on bringing him out here and planning all the things and places to show him. The children would be excited to know they would finally be going to meet their half-brother coming all the way from your fishing village in a country they don't know. And I'd get to see my man smiling more often, perhaps even whistling at breakfast time again. What do you say?"

"Sounds like a wonderful idea, my love. You are right. It's time. Thank you for putting it all in perspective. Now lets' catch some fish and hurry home so we can tell the kids. They'll be just as excited as you've made me feel."

33. A Visitor

Since international letters still took four months on ships sailing directly between London and Sydney, Laura got to work immediately.

July 1822

Dear Thomas, Mike, and Betsy:

It seems that for years Tim has talked about having Thomas come visit us here. We're hoping this letter will set some things in motion to finally make that happen. Thomas, your twentieth birthday comes up next May. As a gift, your birth father and I would like to buy you a return ticket from London to Sydney. I have just written to our bank back in Plymouth with instructions. That letter will be posted along with this one. Happy Birthday way in advance!!!

You have no idea how much it thrills us to finally be making this happen. Tim and I are very excited, as are the children. I know it will require several letters back and forth to organize everything so let's hope our letters cross the oceans quickly. But, because there are no guarantees with the mail, let me write out some information here and now in case for some reason this is the only letter you get before leaving.

It's pretty certain you will be a passenger on a convict boat. Those boats go either to Sydney, or Hobart in Van Diemen's Land. In some cases the ones that go to Hobart often come to Sydney afterwards. Whatever you do, please make sure your boat has Sydney as its final destination. I know Tim will want to meet you in Sydney but there is no way to know in advance when a boat will actually arrive there. So there is a good chance he may not be present when you finally turn up. It usually takes several days for all the convicts to disembark but passengers usually are the first off once the authorities have come aboard and met with the captain and surgeon. You will be taken ashore and checked by the immigration officials.

Now, should you arrive and there is no sign of Tim, please go and book a room at the Dog and Duck hotel. He will come looking for you there should he miss you at the boat. If after two days he still hasn't turned up please catch the small ferry to Parramatta and once there, ask how to get the coach to Windsor. We will make sure the bank provides you with enough money for those tickets as well. In Windsor go to the Commandant's house and ask how to get to the Bartletts' in Richmond. Everyone knows us and it's quite possible someone may give you a ride on horseback or possibly bring you by boat.

I think your birth father would have to have broken a leg before you would need to resort to any of these back-up plans, but now you have them just in case.

Mike and Betsy. Please know we plan to spoil Thomas rotten when he gets here, but we will send him back to you. Make sure he buys that return ticket and not a single. We understand of course that he will be travelling under the name Morrisey. He's welcome to stay with us as long as he likes or until he tires of us, but no more than a year, as his ticket will expire. Of course we are taking it for granted that you approve of his coming out. If that is not the case please let us know quickly.

I know how thankful Tim is that you have raised Thomas as your own. We understand that he considers you as his mother and father and Tim would have it no other way. You have been wonderful to him all these years. I am happy to be his half mother. Plus, there are two half sisters and one half brother here anxious to see if he really is as we've told them. They are fascinated by the thought of someone they are related to coming to see them from so far away.

Please reply quickly and let us know what else we have to organize.

Thank you again for sharing your son.

Yours always

Laura

November 1822

Dear Tim and Laura:

You are both wonderful people. Thomas can hardly sit still these days. I don't think there's a single person in the village who doesn't know he's going to Australia! He's been trying to find out more information about the oceans he'll be crossing and the countries that border them. We have a bunch of old charts now decorating the lounge room floor. He's scrounged them from the older folks in the village who had them stored away and had all but forgotten them until he came knocking. I hope that whatever ship he travels on has an adaptable, patient captain, because I think Thomas will have a persistent, inquiring mind and voice.

Both Mike and Ben have been out on the seas with Thomas and speak well of his capabilities. I think he must take after you Tim. Can be a little impatient at times and Mike is trying to ease that out of him. You may have to reinforce it once he arrives.

It's a little early to know what ship he might travel on yet as the authorities have to see what's available and decide whether they have to commandeer more merchantmen for the task. It also would be a lot more convenient if he could be on one that stops in nearby Plymouth, instead of having to go all the way to London to embark. But he's young and will manage I'm sure. We hear that some boats go directly from Cork, Ireland, but I don't think he'd enjoy being on a ship full of Irish convicts. You've mentioned their reputation in New South Wales. It has changed here as well in the last ten years and is somewhat similar. They are men not to be trusted who would sell their wives for a flagon of ale. I'm sorry to be so crude but they are becoming less and less liked by the English, Welsh and Scots. They seem to have rebellion and a distaste for authority in their blood.

We understand what Thomas will need to do if for some reason Tim is not at the docks in Sydney. He's been questioned about it several times and he can repeat your words verbatim, Laura. It's too bad there isn't a reasonable map of New South Wales yet. I'm sure one will come eventually – maybe during the period Thomas will be there.

I only have one request of you, and I'm grinning as I write. Please make sure he doesn't meet any nice eligible girls there. We'd hate for him to be enticed to stay by someone as smart and as pretty as you must be Laura, to have captured Tim's heart. We want to make sure he comes home.

Thank you again. We don't know how we'll ever repay your kindness.

Yours affectionately

Betsy Anne

March 1823

Dear Thomas, Mike and Betsy:

By the time you get this Thomas will probably know what ship he'll be travelling on. At least we hope so. I do want to warn you of one thing I've noticed here. Even though it's still early times in the colony—we're not even fifty years old yet—there are certain phrases and words and speech habits that seem to be purely Australian. Some of it is maybe because convicts come from towns all over the British Isles, and adjust their accents talking to one another. Some of it is because aborigine words are used to describe animals and places especially, so that our tongues struggle with pronunciation. Finally there are simply phrases and words that wouldn't make sense back home. Aborigines 'go walkabout' and their ancestry is tied up in the 'Dreamtime'. Convicts who have escaped and become rogues are called 'bushrangers' because they live and hide in the forests. Friends can be called 'cobbers' and men often refer to their 'mates' which usually means 'best friends' but can sometimes just mean 'others'. It's one of the hardest words for me to learn to use appropriately. Used much more by men than women and is far more colloquial than the rare times one hears it in England. I'm sure Thomas will wonder about some of the sounds he hears when he first comes across them, and that when he comes home he will use some of them without thinking and you'll have to ask for an explanation. The speech is also often lazy here. I think there's little doubt that he will be called Tom far more than Thomas once here.

As for repaying our kindness, our gift has no conditions associated with it. We want nothing in return so you can never repay it. Perhaps in the future, when you have the chance to do someone some good you can just do it and also not worry about any repayment.

Besides which, I think of this one birthday present as making up for the previous nineteen birthdays where there were no gifts.

Come on, Thomas!

Yours

Laura

Late May 1823

Dear Tim and Laura:

I'm not a good writer, but mother is making me do this. If everything goes to plan, I will be travelling out on the convict ship *Medina*. It is planned to leave The Downs in the first week of August, then travel to Cork and pick up some Irish convicts, leaving there at the end of August or the start of September.

As mother wrote, I'm not keen to be travelling with Irish convicts, but have no choice. At least the ship is planned to go directly to Sydney from Cork without stopping in Rio de Janeiro or Capetown. Although I think it would be great to see both cities. I know timing can change depending on the winds and storms and any damage to the ship. I imagine if we leave Cork on September 1 we should be in Sydney around Christmastime.

Another ship named *Jupiter* is planned to leave London on June 2 and I will be rushing to London to get this letter on it. It is not a convict ship but will carry a number of women and families sent out by the government, and a number of officers and soldiers to occupy administrative positions in Australia. It will be taking a lot of cargo for the colony. I cannot catch it unfortunately as I am not scheduled to get my final travel documents until the middle of June. The boat will also be fairly slow as it will stop in Capetown and Hobart before going on to Sydney. Hopefully this letter will arrive before I do on the *Medina*.

I can hardly wait till I meet all of you. It's been fun already getting approval and arranging the paperwork. Our lawyer has been a wonderful help.

Thank you for my birthday gift. I hope my arrival in Australia will be a unique Christmas gift for us all.

Yours

Thomas (Bartlett) Morrisey

Tim had been worrying about learning Thomas' plans in time, and was relieved when his letter arrived on the last day of November. So, it would be around Christmas when he arrived. Christmas always had been a special occasion. He'd proposed to Laura on Christmas Day in 1804, and they'd be wed on Christmas Day five years later. Two of the children who had birthdays in late September had probably been conceived around Christmas time.

He didn't really want to be away from home at Christmas, so at dinner one evening he asked for advice from all the family members. Eliza, who had just turned thirteen, in her charming, intelligent way, came up with a suggestion. "From what I read Father, ships usually are delayed at departure, and take at least one hundred fifteen days to get here, depending where they leave from. I spent some time working with the calendar. If the *Medina* leaves from Cork September 1 and takes the minimum sailing time, at best she would arrive here on December 23. If she's three days late leaving, or takes three days extra to cross the oceans she would arrive the day after Christmas. I suspect she'll both leave late and take longer than the minimum crossing time. So I think you should stay here for Christmas Day and be with us, then go to Sydney the next day in case the boat arrives on the twenty-seventh. I think even then you may have to wait."

"I can see you have learned well from your mother's lessons in arithmetic, Eliza. How did I raise a daughter who is so logical at such a young age? I like your analysis and suggestion. Charles and Mary, did you understand all that?"

Heads nodded, and Charles spoke up. "Father, when Thomas is here, is that going to make you want to go back to Polperro with him, even though you can't?"

"Well, I can see you children have been doing a lot of talking about your half-brother's visit. And I'm thinking your mother must have been involved a lot too. You ask a very good question, Charles, and I'm not sure I have a simple answer, because I've also been wondering about some things. If this is too hard to understand we can talk about it later again. You know how your father loves the sea. I've given up taking long dangerous adventures as the risks are too great. But I still love sailing, which is why I keep building boats. I'm sure Thomas' visit will remind me of things I did and loved back in Polperro. Perhaps one day when I'm older and you children are all married and gone I may not want to live in this place anymore but would rather live by the sea. That's something your mother and I will have to discuss in the years ahead. But we're not even thinking of moving yet, so don't think too much about it, OK? It would be years away."

Laura chimed in, "Your father has heard about a little spot way down south on the coast where the fishing is great. It might be somewhere to consider going in years hence. There isn't even a settlement there at the moment. The Yuin aborigines who live in the region there call it *Ngulla-dulla*, meaning 'safe harbour.' The famous Captain Cook noted the place in his log book in 1770 as he charted the coastline. I think it's the 'safe harbour' title that gives it appeal. Maybe when Thomas is here, he and your father will make a trip to learn more. That way, if indeed we ever settle there, Thomas will be able to tell everyone about it back in Polperro."

"I don't want to move, Mother," Mary piped up.

"It wouldn't be for a long time yet, sweetheart," Laura responded. "Your father has so many boats still to make – have you seen all the ones under construction down at the boatyard? I'll take you there tomorrow – we haven't been in a while, and I want you to help me choose some ribbons for your hair at the new store in Windsor. Does that sound good?"

"Oooh yes. Thank you Mother," was the happy reply.

Eliza spoke up again. "Father, how will you and Thomas travel back from Sydney? Will you take a horse for him down to Parramatta."

"My gosh, I am very impressed with how much you have been thinking ahead. I think Thomas is going to love meeting you all.

"But to answer the question. First I will check if there's a cargo boat that is planning to travel up the Hawkesbury. None of my boats will be there at that time, but maybe Mr. Grono will have one, or someone else we know. That takes more time but it would be a great way for Thomas to see the northern coast and the river. Now, if there's no boat we'll take the ferry to Parramatta. I will indeed take an extra horse with me when I go down there. I'm sure Thomas can ride based on what he wrote about getting that last letter of his posted in London. Does that seem reasonable?"

Heads nodded again, and it was clear that Thomas' pending arrival was the most exciting topic the children had had to think about in ages. Tim acknowledged internally how thankful he was for their attitude. They could easily have felt resentment at a half-brother coming into their lives. He made a mental note to doubly thank Laura later for her efforts behind the scene.

Christmas dinner was a happy, boisterous affair. The kids were now old enough to help with all the preparations and while the day had dawned hot, the humidity stayed low. The sacrificial turkey was eaten with gusto and the leftovers carefully wrapped in the hope Thomas may arrive quickly enough to partake. Laura promised the children that if he didn't make it in time, they would cook another bird for the New Year holiday.

Tim had arranged for Jacob down in Parramatta to carve replicas of boats and native animals from wood offcuts he provided, as Christmas presents for all the children. They were thrilled as they unwrapped the items and the new toys littered the dining table all through the meal.

On Boxing Day morning Tim readied the horses for the trip to Parramatta. He was excited and a little nervous at the same time. The kids all kissed him goodbye, Laura gave him an extra long hug.

But it was little Eliza who smacked his horse on the rump and yelled, "Go get him, Father." She waved all the way until he disappeared out of sight.

There was no big barque in the harbour so Tim took himself around to Samuel Thorley's Black Dog tavern, where patrons were heartily celebrating the season. Samuel wasn't there, as he was in Newcastle visiting with a cousin. Tim was more lonely than he had expected. Up early next day, the 27th, he wandered along the shore east of the Quay waiting to see if tall masts appeared in the distance. None came in view. Darn, he thought. Eliza looked like being right. How smart she was. He walked to the commercial wharves to see if any boat was planned to leave for the Hawkesbury in the next few days, and was disappointed to learn no one was traveling upstream in the holiday week.

Early Sunday morning on the 28th Tim attended service in St. Phillips Anglican church and prayed for the safe arrival of his son. A Presbyterian church, Scots Kirk, was going through the process of approval but wouldn't come into being for another three years. Spiritually refreshed and anxious, he roamed along the foreshores until he could clearly see the Heads defining the entrance to the Cove. A small schooner headed out to sea with fishing nets dangling from its spars, but nothing else filled the watery gap between the sandstone cliffs.

On Monday, he was woken before daybreak by cannon noise and church bells. He joined a crowd of eye-rubbing citizens walking towards the Quay. The sun was just peeking above the horizon lighting the sky as they gathered by the immigration office and parked themselves on the gentle slopes above the water line. There was always tremendous excitement and joy when a major boat arrived. Boats brought people, goods, and letters from home. And their size and majesty were awesome to those on shore.

The unknown ship had pulled through the Heads in the dark and anchored, waiting until just before dawn to fire her welcoming cannon signaling her arrival. Wharfmen, soldiers, officials, and bell-ringers responded in kind. As did onlookers of all persuasions. Tim was far from alone. He was smart enough to take up a position near the immigration hut, as he knew officials there would be looking up the cove through telescopes trying to read the ship's name as she came into view. Would it be the *Medina*?

The pilot ship had already left to go guide the new arrival into port, but it would still take time until the big ship appeared, especially as the breeze was blowing head-on from the west. Tim eavesdropped on the men with the long-view glasses. One of them could see the ship but not make out its name. He sensed Tim's curiosity and asked, "Are you waiting for a particular ship, mate?"

"The *Medina*," Tim replied.

"Can't tell yet if this is her, mate. Someone you know supposed to be on board?"

"My son," Tim choked out. "As passenger, not convict."

"Well, good luck to you then. Shouldn't be long before we know."

He found his nerves jangling again. How surprising. His senses told him there was no way it could be any boat but the *Medina*. The timing was perfect. Clearly his unseen son meant far more to him than he'd ever imagined. What would he look like? Would he be able to identify him easily? The questions flittered back and forth through his mind.

Finally he could see the ship for himself. A smaller sized barque by the look of her. But darned if he, or even the men with the glasses, could see the name. She was pointed directly towards them managing the wind. There was one last turn remaining to the north that she had to manage before the final leg due west. And suddenly the shouts went up.

"It's the *Medina*. Out of London and Cork!"

"*Medina*, London, Cork, convict ship!"

News of the boat's name and passage up the harbor passed through the crowd like wildfire and Tim found tears at the corners of his eyes. At last, at very long last. The son he'd never seen was only five hundred yards away on the boat sailing majestically towards them. How many years had he waited for this moment? Not years, but a lifetime. Unbelievable! His boy was almost here.

Now they could see figures at the railing. Was Thomas among them? Too far away to tell. They looked more like sailors pushing the rope climbing-nets over the side, and moving the rail pieces for access. Where was he? The crowd onshore started cheering but there was no response from the boat. Which meant that it mainly held convicts and possibly just a few passengers.

She slowly came to a stop in the middle of the cove directly opposite the quay and everyone heard the rattle of the anchor chain finalizing her position. She fired off a three-cannon salute again. The crowd cheered, and Tim leaned against the wooden hut for support. His body shook slightly and once again he felt an apprehension that he'd never anticipated.

Four officials and two oarsmen pushed a longboat into the water and it quickly moved out to the gently rocking brig which now had a stern anchor in place as well. A group of men on deck welcomed the boarding party and they all quickly disappeared towards the aft cabins. Sailors furled the sails and opened the hatches, but there was no distinct sign of any group of passengers. Maybe they'd been taken inside with the officials.

It was a long trying hour before the officials appeared on deck again. Tim's impatience had grown, but now he struggled to calm down and prepare for an event he'd yearned for for eons. He borrowed the telescope again and focused on the men climbing back down into the longboat. Seven, one more than had gone out. A sailor was handing down a carpet traveler bag. Could it be that there was only one non-convict passenger on the boat? The longboat was big enough that it could have brought ten or more extra people ashore.

And then suddenly it was all too real. That was Thomas. Red hair, Clarinda's hair. It flashed in the sunlight. No-one had mentioned his son's hair colour beyond babyhood in any of the letters, and he'd never thought to ask. What a wonderful sight. He handed the telescope to its owner and hurried down to the longboat's landing spot. He waved both hands back and forth above his head, and the man that was his son waved vigorously back.

Joy flooded his soul. After twenty and a half years apart his son stood before him.

Summoning up every ounce of courage, determined not to cry, he clasped Thomas tightly around the shoulders with his left arm and extended his right for a handshake. His smile stretched from ear to ear.

"Welcome to Australia, my son. It is so incredible to see and touch you at last. I've waited years and years for this moment. We have so much to catch up on and share, and I can't wait.

"Come walk this land with me...."

Author's Biography

Having a convict ancestor, Warren has extensively researched the history of convict times, writing about the trials, tribulations and trepidation faced by normal English citizens who were trapped into poverty and crime, convicted, and sent to the Antipodes. They experienced terrible prison conditions in old ships crossing turbulent oceans, arriving in an alien land totally mismanaged by authorities. Forming unions with Free Settlers, these dispossessed folks became the physical and social pioneers that transformed a penal colony into a civilized society, creating a unique culture and way of life. Warren's goal is to make sure their efforts, their beliefs, and their dedication in forging new lives, are not forgotten. His stories are known for their seamless integration of true historical events.

www.ingramcontent.com/pod-product-compliance
Lightning Source LLC
Chambersburg PA
CBHW060247100426
42742CB00011B/1667